MIAMI NOW!

MIAMI NOW!

Immigration, Ethnicity, and Social Change

EDITED BY

Guillermo J. Grenier

and Alex Stepick III

University Press of Florida

Gainesville / Tallahassee / Tampa / Boca Raton
Pensacola / Orlando / Miami / Jacksonville

Copyright 1992 by the Board of Regents of the State of Florida

Printed in the United States on acid-free paper ∞

All rights reserved

The University Press of Florida is the scholarly publishing agency for the State
University System of Florida, comprised of Florida A & M University, Florida Atlantic
University, Florida International University, Florida State University, University of Central
Florida, University of Florida, University of North Florida, University of South Florida,
University of West Florida.

University Press of Florida, 15 NW 15th Street, Gainesville, FL 32611

Photographs by Peggy Nolan

Library of Congress Cataloging in Publication data are located on the
last printed page of the book.

To
S, C, and A
and
C, A, and MC

CONTENTS

FIGURES

TABLES

ILLUSTRATIONS

FOREWORD

In January 1992, articles in the *National Geographic, Esquire,* and *New York* magazines converged on a single theme. The topic was not the country's economic troubles or the political battles of an election year but the remarkable events taking place in an American city. The city is not one of the nation's largest or one of the most centrally located. For many years, its familiar profile was that of a semitropical playground with southern-style race relations. But in the last quarter of a century, Miami has been transformed in ways never before experienced by an American city, and journalists and *literati* elsewhere have taken note.

On February 27, 1992, President George Bush published an editorial piece in the *Miami Herald.* It is extraordinary for any city for the president of the United States to submit an op-ed article to the local newspaper. What made the event even more remarkable is that the president did not discuss what his administration had done or would do for Miami but rather what it had done and would do toward a foreign country. The president sought to reassure his readers that he would continue to stand tough against Castro's Cuba. His was an electioneering gesture toward the Cuban-American community, concentrated in Miami, which has come to play a pivotal role in Florida's Republican party politics.

The episode illustrates the unparalleled happenings in what is arguably the most internationalized American city. What makes Miami distinct is not the large number of foreigners, for other cities like New York and Los Angeles have even more immigrants. It is rather the rupture of an established cultural outlook and a unified social hierarchy in which every group of newcomers takes its preordained place. Instead of an ethnic queue dictated by the familiar views and prejudices of white Protestants, Miami has developed an unexpected and virulent case of cultural pluralism. In the process, southern-style race relations were torn asunder to open space for some groups to reaffirm their own definitions of the situation and for others to fall farther behind.

The central event that ushered in this remarkable transformation was without doubt the Cuban Revolution. The displaced Cuban bourgeoisie resettled en masse in Miami, resisting early efforts of the federal government to disperse it to other localities around the country. Most of the refugees officially resettled elsewhere eventually found their way to South Florida. The choice was not casual, nor was it determined solely by climate. Miami and Havana had long been linked by two-way tourist trade and by a long tradition in which the defeated side in Cuba's political struggles found temporary refuge in South Florida. The Cuban upper and middle classes displaced by Fidel Castro's Revolution followed the same familiar course. Once they had regained their economic footing in Miami, the city became the obvious choice for other Caribbean and South American inflows.

For Latin America's wealthy seeking a safe haven for their capital or a foothold in the U.S. market, there could be no better place: the stability of North American institutions was coupled with transactions in their own language. The same was true, of course, for money launderers. Migration flows from South American countries—Colombia, Peru, Ecuador—were soon partially diverted from New York and rechanneled toward Miami. Refugees escaping conflicts in the convulsed Caribbean followed the same route. Nicaraguans opposed to the left-wing Sandinista regime sought succor and support from their affluent and increasingly influential Cuban brethren. Bereft of any such assistance, Haitians came anyway aboard barely seaworthy craft in search of opportunity and freedom.

The result of these mass migrations during the last three decades is the emergence of an ethnic kaleidoscope where multiple communities vie for voice and interact with each other in complex ways. Among the new-comers Cubans remain dominant numerically and politically, but there are also large and visible Nicaraguan, Haitian, Colombian, and other national communities. The immigrants' presence has also transformed the native white and black populations both in their self-image and their outlook on the city.

Three such changes deserve mention. First the loss of cultural hege-mony has led to a massive white flight, not only out of the city but out of Dade County (the Miami Metropolitan Area) altogether. Between 1980 and 1990, the area lost almost a third of its native white population and only the large influx of immigrants prevented a net population loss.

Second, a novel process of *acculturation-in-reverse* has set in among the remaining native white and black populations. Today in Miami, it is almost as common to see natives learning Spanish as to observe new immigrants struggling to learn English. Cuban and, to a lesser extent, other Latin customs, foodways, and festivities have also found their way into local lore. In view of these changes, local "Anglo" leaders have changed their tune from preaching immediate assimilation to the newcomers to celebrating Miami's cultural diversity and portraying it as "the City of the Future."[1]

Third, the native black community caught in this sea wave of change has developed a revitalized ethnic discourse that asserts the primacy of its claims over those of recent arrivals and decries the rapid ascent of white Latins while black Americans are left behind. The result is a pattern of rising ethnic tensions and sporadic violence whose root causes remain far from being resolved. Native blacks have made common cause with black Haitian immigrants on a number of occasions, but even this alliance is fraught with tension. Racial solidarity is weakened in this case by cultural differences and by the effort of Haitian leaders to create an entrepreneurial ethnic community patterned consciously after Little Havana.[2]

These multicultural and increasingly complex interactions plus the city's international flavor make Miami exceptional. However, the lessons to be garnered from the study of its transformation have more than a purely local import. The forces that transformed Miami are very much at play elsewhere. They include the ever-growing "boundedness" of the world population through the influence of telecommunications and air transport, the media-led diffusion of life-styles and consumption expectations from the developed countries to the Third World, and the strengthening of transnational social networks created by earlier migrants that facilitate the movement of later ones.

As individuals and groups in the poorer countries seek to satisfy consumption expectations beamed to them from the outside or to escape political persecutions at home, other cities in the developed world are bound to feel the impact. In the United States, Boston is host to a revitalized wave of Irish immigration; Los Angeles is more than half Latin under the influence of massive migration from Mexico, augmented by refugees from the Central American conflicts; Chicago is Poland's third largest city and is also home to large Mexican and Asian communities. Miami may not show to other cities the exact image of their own futures, but the social transformations that have taken place in South Florida contain important lessons for the momentous changes now occurring in American urban life.

Most recent books on Miami have been written by outside intellectuals shocked or impressed by developments in the city.[3] The genre has produced novel insights but also a great deal of casual observation, advanced more for its shock value than for its accuracy. The present collection has the merit of being written by scholars who live and work in the area and hence possess first-hand familiarity with the major events that have shaped Miami's recent past. They are all affiliated with an institution—Florida International University—that has been itself at the center of these transformations. A significant proportion of its faculty and staff, including the university president, are first-generation immigrants. The student body is also formed, to a large extent, by immigrants and children of immigrants.

In contrast with earlier portrayals, then, this book is written by insiders, both to the city and to the groups that have caused its transformation. Their knowledge and involvement in local events are tempered by scholarly discipline, yielding a perhaps less colorful but more accurate portrayal of different aspects of city life. Here is a book packed with information of interest to scholars and the lay public alike. Given the significance of Miami as a harbinger of American's urban future, it was long overdue.

Alejandro Portes

Notes

1. This is the title of Allman's book about the city and of numerous articles and newspaper editorials. See T.D. Allman, *Miami, City of the Future* (New York: Atlantic Monthly Press, 1987).

2. Alex Stepick, "The Business Community of Little Haiti," *Dialogue No. 32*, Occasional Paper Series (Latin American and Caribbean Center, Florida International University, 1984).

3. See, for example, Joan Didion, *Miami* (New York: Simon and Schuster, 1987).

1

Introduction

Guillermo J. Grenier
and Alex Stepick III

Miami is hot. Everyone sweats. All the time. It's sweltering. It's vibrant. It's tense and exotic. The "New Casablanca," says *Time* magazine. Essayists and novelists, the networks and newspapers, all have come to write and comment on Miami, to explore "Paradise Lost," as the *New York Times Magazine* lamented in 1988. People write about Miami as if it were a foreign land. It's not. It's the multicultural crest of the wave of the American future.

Miami is hot in all senses of the word. It is the hottest major city in the mainland United States with an average temperature year-round in the eighties. Its crime rate consistently competes for national honors, as does its college football team. Miami is the only U.S. city to have had four major black riots in the 1980s and the only one to receive, at the initiation of the decade, 125,000 new immigrants, many reputed to be criminals or homosexuals and mental health cases. Miami is the drug import capital of America. It is probably the only city whose entire economy would suffer if the Medellín cartel dissolved tomorrow.

In the beginning, Miami became a significant city precisely because it was hot. The physical climate established its two primary industries— agriculture and tourism. But these are hardly the most important aspects of Miami presently. Winter vegetables and fruits come to the states from Mexico and Chile now. Since the arrival of the jet age in the late 1950s winter tourists easily bypass Miami on their way to the Caribbean and Latin America.

Meanwhile, residents of the Caribbean and Latin America have been

1

coming to Miami, fundamentally transforming it from a secondary U.S. city to the economic, social, and sometimes even political capital of the Caribbean and Latin America. Miami now has the largest proportion of foreign-born residents of any U.S. city, one-third of its population compared to less than one-quarter for either New York or Los Angeles. It ranks second only to New York in foreign banks and international airlines, and Latin America's elite and middle classes shop in Miami more than anywhere else. Candidates for the Colombian presidency campaign in Miami, and the Nicaraguan Contra war was often planned over "tres leches" in Miami restaurants.

Yet, much of the old Miami persists. The largest firms are still owned and managed by Anglos. The most important political bodies are still dominated by Anglos. Most television, radio, and print media still use English predominantly, and most of those who use Spanish are owned by Anglos. Coral Gables, the elite city within the broader metropolitan area, remains principally Anglo while Miami Beach and North Miami continue to be Jewish. There is even a small group of octogenarian Stalinists on the beach, unrepentant Communist party members from the 1930s. Black Americans, Miami's first minority, continue to struggle even as they are forcibly mixed with other ethnic minorities.

If the intensity of diversity is, in fact, so magnified by the social dynamics of immigration and ethnicity, what can we learn about Miami to guide our analysis of society? The intrigue of the new Miami is precisely the same set of questions that has guided analysis of U.S. society throughout this century: Who rules? Who benefits? And how do newcomers fit in? In more precise terms, what is the nature of the local power structure? What are the origin and composition of the different social classes? And what is the situation of domestic and immigrant minorities and their process of assimilation in the urban mainstream?

Perhaps the closest parallel to the challenges faced by the current analysts of Miami can be drawn from the early experiences of the Chicago School of ethnic studies. Analysts of the Chicago experience in the first quarter of this century confronted the challenge of making sense of the urban experience and its relationship with the ethnic experience of immigrants. They applied the traditional tools of social problems analysis and succeeded in elevating the analysis of immigrants from one emphasizing their minority status into one emphasizing the cohesiveness inherent in an ethnic group.

It is the Chicago School of ethnic studies that established many of the terms that reverberated through countless other investigations. Immigrant groups are cohesive and exotic, best studied through case study–participant observation ethnography. Immigrant groups are also relatively powerless in a society dominated by established Americans. Indeed, through its emphasis on the process of assimilation, the Chicago School asserted that only by becoming part of the dominant culture could immigrants hope to exert meaningful influence over the social, political, and economic structures of a community.

Analysis of Miami turns the Chicago School on its head. While the Chicago School emphasized the assimilation and accommodation of immigrants, the budding Miami School highlights the domination of immigrants. While the Chicago School developed its paradigms by portraying the immigrants from the point of view of the established American society, the Miami analysts look at the impact of immigration from the perspective of the immigrant groups. For in Miami, these groups are not powerless in any general sense. Rather, immigrants in Miami exert power over significant aspects of the social structure, including city politics and some sectors of the economy.

Greater Miami has experienced a quarter century of profound changes that have transformed the city from a middle-sized tourist haven into a socially and economically complex metropolis. Miami has undergone the most dramatic ethnic transformation of any major American city in this century. The history of Miami since the early 1960s has been affected thoroughly by one particular phenomenon—immigration. In fact, the latter half of the twentieth century can be divided into two basic parts: before the immigrants and after the immigrants.

Before the 1960s, Miami's population consisted largely of black and white southern in-migrants and their descendants, transplanted northerners, including many Jews, and Bahamian and other Caribbean blacks and their descendants (Mohl 1983, 1986). In the past thirty years, a large number of Latins (primarily Cubans) and a substantial Haitian population have been added forcefully to the mix. As shown in figure 1.1, by 1980 Miami had the highest proportion of foreign-born population of the major metropolitan areas in the United States. Their impact has been so dramatic that it is doubtful that there is another urban area in the United States in which the theme of immigration has such a major presence in both private conversations and public discourse.

The two most striking changes since 1960 in Miami are a demographic shift from having virtually no immigrants at the end of the 1950s to a

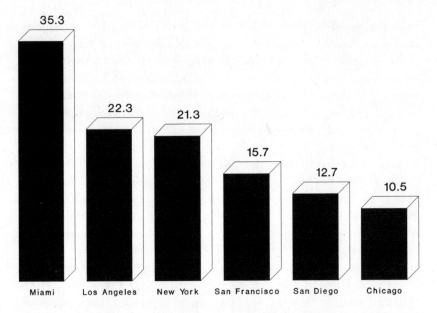

Fig. 1.1. Percent foreign-born population in major U.S. cities. *Source*: U.S. Census 1980.

plurality of immigrants by the mid 1980s, and an economic reorientation away from domestic tourism and toward a service- and finance-oriented economy that includes significant Latin American trade. The two transformations are associated, and that association amplifies their effects on the social structure of the area. Particularly critical demographic and economic considerations are the rapidity of the change; the racial composition of the two main immigrant flows, black Haitians and white Cubans; and the coincident timing of the civil rights movement and the arrival of the Cubans.

Demographics

Miami was incorporated in 1896, soon after Henry Flagler completed a railroad linking it to northern Florida and the rest of the East Coast. When the vote was taken to incorporate the city, 162 of the 368 persons who participated were black. All the officials elected at the time were white. In the early days, at the turn of the century, Bahamian immigrants provided the local, unskilled labor, and they outnumbered black Americans, who came to Miami primarily from northern Florida and Georgia.

But neither Bahamian blacks nor black Americans had significant political or economic power in early Miami. It was a southern city, one in which blacks were denied most basic rights: whites, including the police and the Ku Klux Klan, could harass and even kill blacks with impunity. Blacks could not swim in the ocean or in the public parks. They could not eat at the downtown lunch counters. They could not live in white areas.

Cubans fleeing Castro's Cuba, Miami's principal immigrant group, began arriving in significant numbers in the 1960s following the failure of the Bay of Pigs invasion. The flow has been largely one way. Once Cubans come to Miami, few return. The U.S. government encouraged and aided the flow by providing special immigration status and federal aid. While significant numbers of Cubans settled in New York and New Jersey, Miami was the preferred destination of the vast majority, making Cubans Miami's most visible minority. Their numbers were considerably increased by the Mariel boatlift of 1980, which brought 125,000 Cubans, the majority of whom settled in Miami. By 1990, there were nearly one million Latins in the area, just over 49 percent of the entire metropolitan population (see figs. 1.2 and 1.3). Latins outnumber all other groups in both the city of Miami and in Greater Miami, and in all likelihood they have already established an absolute demographic majority in Dade County since the census count. In contrast, the population of established resident white Americans has been decreasing relatively since 1960 and absolutely since 1970. From a 1950s peak of 85 percent, it will decline by 2,000 to around 30 percent of the total, barely more than blacks (fig. 1.2). This decrease will occur not just in the inner city, where the change is even more dramatic, but throughout the metropolitan area, including all of the suburbs and Miami's elite residential areas.

A second major immigrant group consists of blacks from various Caribbean islands. The largest concentration is of Haitians, who number approximately 70,000 in the Greater Miami area. There are also significant numbers of Bahamians, Jamaicans, and others from additional Caribbean islands. While the numbers of these immigrants are significantly fewer than those of Latins, they have contributed to the relative and absolute growth of Miami's black population. Between 1970 and 1980, Dade's black population grew by 47 percent, a growth rate exceeded only by Atlanta, making it one of only sixteen metropolitan areas with more than 300,000 blacks.

Just as the civil rights movement was beginning to be translated into

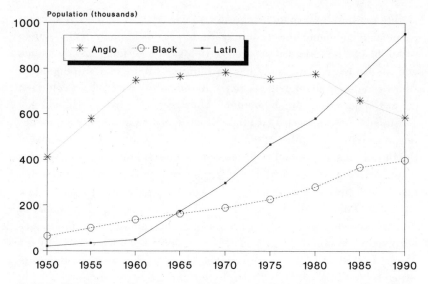

Fig. 1.2. Population and ethnicity in Dade County, 1950–90. *Sources*: Metro–Dade County Planning Department 1984; Wallace 1991.

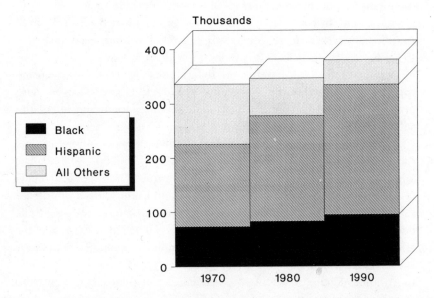

Fig. 1.3. Population of the City of Miami, 1970–90. *Sources*: Metro–Dade County Planning Department estimates 1988; Wallace 1991.

significant gains for blacks, Fidel Castro came to power in Cuba in 1960. In most cities blacks occupied center stage in the desegregation process. Their social and economic problems were given space in the press; they were of concern to public officials; they were discussed by black leaders; whites listened. And in most cities, blacks received much of the anti-poverty and community development money allocated to help relieve the situation. In Miami, however, the process of integrating blacks into the dominant culture was greatly complicated by the arrival of hundreds of thousands of Cubans and other Hispanics from Latin America and the islands of the Caribbean, many of them middle-class and looking as white as the resident white population.

The new arrivals were considered to be members of a minority group by virtue only of their foreign language. Given this status, however, they succeeded not only in diverting attention from Miami blacks during the crucial integration period but also, by virtue of their greater social acceptability and entrepreneurial skills, in winning the lion's share of public and private money available for minority economic development. The issue of what to do about black demands for inclusion and equality was preempted. For Miami, the major question became what to do about the Cubans.

This diverse ethnic mix has produced a confusing ethnic profile and labels as language, race, and nationality all independently vary. The majority of Cubans is phenotypically white and refuses to be contrasted with "white" Americans. Moreover, a high percentage of Cubans are U.S. citizens, and even for those who are not, Cuba is still geographically a part of the Americas. Hispanic is emerging as an ethnic identity among some, but these are primarily highly educated and politicized Cuban-Americans who seek affiliations outside of the Miami Cuban community. The term Latin is used almost exclusively by the Anglo elite, and virtually no one uses "Latino." Their predominant self-identification is as Cubans, just as Nicaraguans and other Latins commonly refer to themselves by a national label.

In contrast, native white Americans do not wish to be identified by the residual category "non-Hispanic whites." Anglo is a problematic category because a high percentage of this category is Jewish.

Similar categorical difficulties exist among African-Americans. The term African-American has the same problem as white American, since virtually all blacks in Miami are from the United States, the Caribbean, or Central America, all a part of the Americas. As with Latins, national identities predominate, such as Haitian or Jamaican. As mentioned, even those descended from Bahamians still recognize themselves as different even if they and their parents were born in the United States. Those who may be black and Latin tend to identify themselves as blacks from a particular country, e.g., black Cubans.

Because of this complexity, whatever labels we use will be either confusing or arbitrarily simple. Many times the source of data dictates the label. The United States Census, for example, refers to blacks and whites, which in Miami newspapers becomes non-Hispanic whites. We let the authors of each chapter determine what terms they want to use. Usually they have chosen non-Hispanic white, black, and Hispanic. When other terms are chosen, we hope that this brief discussion will clarify some of the confusion. But in fact not all of the confusion can be illuminated. The reality of Miami is simply complex, no matter what terms are used.

Economics

Miami's demographic growth has been closely associated with its economic cycles. The boom produced by the 1898 Spanish-American War was followed by a bust when the war concluded later that same year. Another boom began in the mid-1920s when developers hailed Miami throughout the northeastern United States as a tropical paradise. The devastating hurricane of 1926, which swept through Miami's flat, former swamplands and destroyed much of the rapidly constructed developments, initiated another bust. A few years later, Miami began to resurface as a favorite winter tourist spot and following World War II Miami was the most noted winter vacation resort for the eastern United States as show business personalities such as Arthur Godfrey and Jackie Gleason championed it on national television. Throughout this period, more and more people, most from the northeastern region of the country, and many retirees, made Miami their permanent home. As the proportion of tourists declined and that of retirees increased, Miami became more of a settled community. Those directly involved in the tourist industry declined, but the economy still remained service-oriented. Some light, locally oriented industry emerged, but the focus remained firmly on attracting more northerners and providing services for those who came bringing money from elsewhere.

At the end of the 1950s, direct air service to the Caribbean islands began to undermine Miami's tourism. The winter of 1958 brought both a national recession and a record cold spell in southern Florida. Tourists stayed away, many hotels went bankrupt, and the area began to wonder about its economic future. The Cuban Revolution in 1959 could not have come at a better time for the Miami economy.

Miami has been characterized by some as the vortex of the Caribbean (Garreau 1981) and even of the entire Latin American economies (Levine 1985). It always had a service-centered economy, but after the arrival of the Cubans, the focus of those services shifted from tourists and sojourners toward providing Latin America with financial services. During the 1960s, Miami displaced New Orleans as the country's principal trade outlet with Latin America. In 1980 one hundred multinational corporations had their Latin American headquarters in Miami. By 1982, it stood second only to New York as an international banking center. By the mid-1980s, its International Airport was the ninth busiest airport in the world in passengers and the sixth largest in air cargo tonnage. About 160,000 workers, one-fifth of its labor force, were directly or indirectly employed in airport and aviation activities. Moreover, the Port of Miami provided a base for over eighty-five steamship companies and was the largest cruise ship port in the world (Mohl 1985).

The recession of the early 1980s hit Miami, as it did the rest of the United States, and those sectors tied to Latin America were severely affected because the national recession coincided with even more severe difficulties in Miami's backyard, i.e., the Caribbean and Latin American economies. Nevertheless, partially because of the rise of the Cuban enclave, the area's economy has proven resilient in the face of shocks such as the Latin American debt crisis. The unemployment rate for Dade County was a relatively low 5.2 percent in late 1988.

By the late 1980s, Miami's industrial profile was similar to other newer American cities in which the economy was led by services, wholesale trade, finance, insurance, and real estate. The biggest occupational increases came among executives and in sales (Metro-Dade 1988). Overall white-collar jobs were increasing, while blue-collar jobs declined (Cruz 1990).

The only difference in Miami is in the answers to the basic questions posed above: Who rules? Who benefits? And how do newcomers fit in? Miami's Latins rule and benefit much more than Latins do in any other major U.S. city, although Anglos still exercise the most economic and political power.

Cubans played a pivotal role in Miami's economic transformation. They frequently headed the import and export companies, the banks that financed the transactions, and the smaller transportation and service companies that allowed goods and services to migrate. There are over 25,000 Hispanic businesses in Dade County. While the vast majority are small businesses that are the true engines of Miami's economic growth (Satterfield 1987), many of the most powerful economic corporations are Latin-owned and -operated. While Miami has only 5 percent of the U.S. Hispanic population, it has close to half of the forty largest Hispanic-owned industrial and commercial firms in the country. By the mid-1980s, 40 percent of Miami's banks were owned by Latins (Botifol 1985). There were Latin insurance companies, shipping firms, and innumerable import and export establishments. Some of the most important developers were Latins, one, Armando Codina, having become in the late 1980s the first Latin head of the Greater Miami Chamber of Commerce.

During the 1980s Cubans in Miami established pivotal local power, exercised through the increasing number of elected officials and such organizations as the Cuban American National Foundation, the Latin Builders Association and the Hispanic Builders Association, and the Latin Chamber of Commerce.[1] By the late 1980s, the city of Miami, along with numerous smaller municipalities in the metropolitan area, had Cuban-born mayors. The city manager and the county manager were Cubans. Cubans controlled the City Commission and constituted more than one-third of the Dade delegation to the state legislature. After Claude Pepper died, a Cuban, Ileana Ros-Lehtinen, won his U.S. House of Representatives seat. The authors of chapters 8 and 9 detail how and why these events came about. Our point here is simply to indicate that nowhere else in America, or even in American history, have first-generation immigrants so quickly, so thoroughly appropriated political power.

Three factors have been identified as promoting Miami Cuban economic and political activity: structural factors arising from the human capital Cubans brought with them and their geographical concentration in Miami (Portes and Bach 1985); the role of the U.S. government in providing aid to the arriving Cuban refugees (Pedraza-Bailey 1985); and the creation of a collective Cuban-American identity arising from the interplay of the U.S., state, and Cuban exile counterrevolutionary organizations (Forment, 1989).

Cubans did have a presence in Florida before the Cuban Revolution, as Lisandro Pérez discusses in chapter 5. Tampa has had a significant Cuban community since the turn of the century and the Spanish-American War, but as Miami grew after World War II, it became more of a focal point than Tampa. There was even a settled community of middle-class Cubans in Miami before the revolution.

The first wave of Cubans has been labeled the "Golden Exiles," the top level of Cuban society, who were most immediately threatened by a socialist revolution. Many had already established a footing in the United States, and when the revolution came, they simply abandoned one of their residences for another across the Straits of Florida. A Cuban shoe manufacturer, of Suave Shoes, for example, produced footwear for Sears, a major U.S. retail chain, before the revolution. He obtained his working capital from New York financial houses. After the revolution, the only change that occurred was that the manufacturing was done in Miami rather than Havana (Stepick and Fernandez-Kelly 1987). The Cuban Revolution made success available for him and many other exiles in a way that has not occurred for upper-class Mexicans or Puerto Ricans. The revolution thus biased upwardly the socioeconomic profile of Miami's Cuban population. Even if they could not transfer their investments, their human capital— their knowledge and experience—came with them.

Second, the U.S. government created an unprecedented direct and indirect assistance program for the arriving Cubans. The Cuban Refugee Program spent nearly $1 billion between 1965 and 1976 (Pedraza-Bailey 1985:41). The federal government provided transportation costs from Cuba, financial assistance to needy refugees and to state and local public agencies that provided services for refugees, and employment and professional training courses for refugees. Even in programs not especially designed for them, Cubans seemed to benefit. From 1968 to 1980, Latinos (almost all Cubans) received 46.9 percent of all Small Business Administration loans in Dade County (Porter and Dunn 1984:196).

Even more important was indirect assistance. Throughout the 1960s, the University of Miami had the largest CIA station in the world outside of the organization's headquarters in Virginia. With perhaps as many as 12,000 Cubans in Miami on their payroll at one point in the early 1960s, the CIA was one of the largest employers in Florida. It supported what was described as the third largest navy in the world and over fifty front businesses: CIA boat shops, CIA gun shops, CIA travel agencies, CIA detective agencies, and CIA real-estate agencies (Rich 1974:7–9; Didion 1987:90–91; Rieff 1987:193–207). This investment served far more to boost the Cubans in Miami economically than it did to destabilize the Castro regime.

This favorable reception by the U.S. government translated itself not only into millions of dollars of resettlement assistance but also into a "direct line" of Cuban exile leaders to the centers of political power in Washington. Unlike other immigrant and ethnic minorities who had to struggle painfully for years or even generations to gain "access" to the corridors of power, this access was available to Cuban leaders almost from the start.

This window of opportunity greatly boosted the Cubans in the 1960s and the Miami economy in general. Waves of Cuban immigrants stimulated demand and received substantial subsidies from the federal government. With a high rate of labor force participation, especially among women, the Cubans also contributed significantly to productivity growth. The recession of 1973–74 even had an indirect benefit for Cubans. Construction, one of the growth sectors during the boom, almost completely collapsed, spurring many American residents to flee Dade County. In the subsequent recovery of the late 1970s a de facto segmentation of the industry emerged, with Latins becoming the leaders in home construction and American resident whites maintaining dominance in large-scale commercial construction. This division reflected an even more important development within the community: the emergence of the Cuban enclave or institutionally complete community, discussed by Lisandro Pérez. Compared to American blacks, Cubans in Miami have a far greater likelihood of being able to work with coethnics, shop in stores owned and operated by coethnics, and obtain professional services from coethnics.

There is equally no doubt that not all Miami Cubans are rich and powerful businesspersons, as indicated in figures 1.4 and 1.5, and Guillermo Grenier discusses this in his contribution. Even the fact of business ownership is somewhat misleading. Of the nearly 25,000 Latino-owned and -operated businesses in 1982, only 12 percent had paid employees and together they generated a total of only 18,199 paid jobs (Diaz-Briquets 1984), a number only slightly higher than the number of Latins in Dade County who belong to unions. Moreover, most of the Latin employment growth during the 1970s was directly attributable to population growth. Latins (as well as blacks) were underrepresented in Miami's fastest growing industries, especially financial services, which were dominated by white Americans (Cruz 1990:17). As shown in figure 1.4, the non-Hispanic white abandonment of Dade County that began in the 1970s was class-selective. Non-Hispanic white laborers and production workers left in great numbers, while higher-class workers, notably executives and

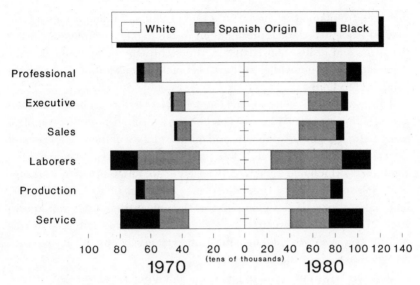

Fig. 1.4. Occupations of employed persons, Dade County, 1970 and 1980. *Source*: Metro–Dade County Planning Department 1984.

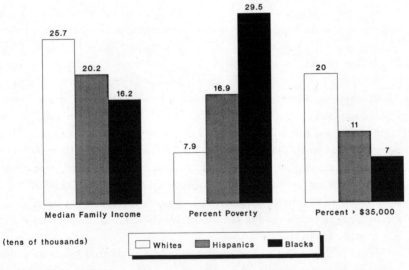

Fig. 1.5. Income, affluence, and poverty, Dade County, 1980. *Source*: Metro–Dade Planning Department 1984.

managers, remained or moved into Dade County. Although Latins (and blacks) expanded their representation in the higher occupations during the 1970s and 1980s, non-Hispanic whites still outnumbered them. Similarly, non-Hispanic whites still are economically advantaged as a group compared to Latins.

The region's emergence as the capital of the Caribbean has reinforced demographic trends. Miami is now the most desired migration point of many Latins, especially the elite and middle classes of the Caribbean and Central America. In the late 1980s, as the United States abandoned the Contra war (which had been largely based in Miami), a broader, working-class flow emerged, first from Nicaragua, then from other Central American nations as well as Colombia, the Dominican Republic, and Puerto Rico. Meanwhile, the frustrations of democracy in Haiti increased migration pressures there, although the United States continued its policies designed to repress the Haitian flow.

In summary, in the span of just one generation Miami has gone from a declining tourist and retirement center with few foreigners to the capital of the Caribbean with proportionately more foreigners than any other U.S. city. This transformation occurred precisely as black Americans were beginning to achieve civil rights that had been denied them since the city's founding at the end of the last century. The new white immigrants, the Cubans, soon received the benefits of being a minority. While blacks have experienced some progress, the white Cuban immigrants have leaped over blacks, quickly garnering political and economic gains that still elude black Americans.

The response by many white Americans has been to abandon the city, while others fight to reestablish the old order in which U.S.-born Americans completely dominate socially, politically, and economically. White flight decreased the number of non-Latin whites in Dade County by 24.4 percent between 1980 and 1990 (U.S. Census 1990, in Wallace 1991).

While Haitians are new immigrants, too, and have received some special attention because they are also defined as a minority, they have been nowhere nearly as fortunate as Cubans. Black Haitians have struggled simply to be allowed to remain in the United States and to have the opportunity to survive.

Miami is thus riven by two fundamental divisions: black versus white and U.S.-born Americans versus immigrants. The former was established at the city's founding and persists in spite of the recent transformations. The latter emerged only recently but is nonetheless profound as it provides new answers to the old questions of who rules, who benefits, and how immigrants fit in.

Miami, like most large urban areas, is hardly a coherent, harmonious, integrated community. Struggle, diversity, and social change mark it and its constituent components: Anglos, black Americans, Cubans, Haitians, and all the others. In this book we examine the diversity of Miami's constituent communities, the economic and demographic differences, the class differences, the political struggles, and the symbolic and linguistic battles. The authors all live and work in Miami. They all study Miami partly out of professional curiosity and partly out of the conviction that in a significant way they are looking into the future. Miami now gives us a glimpse of America tomorrow.

Anthony Maingot's article details Miami's function as the unofficial capital of the Caribbean. Like all capitals, Miami serves as the hub of the flow of capital, goods, and people throughout the region. Maingot explores the social, economic, and moral implications of this pivotal position.

Marvin Dunn and Alex Stepick explore the history, experience, and frustration of American blacks in Miami. As in many communities throughout America, blacks served as the economic backbone of the nascent city. The early struggles served to establish the solid foundations of a community ready to embrace the rewards promised by the civil rights victories of the 1960s. Instead, the community confronted the first massive immigrant influx of a predominantly white minority, the Cubans, who used the political openings of the civil rights movement to advance over the blacks.

Lisandro Pérez explores the economic, political, cultural, and social dynamics of the Cuban community, a community that serves as the axis of Miami's transformation. The Cubans transpose many common stereotypes of Hispanic immigrants: they are white, primarily middle class, and politically conservative. They are America's most successful Hispanic group, and unlike almost all other American immigrants they have achieved success in one generation.

Alex Stepick provides a detailed analysis of the immigrant experience of a black ethnic group, the Haitians. Unlike the Cuban immigrant experience, the Haitians were victims of persecution and discrimination. Yet, perseverance and alliances allowed formation of a growing and deceptively diverse community. Although not politically strong, the Haitians are a significant symbol of the diversity of Miami, what Stepick terms a triple minority: black, foreign, and linguistically creole.

Max Castro analyzes the significance of Miami as the wellspring of both bilingualism and antibilingualism. In Miami, language is an emotional and symbolic issue that encapsulates social and political struggles and changes. Castro identifies how white, working-class Americans attempt to reestablish cultural hegemony in the name of American values through the politics of language. He contrasts the response of white American elites who would rather switch than fight but still resent the public use of Spanish in Miami.

Guillermo Grenier explores the little-known differentiation within the Cuban community revealing that, despite their success, most Cubans are not successful entrepreneurs but rather working-class people with working-class interests who are active in the labor movement. Yet, anticommunism remains hegemonic, a fact to which other interests must adapt.

John Stack and Christopher Warren present a unique analysis of the reality of thoroughly ethnic politics in Miami. They detail how formal political structures change under pressure in the name of fairness and equity but remain a method through which white Americans attempt to retain power.

Dario Moreno and Nicol Rae describe the dynamics of a specific political campaign in which the elements of ethnic solidarity and party politics interact to polarize the community. The campaign that saw Ileana Ros-Lehtinen become the first Cuban-American congressional representative is a case study of politics that became ethnically polarized in spite of the elite's efforts to neutralize the issue of ethnicity.

Note

1. Incidentally, the Cuban-American members of Miami's power structure appear to have class, economic, and even sectoral interests similar to those of the local non-Cuban and elites in other cities. They are substantial businesspersons or executives, especially those concerned with real estate and development. See Stepick, Castro, Dunn, and Grenier 1990.

References

Botifol, Luis J. 1985. "How Miami's New Image Was Created." Occasional Paper Number 1985-1, Institute of Interamerican Studies, University of Miami.

Cruz, Robert David. 1990. "The Industry Composition of Production and the Distribution of Income by Race and Ethnicity in Miami." Unpublished paper, Department of Economics, Florida International University, Miami.

Diaz-Briquets, Sergio. 1984. "Cuban-Owned Businesses in the United States." *Cuban Studies* 14, no. 2 (Summer): 57–68.

Didion, Joan. 1987. *Miami*. New York: Simon and Schuster.

Forment, Carlos A. 1989. "Political Practice and the Rise of an Ethnic Enclave: The Cuban American Case, 1959–1979." *Theory and Society* 18: 47–81.

Garreau, Joel. 1981. *The Nine Nations of North America*. New York: Houghton-Mifflin.

Levine, Barry B. 1985. "The Capital of Latin America." *Wilson Quarterly* (Winter): 46–73.

Metro–Dade County Planning Department. 1984. *Profile of the Black Population*. Miami: Research Division, Metro–Dade County Planning Department.

————. 1988. "Changes in Employment and Occupations: Dade County, Florida: 1980–1987." Unpublished paper (September 14). Miami: Metro–Dade County Planning Department.

Mohl, Raymond. 1983. "Miami: The Ethnic Cauldron." In *Sunbelt Cities: Politics and Growth since World War II*, edited by R.M. Bernard and B.R. Rice, 67–72. Austin: University of Texas Press.

————. 1985. "An Ethnic 'Boiling Pot': Cubans and Haitians in Miami." *Journal of Ethnic Studies* 13, no. 2 (Summer): 51–74.

————. 1986. "The Politics of Ethnicity in Contemporary Miami." *Migration World* 14, no. 3.

Pedraza-Bailey, Silvia. 1985. *Political and Economic Migrants in America: Cubans and Mexicans*. Austin: University of Texas Press.

Porter, Bruce, and Marvin Dunn. 1984. *The Miami Riot of 1980: Crossing the Bounds*. Lexington, Mass.: Lexington Books, D.C. Heath and Company.

Portes, Alejandro, and Robert L. Bach. 1985. *Latin Journey: Cuban and Mexican Immigrants in the United States*. Berkeley: University of California Press.

Rich, Cynthia Jo. 1974. "Pondering the Future: Miami's Cubans after 15 Years." *Race Relations Reporter* 5, no. 21 (November): 7–9.

Rieff, David. 1987. *Going to Miami: Exiles, Tourists, and Refugees in the New America*. Boston: Little, Brown.

Satterfield, David. 1987. "Growth Is on Rise; Focus Is in Dade." Special Report, Outlook '87, *Miami Herald*, January 19: 29–31.

Stepick, Alex, and Maria Patricia Fernandez-Kelly. 1987. Unpublished fieldnotes from interviews on informal sector in Miami.

Stepick, Alex, Max Castro, Marvin Dunn, and Guillermo Grenier. 1990. "Changing Relations among Newcomers and Established Residents: The Case of Miami, Final Report." Center for Labor Research and Studies, Florida International University, Miami.

U.S. Bureau of the Census. 1984. *Detailed Population Characteristics, Florida*. Series PC80 = 1-D1-A. Washington: U.S. Government Printing Office.

Wallace, Richard, 1991. "South Florida Grows to a Latin Beat." *Miami Herald*, March 6, 1A.

2

Immigration from the Caribbean Basin

Anthony P. Maingot

Legal and constitutional responsibility for immigration policy resides with the federal government. Living with the immigrants—their contributions and their problems—occurs, however, on a regional and local level. Moreover, each region of the United States contains different immigrant groups and thus different problems. Florida is no exception. This state faces America's "Third Frontier," the Caribbean Basin, and is most intimately involved with the challenges facing that area. Along with all other regions, Florida confronts the fact that immigration is a problem of law, economics, and heart or attitudes.

The third matter is not as intangible as one would suspect: the whole history of the United States has been one of "opening its heart" to immigrants. "Once I thought to write a history of the immigrants in America," wrote Oscar Handlin, "then I discovered that the immigrants *were* American history" (Handlin 1951:3). What has varied is the degree of openness and the groups to whom that heart has been open. Milton Gordon has described well the various "theories" of assimilation that have dominated different periods of American history and the prejudices and discriminations that accompanied each (Gordon 1964). On the one hand, the United States has long been antagonistic, if not consistently repressive, toward aliens deemed "radicals," regardless of the interpretation of that term (Higham 1963). But it has also been the American experience that both the host society and the immigrant soon realize whether the atmosphere is an understanding and generous one or not. In this sense the "host society" is not some vague semi-anthropomorphic allusion. It refers to a dominant American societal sentiment. As Milton Gordon noted: "The white Protestant American is rarely conscious of the fact that he inhabits a group at all. He inhabits America. The others live in groups" (Gordon 1964:5). In other words, it is this dominant host group that makes evident whether immigrants are seen to represent an opportunity—for them and for the host society—or a problem for both.

This process begins, at least analytically, at the national level where, as figure 2.1 indicates, a complex array of federal agencies sets immigration policy. These agencies think and act with more than heart and respond to more than just regional attitudes, wishes, and interests. Their primary concerns, more often than not, are national constitutional, political, and geopolitical realities of immigration.

There have been three structural changes in the nature of immigration to the United States since 1960. First, the 1965 changes to the Immigration and Nationality Act of 1952 brought about a substantial increase in legal immigration. Abolishing the national origin quotas and giving priority to the principle of family reunification contributed to the increased numbers of immigrants. Along with this increase came a shift in the national origin of the immigrants. Both these changes in turn had profound impacts on immigration to south Florida. Between 1960 and 1980 the share of European immigration declined from 70 percent to 15 percent, while that of Asians and Hispanics increased from 25 percent to 80 percent. The third structural change was the substantial increase in illegal immigration.

It is clear that each of these structural changes was enough to affect the host society's perceptions and attitudes. Yet, it was a series of dramatic events in 1980 that influenced the federal government's decision to again reform immigration policy in the mid-1980s. No sooner had Congress passed the Refugee Act in 1980 in an attempt to eliminate geopolitical considerations from refugee and asylum decisions, than thousands of Cubans and Haitians began arriving on the shores of south Florida. The government, unable to say that all the Cubans were legitimate refugees and/or none of the Haitians were, sidestepped the "refugee" issue and created a one-time status entitled "Cuban-Haitian Special Entrant" (Gonzalez Baker, 1990). No policy area as important as immigration can be managed on exceptions, however. The need for some clarity was evident in the mid-1980s. Pushed by a growing public perception that the nation's immigration policy was out of control, Congress began debating a reform to the law.

The Immigration Reform and Control Act (IRCA) was finally passed in

Department of Justice	Department of State		
Immigration and Naturalization Service (INS)	Bureau of Consular Affairs	Bureau of Refugee Affairs	Bureau of Human Rights and Humanitarian Affairs
Inspections, Adjudications, Admissions, Enforcement	Immigrant and Non-Immigrant Visas: U.S. Passports	Refugee Admissions, Relief, Aid, Crisis Planning and Response	Asylum Advisories

Department of Labor	Department of Health and Human Services	Department of Treasury	
Employment and Training Administration	Family Support Administration	Bureau of Customs	U.S. Coast Guard
Labor Certification for Immigrants	Refugee Resettlement (in the U.S.)	Enforcement (Ports of Entry)	Enforcement (Interdiction)

Fig. 2.1. Current government organizational structure for migration affairs. *Source*: Commission for the Study of International Migration and Cooperative Economic Development 1990:28.

October 1986. Put in the starkest terms, the intent of IRCA was to reduce illegal immigration. It proposed to do so by, first, legalizing illegals through two mechanisms—providing amnesty to illegals who could demonstrate continuous residence in the United States since January 1, 1982, and allowing the adjustment of immigration status of certain illegals who had worked in agriculture—and second, imposing sanctions on employers who knowingly hired illegal workers.

By late 1990 there was evidence that the amnesty part of IRCA worked: approval rates for the approximately 3 million illegals who applied for legalization were running above 95 percent. As an authoritative study on the issue notes, "it is not unreasonable to expect that more than 2.7 million undocumented aliens will eventually be approved for temporary residence" (Bean, Vernez, and Keely 1989:68). As far as slowing down illegal migration to the United States, however, there is no evidence that employer sanctions had any impact.

These, then, are the broad outlines of the national legal and sociological context of immigration policy in the 1990s. In terms of practical results, we can sum up the policy as follows: expansion of the flow of legal immigrants through the legalization measures and continuance of family reunification preferences. This trend was given additional vigor when in late 1990 President George Bush signed into law an expansion of the quota of legal immigrants from 500,000 to 700,000 per year. Additionally, the number of skilled worker visas was increased from 55,000 to 140,000 per year. The latter change reflects the pressure to secure the kind of talent required by the postindustrial society, talent that is not being produced by U.S. universities. There is no expectation that these increases in legal immigration will reduce the large flows of undocumented aliens. It is also a plausible assumption that a good proportion of both legal and illegal immigrants will continue to come from Latin America and the Caribbean. This is the context that Florida decision makers should keep in mind as they confront a series of public queries, in which the question of "how many?" will probably be uppermost.

How Many? A Question of Perceptions

Each region tends to feel overwhelmed by the immigration problem. In south Florida immigration is a matter of constant debate. Nervous glances are cast at the nearby Caribbean Basin: Mexico, Central America, the insular Caribbean, Colombia, and Venezuela. The historical records show two relevant trends in this region. First, there is an extremely fast rate of population growth, from a population of 55 million in 1940 to 166 million in 1980. Second, the Caribbean Basin's share of total immigration to the United States has been increasing, from 19.3 percent between 1951 and 1960 to 35.5 percent between 1971 and 1980 and 30.6 percent between 1981 and 1985 (see table 2.1). From 1971 to 1980, Caribbean Basin immigrants represented 86.6 percent of all immigrants from Latin America (Pastor 1989:6).

Certainly, all this sounds ominous to those concerned with the question, "how many?" And yet, if we disregard unusual circumstances such as the Mariel boatlift of 1980, we note that Florida is not the intended residence of most immigrants. In fact, in 1985 Florida ranked a distant fourth in terms of the intended residence of immigrants to the United

Table 2.1. Caribbean Migration to the United States: The Reciprocal Impact

Country	Population	Total immigration, 1950–83	Estimated illegal population in the U.S.	Migrants to the U.S. as % of home population
Cuba	9,771,000	910,867	—	9.3
Dominican Republic	5,762,000	318,644	225,000	9.4
Haiti	6,000,000	132,610	400,000	8.9
Commonwealth Caribbean				
Barbados	252,000	38,183	25,000	25.1
Guyana	795,000	80,462	—	10.1
Jamaica	2,225,000	288,464	250,000	21.4
Trinidad and Tobago	1,176,000	100,305	60,000	13.6
Total Caribbean	25,981,000	1,869,535	960,000	10.0

Source: Pastor 1985: 12.

States: only 6.5 percent (36,833) intended to reside in Florida compared to 27.3 percent (155,403) in California, 18.4 percent (104,734) in New York, and 7.7 percent (43,915) in Texas (U.S. Bureau of Census 1986).

Additionally, in per capita terms, the Miami-Hialeah area, the area of Florida with the greatest concentration of immigrants, ranked sixth in terms of immigrants (7.9 per thousand inhabitants) after Jersey City (13.5 per thousand), San Francisco (11.2 per thousand), New York (10.8 per thousand), San Jose (9.2 per thousand), and Honolulu (8.1 per thousand).

But what about illegal aliens? While it is exceedingly difficult to measure the number of illegal immigrants in the United States or any of its regions, the existing studies do indicate that Florida is low on the list (Passel and Woodrow 1984). The 1980 census calculated that Florida had 3.9 percent of all illegal immigrants in the United States, fifth behind California (49.8 percent), New York (11.4 percent), Texas (9.0 percent), and Illinois (6.6 percent). Florida also ranked sixth in terms of numbers of applicants seeking legalization under IRCA (Bean, Vernez, and Keely 1989).

What, then, accounts for the perception of a threat from massive immigration in the state of Florida and particularly in the Miami area? One approach is to understand the difference between those immigrant flows that are constant and continuous ("structural") and those that are occasional, dramatic, and responsive to particular crises in a sending country. The former type is by far the more important because it is the flow that establishes the social networks that make the area a desirable destination. This structural flow is discussed below.

It is the occasional, "catastrophic" flow that engenders the greatest fear and generates the most problems. One of the basic problems created by this type of flow is legal: the migration that results from such calamities often does not fall under any legal category. Yet precisely because it results from some calamity—political or economic—the immigrants cannot be easily dismissed as "illegal" or deportable aliens.

These sudden and unexpected "catastrophic" flows also tend to impact individual communities much more than states or even regions. Thus, south Florida (and in particular Miami) has taken the brunt of the Cuban, Haitian, and Nicaraguan migrations. Invariably these movements tend to reflect unstable—political and/or economic—circumstances in the home countries. Evidence of this phenomenon can be obtained from the statistics on nonimmigrant "overstays": illegal actions by people who have already gone through the rigorous in-country screening that precedes the granting of any kind of visa to enter the United States.

The statistics in table 2.2 are in many ways a measure of the instability of Caribbean Basin societies; their overstay rates are invariably much higher than the overall average. Florida officials do have to take note that these overstays are not purely a matter of perceptions: Florida does rank third as a destination of overstays, after New York and California (Bean, Edmonston, and Passel 1990).

There is an important regional difference here. Caribbean Basin illegals tend to overstay legal nonimmigrant visas, whereas Mexicans predominate among those who enter without inspection (EWIs). Certainly this is largely a matter of geography and accessibility: the difference between a land boundary and dangerous ocean currents. But there are other differences. Visa overstays put pressure on the legal channels, bringing the whole process of nonimmigrant visa granting under a cloud of suspicion. Because these trends in immigration from the Caribbean appear to be ongoing rather than crisis-driven, it is important that the processes underlying these trends be understood.

Structural Aspects of Migration from the Caribbean

At least as regards the Caribbean, demographic and economic conditions have combined with social and cultural factors to create a history of migration best called "structural," as distinct from time- or event-fixed. The direction of the flow and the magnitude might have varied occasionally, but the general "push" factors in the Caribbean have been constant, and the general movement will continue to be constant until such pressures subside. Because it is driven by both material forces (geography, demography, and economics) and because it is now an integral part of Caribbean consciousness, high rates of migration will most probably continue into the near future (Kritz, Keely, and Tomasi 1981).

Given this reality, it seems reasonable to look at the factors that led initially and sustain today this condition of structural migration. The analysis here is limited to legal migration, which as an important part of Caribbean Basin migration gives us more accurate figures as well as being a window onto official U.S. policy. It is fair to assume, however, that where the pressures for legal migration are great so are the pressures for illegal movements.

It is calculated that during the late 1970s and early 1980s, some 80

Table 2.2. Estimated Legally Resident Foreign-Born Population by Country of Birth, June 1988
(populations in thousands, all numbers rounded independently)

| Country or region of birth | Legally resident foreign-born | | | Legal immigration, April 1980– June 1988 | Applicants for legal status (I-687s) | Emigration, 1980–88 |
	Total (1) = (2) + (3)	Alien (2)	Citizen (3)			
All countries	12,084	5,965	6,119	4,991	1,745	1,097
North America	3,666	2,433	1,233	1,665	1,521	414
Mexico	1,400	1,195	205	565	1,219	107
Other North America	2,266	1,238	1,028	1,100	303	307
South America	466	335	131	330	74	73
Europe	5,283	1,450	3,833	544	33	267
Asia (total)	2,460	1,629	831	2,282	82	272
China and Korea	744	454	290	643	21	X
Philippine Islands	515	292	223	394	19	X
Other Asia	1,201	882	318	1,244	42	X
Africa and Oceania	209	119	90	171	36	71

Source: Bureau of the Census, Population Division, 1989.
Note: Data on I-687 applications for legal status were provided by Michael Hoefer, Immigration and Naturalization Service, Statistical Office, and are based on applications filed and processed as of May 9, 1989.

Table 2.3. Estimated Nonimmigrant Overstays, by Area and Selected Country of Citizenship, 1985–88
(numbers rounded independently)

Area or Country	Estimated overstays				Percentage overstay			
	1985	1986	1987	1988	1985	1986	1987	1988
Total	217,300	242,700	226,500	254,200	2.4	2.4	1.9	1.9
North America	79,300	94,900	98,600	117,700	4.1	5.1	4.7	5.1
Canada	9,400	6,800	6,400	6,300	18.8	15.4	15.2	17.7
Mexico	24,700	32,900	41,200	55,800	2.8	4.3	4.7	5.9
Bahamas	5,200	7,100	5,400	2,300	2.6	3.2	2.1	0.8
Barbados	700	600	1,200	1,000	3.3	2.8	4.1	3.0
Bermuda	300	400	500	500	17.7	23.4	21.7	29.4
Cuba	1,600	1,000	700	300	13.1	25.7	17.8	11.5
Dominica	600	1,600	2,200	3,000	6.3	4.8	3.4	3.9
Dominican Republic	2,900	2,900	1,700	3,000	3.8	4.2	3.2	4.8
Grenada	300	400	600	500	11.7	11.6	13.9	11.4
Haiti	12,800	14,300	11,800	14,300	15.0	16.6	13.8	16.0
Jamaica	5,800	5,900	4,500	3,600	4.6	4.0	2.6	1.8
Trinidad and Tobago	1,100	2,500	5,500	7,500	1.3	3.5	6.8	8.4
Total, Central America	10,100	15,200	12,500	16,100	3.6	4.9	3.7	4.4
Belize	800	900	700	900	8.2	8.8	6.1	7.3
Costa Rica	100	300	200	100	0.3	0.5	0.3	0.1
El Salvador	2,100	3,000	2,200	2,300	4.1	5.7	3.9	4.1
Guatemala	2,900	4,400	3,400	4,000	4.4	6.4	4.1	4.1
Honduras	1,800	2,800	2,000	2,100	3.6	5.1	3.3	3.2
Nicaragua	2,500	2,700	2,900	4,500	12.2	14.2	14.0	18.3
Panama	300	1,100	1,200	2,300	0.6	2.3	2.4	4.3
Other North America	3,200	3,300	4,600	3,500	4.8	4.3	4.9	3.5
South America	15,300	18,100	13,800	18,800	1.9	1.9	1.4	1.9

percent of all immigrants to the United States came from Latin America and Asia. Proportionally, however, the nations of the Caribbean Basin— and the insular Caribbean in particular—provided the largest share. Korea, with 41 million people, sent 29,248 immigrants to the United States in 1979; the nations of the insular Caribbean (excluding Mexico, Venezuela, and Colombia) represent 39 million people but sent 92,000 legal immigrants to the United States that same year. Korea sent 711 per million, the average for Europe was 125 per million, while for the Caribbean Basin it was 1150 per million and much higher than that from the island states. While the European share of total legal immigrants went from 59 percent from 1951 to 1960 to 19 percent from 1971 to 1980, the West Indian share climbed from 5 percent to 18 percent. The Haitian share went up from 0.7 percent from 1957 to 1961 to 3.6 percent from 1967 to 1971 and then declined a bit to 3 percent from 1972 to 1976 (Pastor 1985).

The important thing to keep in mind is that the movement of Caribbean people to the United States has been constant and from the area as a whole, regardless of economic system or political regime. This is where perceptions need correcting. While it is true that close to 10 percent of the Cuban population left Cuba, the same percentage has left the Dominican Republic and much larger percentages have migrated from Barbados and Jamaica. There are, of course, important differences between these populations and the reasons for their immigration. But, if the question is "how many?," the answer is that since they come from the whole area, regardless of political-economic system, chances are that the "push" factors will continue to operate. It is impossible to predict an end to this movement.

Clearly and evidently, the more vicious aspects of the racial bias that characterized so much of U.S. immigration policy up to 1965 have abated visibly, while other less desirable legacies also appear to be in fast retreat today. Caribbean people visit the United States in extraordinary numbers, demonstrating voluntarily a preference for the United States over other possible destinations.

It is good to remember, however, that despite this past racial bias and despite the fact that the numbers of Caribbean people arriving now are greater, the movement has a long history. It takes time for any such movement to assume the structural features that Caribbean migration has today. We can identify five important dimensions to that structural reality that are best characterized as giving shape to a "pull" syndrome.

1. *The Caribbean is a self-contained geographical space.* No major

mountain barriers or unmanageable bodies of water separate potential immigrants from their North American destinies. Even the Caribbean Sea flows like a river from south to north, as do the constant winds that are part of this stream. Historically, when and where Caribbean men and women could not walk to their destinations, they rowed or sailed. That they still do is evident in the fantastic trek of Haitian sailboats from the island through the Bahamas to Florida and—even more spectacularly—to as far as Guadeloupe. The Haitian case is particularly poignant. Despite an active interdiction program enacted in September 1981 by the U.S. Coast Guard, Haitians keep attempting the perilous crossing. Similarly, the numbers making the very dangerous crossing from the Dominican Republic to Puerto Rico have been increasing, as have the numbers perishing in the attempts.

2. *The movement to the United States tends to be preceded by earlier moves, very often to sites of U.S.-financed or -managed job opportunities.* For instance, the building of the Panama Canal drew large numbers of West Indians to that site. Just from Barbados, 20,000 men were recruited, which was 10 percent of the island population and 40 percent of all adult males. But as David McCullough writes, "for every man who was picked to go to Panama there were five or more others eager for the chance" (McCullough 1977:475). From Panama, the West Indians moved to work in American-owned banana plantations and build British or American-owned railroads in the rest of Central America. West Indians also worked on U.S.-owned plantations in Cuba and the Dominican Republic (Del Castillo n.d.). It is an interesting footnote to the story of Caribbean migration that three of the significant protagonists of Grenadian politics in the 1960s, 1970s, and 1980s (Eric Gairy, Maurice Bishop, and Herbert Blaize) all either grew up or worked at the same time at the U.S.-owned oil refinery in Aruba. The man accused of murdering Bishop, Bernard Coard, was a graduate of Brandeis University.

This historical experience of West Indians with migration and with U.S. capital and business abroad created three additional characteristics, each critical for an understanding of the "structural" nature of Caribbean migration.

a. The very nature of the "open," export-oriented economies of the area familiarized Caribbean people with alien—especially American—people and customs. Even the lamentable U.S. expansionism and military interventions in the Caribbean, which have resulted in definitely negative ideological legacies and reverberations, ironically also generated contacts and familiarity. It is a Caribbean-wide fact that the often virulent anti-Americanism of the intellectuals is rarely shared wholeheartedly by the majority and certainly not by the skilled workers and middle classes who are unambiguous in their preference for the United States as a destination. In the 1970s, between 60 percent and 70 percent of the Caribbean emigrants were professionals, managers, and skilled workers. Contemporary development policies in the Caribbean Basin have done nothing to change the "open" nature of economies and thus of immigration flows.

   b. An attitude developed that migrating was the best avenue for success and that exercising such an option was a "right." There was and is today group approval for individual decisions to migrate, and there are group expectations about remittances and future sponsorships of others. The immigrant's so-called "guilt of abandonment" complex about which sociologists hypothesize is nonexistent in the Caribbean.

   It makes no sense for Caribbean governments to ridicule or lament the "visa mentality" of their people, much less to attempt to curtail its exercise. This was a lesson learned by some of the more totalitarian-minded of the People's Revolutionary Government (PRG) in Grenada, who toyed briefly in the early 1980s with the idea of restricting immigration by creating a Cuban-style "army of work." The public's response quickly disabused them of any such plans.

   c. Because it is a relatively old migration, there exist—in Miami and other regions—in the 1980s the necessary social-cultural enclaves. Enclaves are those social networks that attract others and facilitate their entry and success. These enclaves were built either directly in the United States or in the intermediate, U.S.-controlled areas in the Caribbean. As important as these latter "stepping-stone" migrations to the United States were, there was of course a significant direct movement from the West Indies to the United States, despite the racially biased immigration system in operation from 1900 to 1910. During that decade, 30,000 West Indians arrived; from 1910 to 1920, some 60,000; and during the 1920s an additional 40,000. By 1930, West Indian blacks were about 1 percent of the U.S. black population and about 25 percent of the population of Harlem. As shown in table 2.3, the numbers of Caribbean Basin—including especially insular Caribbean—immigrants legally in the United States (listed under "Other North America") are large in absolute and relative terms. Additionally, their rates of naturalization are very high: four times higher than that of Mexican immigrants for instance. This naturalization rate is an indication of Caribbean Basin immigrants' integration into the U.S. system. Caribbean networks are strong; they operate to attract other immigrants. The presence of such "critical masses" was both cause and effect of the third structural feature of Caribbean migration.

3. *Caribbean men and women have been successfully assimilated into the United States.* Thomas Sowell notes that as early as 1901, West Indians owned 20 percent of the black businesses in Manhattan and were represented beyond their numbers in the professions, while second-generation West Indians have higher incomes than U.S. blacks and whites and have below average unemployment rates. West Indians also have lower rates of fertility and crime than either black or white Americans. Sowell's explanation that "West Indians were much more frugal, hard working and entrepreneurial," and that "their children worked harder and out-performed native black children in school" (Sowell 1981:219) describes many other immigrant groups.

The Harlem story has parallels all over the United States and not the least in Miami where immigrant success stories are well-known, a fact demonstrated by the relative success of more recent Caribbean migrants: Cubans and Haitians.[1] The important point is that these success stories tend to have two effects: they act as powerful incentives to the immigrant's compatriots to move to the United States, and they propagate a favorable image of the immigrant in the host country. Assimilative capacity interacts positively with host society absorbability. It has been a positively reinforcing cycle insofar as much of Caribbean migration is concerned. The same does not hold for Mexican and Puerto Rican migrants, who, recent studies indicate, are not doing well in American society (Smith 1991).

4. *Ethnicity continues to have a role in international relations.* Ethnicity is important both in official policy as well as in what is today known as transnational forces: forces that operate independently from official or governmental actions. Ethnicity is one of the most difficult areas to analyze. While we are dealing with attitudes and perceptions as realities, there can be no doubt that official policy formulation also continues to be important.

It is evident for instance that the 1965 changes in immigration law were strongly influenced by the ideas of Lyndon Johnson's Great Society, which in turn had been influenced by the civil rights movement. American blacks made the linkage between their gains in civil rights with the rights of foreign blacks to equal access to U.S. residence through immigration reform. This tendency to link civil rights to foreign policy and both to immigration policy continues.

As far as Miami goes, two fundamental aspects of that linkage deserve attention. The first deals with race as it relates to internal U.S. politics. Caribbean migrants (both black and white) have been quick to recognize that while the "immigration problem" is a secular one in this society, race and ethnic problems are very much also moral problems. Even before they become citizens, immigrants learn the value of ethnic bargaining; they have made great strides on their own behalf through the use of U.S. laws generally and the civil rights movement specifically (Maingot 1981). It is important that the Caribbean Basin is predominantly black, mestizo, or mixed. Race and ethnicity will continue to play an important role in international politics and therefore also in U.S. thinking and actions on immigration policy.

The second issue is geopolitical. The Caribbean Basin has been a traditional U.S. sphere of influence in which particular responsibilities and obligations transcend issues of immigration. The point is, of course, that these obligations have direct effects on immigration policy. Whether they are Cubans, Haitians, or Nicaraguans, the decision as to whether these persons are immigrants or refugees is never removed from political and geopolitical considerations (Weiner 1965; Teitelbaum 1983). Geopolitical considerations made by the federal government are particularly tricky for local governments since these governments suffer the consequences if the decisions go awry.

5. *In the United States, both pragmatism and sentiment seem to provide strong and enduring support for the principle of family reunification as one of the centerpieces of immigration law.* The principle of family reunification is less permanent than the previous four features. However, it appears to have become enough of a part of United States thinking on immigration to be considered structural. Family reunification takes on a mathematical dimension when we observe that the number of Caribbean people already in the legal immigration pipeline in the mid-1980s was substantial: 438,841 in all seven preference categories in 1982. Again, we note the demand from the islands by observing that the Hispanic Caribbean (with thirty-two times more population than the insular Caribbean) has fewer than five times the active visa applicants. The number of applicants under preference categories two (spouses and unmarried sons and daughters of permanent residents) and five (brothers and sisters of U.S. citizens) is a good indication of the strength of both the immediate and extended Caribbean family systems. These strengths become part of the "structure" through immigrants' contributions to their networks, their success, and their sense of "right" to migrate.[2]

These five features, therefore, are parts of a "pull" syndrome. These features are mutually reinforcing, gaining strength as they interact over time.

To this point, I have considered only one-half of any migration equation: the "pull" of the targeted area of settlement. We must also consider the "push" factors. These range from being purely voluntary, to merely persuasive of out-migration, to fully compelling. As it turns out, these factors also represent structural features in the "sending" countries that are not easily solved. As I have already noted and as illustrated in table 2.3, the "push" factors operate in one form or other throughout the whole Caribbean Basin.

The Structure of Caribbean "Push" Factors

In his influential 1950 treatise on economic development in the West Indies, W. Arthur Lewis asserted that "the case for rapid industrialization in the West Indies rests chiefly on overpopulation." Agriculture could not provide the answer to the employment needs; industrialization and manufacturing had to be major parts of the solution. As Lewis understood it, there were other parts: "There are two other principal opportunities, namely the development of the tourist industry, and emigration."

Even before Lewis's treatise, and certainly after it, the assumption of continued and uninterrupted high rates of out-migration had become an integral part of West Indian development thinking and planning. The *Barbados Development Plan, 1979–1983*, for instance, makes projections for population and employment based on three assumptions: a stable pattern of mortality, a marginal decline in fertility, and "a continuation of the level of emigration experienced in the post censal period." Barbadians also project—just as Lewis had theorized three decades earlier—that while the level of employment in agriculture would remain static, those same numbers would bring about some increase in agricultural productivity. The real growth would be in manufacturing, expected to grow by 4.9 percent, and services (government and tourism), expected to grow by 5 percent.

The problem is that neither in Barbados, where effective family planning has caused fertility rates to drop dramatically, nor in the rest of the Caribbean, where fertility rates have not dropped, are things working out that way. World Bank statistics show that while employment in agriculture has dropped drastically, so has agricultural output. In Jamaica, agricultural employment went from 39 percent of the labor force in 1960 to 29 percent in 1970; agricultural output went from 12 percent of GNP in 1960 to 8 percent in 1970. Similar or larger drops in both agricultural employment and output are being experienced throughout the area. Visits to any farming or fishing community in the region will immediately reveal a dramatic demographic picture: virtually all the people in the field or fishing are older. The young are simply not entering into agriculture.

Except in the cases of Haiti, El Salvador, and some of the smaller islands, land hunger or scarcity is not the central problem. This can be seen in the cases of Guyana, the Dominican Republic, Trinidad, and certainly Cuba, where the government holds large tracts of state or "crown lands" but where many an agricultural scheme has come to naught. The fact is that the move away from the land results from very complex forces in the region that have yet to be fully analyzed. Caribbean leaders continue to be concerned with the low degree of self-sufficiency in foods of the region but are at a loss to find solutions. Despite available land and "surplus" populations, every country in the Caribbean is heavily dependent on food imports.

The Caribbean situation has an even more complex dimension: when people abandon agriculture and migrate to cities or go abroad, migrants from less developed areas frequently take their places. These migrants, many of them illegals, initially work both in subsistence and truck farming as well as in large-scale export crop agriculture. They invariably then drift into urban areas. For instance, Haitians now constitute 90 percent of the labor in Dominican Republic sugar production and 30 percent of that country's coffee work force. Before the economic downturn of the 1980s, Colombians used to stream over the border into Venezuela, replacing Venezuelans who moved to the cities (Kritz and Gurak 1979). In the 1980s and early 1990s, eastern Caribbean "small islanders" replaced (and still replace) agriculturalists moving out of Barbados and Trinidad. Many of these same migrants soon become candidates for another migratory step: to the U.S. mainland. This certainly has been the case with the Haitians who moved to the Bahamas (Marshall 1978), the Leeward Islanders who moved to the U.S. Virgin Islands, and the Dominicans who moved to Puerto Rico. The case of the British Virgin Islands provides an especially poignant picture of the dimensions of the population movements in the area: in 1970 it was calculated that 37.9 percent of the population of the U.S. Virgin Islands had moved to the U.S. mainland and Canada, while the percentage of foreign-born residents in those islands was 34.1 percent. The U.S.V.I. have become a "transshipment" station, as have other islands.

The structure of Caribbean migration to the United States has geographical, historical, and socioeconomic dimensions. Up until the present, the United States in general and south Florida in particular have been receptive to these migrants, in part because immigrants from the Caribbean have enjoyed a good reputation and have shown a good capacity to assimilate in a state (Florida) that has been growing very fast.

Generally speaking, this migration has been a success story; challenges have been turned into opportunities for most people involved. There are, as is to be expected, some real and potential negative aspects to this movement. Unfortunately these negative aspects might overwhelm the positive and have the greatest and most damaging influence on the host society's receptivity to new immigrants. These negative aspects deserve a serious hearing in any analysis on the future of immigration to Florida.

The Dark Side of Caribbean Basin Immigration

Issues surrounding a public's acceptance of immigration flows, especially "structural" ones such as those of the Caribbean, are never divorced from the general concerns of that public. To the extent that people worry about crime, drugs, law and order, and the environment, they are quite capable of making linkages between these concerns and how they are affected by immigration. The linkages are, of course, not always accurate but are invariably powerful.

By far the most damaging to a host society's support for future immigration is any movement that gives the impression of "being out of control": out of control of the federal government and its agents and certainly out of control of the state governments. The classic case was south Florida in 1980: nearly 200,000 Cubans and Haitians landed in Florida, undocumented, unexpected, and uninvited. The event contributed to the defeat of the then incumbent president, and the aftershocks are still being felt in U.S. criminal justice circles. A special legal category, "entrant," was created to handle the crisis and in general, south Florida responded with compassion. However, no state or city can withstand too many such shocks, nor can any successful immigration program be conducted by the creation of extraordinary statuses. A minimum degree of predictability is needed about numbers, community absorptive capacities, privileges, and responsibilities on all sides.

Predictability just might be one of the most serious short-term challenges facing Florida for the simple reason that there is no predictability possible when dealing with the politics of such a large and varied number of countries. Events in Eastern Europe illustrate how the initial joy at the liberation of these authoritarian states has been followed by real fears of a flood of migrants seeking jobs in the West. Is this the proper scenario for a post-Castro period? Will Cuban refugees, rather than return to Cuba, head for the Miami area in large numbers? Similarly, it is said that the European Community (EC) is fast approaching the "intolerance threshold" vis-à-vis migration from the fourteen non-EC countries that have traditionally been its sources of immigrants. The EC—with the same number of people as these fourteen countries—has been an escape valve plus a source of remittances, calculated at $8 billion (in United States currency) in 1989.

These examples are not so hypothetical, as the case of the Nicaraguans in Miami illustrates. In the late 1980s, Miami had some 70,000 Nicaraguans. Their legal status has been in limbo for over a decade, and the recent election of an American-supported political coalition in Nicaragua has done nothing to simplify the situation. Should their status be legalized, will this mean movements of Nicaraguans presently in third countries? Certainly the statistics in table 2.3 indicate that Nicaraguans are overstaying their legal nonimmigrant visas in very large numbers. There are some 200,000 Nicaraguans in Costa Rica and about 75,000 in Honduras. If these Nicaraguans settle in south Florida, will they attract other Nicaraguans presently settling in California? Will the federal government pay for the settlement costs of these victims of a bad geopolitical situation?

Whatever the answers to these question might be, the speed with which Nicaraguans have established their networks in south Florida indicates that there will be an established community long before specific legal answers are given. There were in early 1991 already formal associations of Nicaraguan lawyers, doctors, architects, engineers, pharmacists, teachers, political parties, and even an "Association for the Development of the Atlantic Coast." All claim to retain ties with counterparts in Nicaragua (Maingot 1990).

At a minimum, local communities are entitled to be informed—by federal authorities and through their own research efforts—about regular immigration flows and certainly about the possibility or probability of sudden crisis ones. Closer to home, it is all too evident that recent journalistic reports about the flow of Nicaraguans into south Florida ought to be pursued and explored in much greater depth. We should not wait until the crisis to commission studies on such issues. This is particularly vital in a city such as Miami, where fears of bad publicity and a bad "tourist climate" are real enough. These apprehensions should not, however, keep studies bringing potentially bad news at bay.[3]

On this score, there is a critical need for a study of criminality among south Florida's alien population similar to that which the General Accounting Office prepared about New York in 1986. It is not enough to study common criminals such as Jamaican "posses" and "yardies" or the growing Haitian crack cocaine criminal gangs.[4] We also need to know about the "white collar" criminals, veritable "fifth columns" in the war on drugs. Exposing the rotten apples will be salutary to the community but especially beneficial to the majority of honest immigrants themselves. Stereotypes are nefarious and intractable. Once an immigrant group gets stuck with what is more properly called a "contrast conception," both the receptivity of the host society and the capacity to assimilate of the immigrant are affected. A change of heart takes place, and all the social, economic, and geopolitical facts in the world will be hard put to bring perceptions back to a state propitious to further immigration.

Conclusion

It is difficult to say with absolute clarity what impact migration will have on the parameters of political decision making in the Caribbean and the United States. It is absolutely clear, however, that migration has had and will most probably continue to have an increasing political influence and that this fact cannot be ignored in any planning or policy-making in Caribbean countries or in the United States. Before decision makers can turn to questions of economic development or long-range planning in general, they have to come to grips with the political reality of migration.

It is precisely this fact that led a congressional commission to recommend the establishment of the Agency for Migration Affairs. This agency would rationalize the various agencies described in fig. 2.1 and would provide overall leadership and direction for U.S. immigration policy. As the commission stated: "The reorganization must insure that migration be given a high priority on U.S. domestic and foreign policy agendas, and that migration consequences be carefully considered by policymakers involved in trade, development and other international economic matters" (Commission for the Study of International Migration and Cooperative Economic Development 1990). Although there appears to be little chance that the commission's recommendations will be adopted any time soon, the commission makes a telling point.

Caribbean policymakers should be just as conscious of the overall significance of migration. Socialist reformers—in Cuba or elsewhere—should understand that the propensity to migrate is not, and has never been, limited to the bourgeoisie; free enterprise reformers should understand that they have no particular long-term claim on that bourgeoisie either. The sociopolitical dimension of migration is one of the fundamental characteristics of the area, and no decision—by receiving or sending societies—can be made without addressing this dimension. The costs of ignoring the sociopolitical dimension of migration are too great; the potential benefits from harnessing it for development are too enticing. This can be said about the Caribbean as well as Florida—a fact that has very real implications and that can perhaps be summarized in two crucial points.

First, the social and cultural patterns that make Florida and the Caribbean a sociocultural area will probably be strengthened (Maingot 1985). The very size of the migration assures this strengthening, and the generalization of the U.S. presence through new, export-driven development programs in the area further guarantees it. Shortsighted attempts by Caribbean leaders to minimize the damage done by the outflow of skilled personnel—the so-called brain drain—by restricting their rights and opportunities to migrate will not work. Similarly, anti-immigration movements have never prospered at a national level in the United States, and regional sentiments invariably fall in line with the generalized attitudes of Americans. Attitudes, however, should never be taken for granted. While American and Floridian attitudes have been generous to immigration in the past, there are some ominous signs on the horizon, especially in South Florida. It is a safe bet, however, that if the more glaringly noxious of the spin-offs of the movements from the Caribbean can be controlled, the generosity will continue into the near future.

Second, it is increasingly evident that Caribbean migrants to the United States keep close ties to their homelands. This linkage is not only reflected in the remittances they send back and their frequent return visits, but also in their participation in U.S.-based organizations that deal with issues related to their home islands. Decent, honest immigrants will have beneficial impacts on their former native lands. They will also contribute to the internationalization of their adoptive country, too long content to feel secure in an isolationist cocoon.

In an increasingly competitive world, parochialism is an attitude that can hardly be afforded. The potential for mutually beneficial relationships is great. Because the numbers of Caribbean Basin immigrants involved at present are manageable, because the majority are here legally, and because both hosts and new arrivals share substantial cultural traits, Florida has an excellent opportunity to make its immigration story an important part of the American immigration experience.

Notes

1. Cf. Alex Stepick (1984): "The Haitian business community has self-consciously attempted to repeat the earlier successes of the Cuban immigrant entrepreneurs."

2. It is interesting to see the spirited West Indian defense of the guest worker (H-2) program, which has been in operation since 1942 and which today hires some 16,000 British West Indians to cut Florida sugarcane and pick New England apples. H-2 is generally regarded as "legitimately" a West Indian program, just as movement to the USA is generally regarded as a historically legitimate Mexican experience.

3. Who, for instance, has seen the United Way's Long Range Planning Committee's (1982) sobering report on the future of Dade County? Anglo flight, increasing poverty, increasing ethnic tensions, increasing unemployment among minority youth—all are projected into that future.

4. It is extraordinary to learn that there are forty Jamaican gangs with 10,000 members operating in the United States. They are said to control 40 percent of the crack cocaine trade and to have committed over 1,400 murders since 1985. They are reputed to be led by important members of the Jamaican bourgeoisie (*New York Times* 1988).

References

Bean, Frank D., Barry Edmonston, and Jeffrey S. Passel, eds. 1990. *Undocumented Migration to the United States*. Santa Monica, Calif.: RAND Corporation.

Bean, Frank D., Georges Vernez, and Charles B. Keely. 1989. *Opening and Closing the Doors*. Program for Research on Immigration Policy. Washington: RAND Corporation and Urban Institute.

Commission for the Study of International Migration and Cooperative Economic Development. 1990. Report on "Unauthorized Migration: An Economic Development Response."

Del Castillo, José. n.d. *La inmigración de braceros . . . 1900–1930*. Santo Domingo, Dominican Republic: Cuadernos del ENDIA, no. 7.

Financial Times. 1990. March 12:12.

General Accounting Office (GAO). 1986. "Criminal Aliens: INS' Investigative Efforts in the New York City Area." Report (March). Washington.

Gonzalez Baker, Susan. 1990. *The Cautious Welcome*. Program for Research on Immigration Policy. Washington: RAND Corporation and Urban Institute.

Gordon, Milton M. 1964. *Assimilation in American Life.* New York: Oxford University Press.

Handlin, Oscar. 1951. *The Uprooted: The Epic Story of the Great Migrations that Made the American People.* Boston: Little, Brown.

Higham, John. 1963. *Strangers in the Land: Patterns of American Nativism, 1860–1925.* Reprint. New York: Atheneum.

Kritz, M.M., and D.T. Gurak, eds. 1979. "International Migration Patterns in Latin America." *International Migration Review* (Fall).

Kritz, Mary M., Charles B. Keely, and Silvano M. Tomasi, eds. 1981. *Global Trends in Migration.* New York: Center for Migration Studies.

Lewis, Sir W. Arthur. 1950. "The Industrialization of the British West Indies." *Caribbean Economic Review* 2 (May).

McCullough, David. 1977. *The Path Between the Seas.* New York: Simon and Schuster.

Maingot, Anthony P. 1981. "Ethnic Bargaining and the Non-Citizen: Haitians and Cubans in Miami." Report to the U.S. Coordinator of Refugee Affairs, Miami.

———— 1982. "Ideology, Politics, and Citizenship in the American Debate on Immigration Policy: Beyond Consensus." In *U.S. Immigration and Refugee Policy,* edited by M.M. Kritz. Lexington, Mass.: Lexington Books, D.C. Heath and Co.

———— 1985. "Political Implications of Migration in a Socio-Cultural Area." In *Migration and Development in the Caribbean,* edited by Robert A. Pastor. Boulder, Colo.: Westview Press.

———— 1990. "United States–Caribbean Immigration Relations." In *Immigration International Relations,* edited by Georges Vernez, 167–76. Washington: RAND Corporation and Urban Institute.

Marshall, Dawn. 1978. *The Haitian Problem: Illegal Migration to the Bahamas.* Mona, Jamaica: ISER.

Neda, Read. 1980. "West Indians." In *Harvard Encyclopedia of American Ethnic Groups,* edited by S. Thernstrom. Cambridge, Mass.: Belknap Press.

New York Times. 1988. October 14:5.

Passel, J.S., and K.A. Woodrow. 1984. "Geographic Distribution of Undocumented Aliens Counted in the 1980 Census by State." *International Migration Review* 18, no. 3.

Pastor, Robert A. 1989. "Migration and Development in the Caribbean Basin: Implications and Recommendations for Policy." Working Papers, no. 7 (November). Washington: Commission for the Study of International Migration and Cooperative Economic Development.

————, ed. 1985. *Migration and Development in the Caribbean.* Boulder, Colo.: Westview Press.

Preston, William, Jr. 1963. *Aliens and Dissenters.* Cambridge, Mass.: Harvard University Press.

Sassen-Koob, S. 1979. "Economic Growth and Immigration in Venezuela." In "International Migration Patterns in Latin America," edited by M.M. Kritz and D.T. Gurak. *International Migration Review* (Fall).

Smith, James P. 1991. "Hispanics and the American Dream: An Analysis of Hispanic Male Labor Market Wages, 1940–1980." Santa Monica, Calif.: RAND Corporation. Forthcoming.

Sowell, Thomas. 1981. *Ethnic America*. New York: Basic Books.

Stepick, Alex. 1984. "Haitians Released from Krome: Their Prospects for Adaptation and Integration in South Florida." Dialogue Series No. 24. Latin American and Caribbean Center, Florida International University. Miami.

Teitelbaum, Michael S. 1983. "Immigration, Refugees and Foreign Policy." *International Organization* 38, no. 3 (Summer).

U.N. Caribbean Regional Integration Advisors' Team. 1975. "Planning to Meet the Caribbean's Growing Food Needs." Final report. Port-of-Spain, Trinidad and Tobago.

U.S. Bureau of Census. 1986. *Statistical Abstract of the United States*. Washington.

———, Population Division. 1989. *Post-IRCA Undocumented Immigration to the United States: An Assessment Based on the June 1988 CPS*, by Karen A. Woodrow and Jeffrey S. Passel. Washington.

United Way of Dade County. 1982. Report of the Long-Range Planning Committee. Miami.

Weiner, Myron. 1965. "On International Migration and International Relations." *Population and Development* 2, no. 3 (September).

World Bank. 1978. *The Commonwealth Caribbean*. Baltimore: Johns Hopkins University Press.

———. 1989. *World Development Report—1989*. New York: Oxford University Press.

3

Blacks in Miami

Marvin Dunn
and Alex Stepick III

The 1980s were not kind to Miami's black population. While the Cubans prospered economically and politically, on four separate occasions riots engulfed Miami's primary black neighborhoods, Overtown and Liberty City, causing hundreds of millions of dollars in damage, numerous deaths, and grave reflections on the state of the local black community. In all four cases the immediate cause of the riots was police shootings of blacks, but these occurred against a backdrop of a community that contrasts conspicuously with the rapid growth and prosperity of Miami's immigrant Cuban community. Miami's black community appears to have missed out on Miami's growth and political changes. Instead of dynamic growth and prosperity, the repeated riots create an image of apparent stagnation, desperation, and isolation. Chapter 8 details the political powerlessness of Miami's blacks. In this chapter, we address the community's social and economic status. While desperation and frustration are present, we find that some parts of Miami's black community have prospered and that a more accurate view is one of a community in transition toward greater complexity and stratification.

History

While the riots attracted attention to Miami's black population during the 1980s, the underlying causes of isolation and subjugation were hardly novel phenomena for Miami's blacks. When the city of Miami was chartered in 1896, Florida state law required a petition of 300 citizens. Miami had fewer than 200 whites at the time, so they obtained blacks' signatures (Metro-Dade 1984). It was the last time for more than half a century that blacks played a pivotal political role in Miami. Following incorporation, none of the subsequently elected officials was black.

Many of the original black settlers in Miami came from the Bahamas, but local whites impressed upon them appropriate southern "Negro" behavior standards.[1] In 1910, a Miami municipal court judge, John Grambling, congratulated the Miami police for changing the attitudes of "Nassau Negroes" who "upon their arrival here considered themselves the social equal of white people." In 1917 a race riot nearly occurred after a group of whites dynamited the largest building in Colored Town: Odd Fellows Hall. In 1921 the Klan kidnapped a black minister in Coconut Grove, H.M. Higgs, who preached racial equality. They released him after he promised to return to the Bahamas. Two weeks later, the Klan kidnapped another minister, Phillip Irwin Wright, for the same offense. They beat, tarred, and feathered him, ordered him out of town, and finally threw him from a speeding car onto a street in downtown Miami. Two years later in Homestead, south of Miami, a mob lynched two blacks accused of killing a U.S. marshal (George 1978:445).

The court system reinforced these behaviors by quickly exonerating police and other whites accused of killing blacks. Through the first third of this century the local newspapers, the *Miami Metropolis* and later the *Miami Herald*, regularly referred to blacks as "coons," "fiends," and "hamfats." In the 1930s, the *Miami Herald*, referring to black efforts to settle outside of Overtown, asserted: "The advance of the Negro population is like a plague and carries devastation with it to all surrounding property" (Mohl 1987b:9).

Slow improvements began in 1944 when the U.S. Supreme Court required the local Democratic party to open its registers to blacks. It was also in 1944 that the city trained its first blacks for the police force, but the training took place in secret, due to fear of a white backlash. Once the blacks were trained, they were permitted to patrol only in black neighborhoods, and they could not take whites into custody (Metro-Dade 1984). At the beginning of the 1950s, a black was first allowed to serve on a jury. Dade County also had its first black judge, who had jurisdiction over "Negro districts." The county designated Monday for blacks' use of public golf courses. The NAACP and the Congress on Racial Equality (CORE) filed a suit against the "Monday Only" rule for blacks at public golf courses. Other lawsuits sought to desegregate public facilities, including schools, transportation, and swimming pools. The NAACP and CORE won all these suits, although the elected officials evaded integration as long as possible, usually until the early 1960s.

In the late 1960s, a black (Dewey Knight) was appointed to the county manager's staff and to the city commission (Athalie Range), and blacks were elected to the state legislature (Joe Long Kershaw) and to the county commission (Earl Carroll). In the late 1970s, Miami blacks were appointed to such positions as superintendent of the Dade County schools (Johnny Jones), manager of the City of Miami (Howard Gary), and city attorney (George Knox). Blacks were also elected to the city commission (Miller Dawkins), the state senate (Carrie Meek), and the school board (William "Bill" Turner). In the 1980s, three chiefs of police in the City of Miami were black. A black was appointed a state court judge. Blacks maintained seats in the state legislature, on the county and city commissions, and on the school board.

In all of these bodies, blacks were either a minority or served at the pleasure of a nonblack majority. In contrast with most major U.S. cities twenty years after the civil rights movement, blacks did not exercise political control in any arena.[2] More importantly, police still treated blacks as if they were not the social equal of whites. In 1979 there were two widely reported incidents of black confrontations with police that required up to twenty extra squad cars to control. In another highly publicized incident, police raided the wrong house in search of drugs. The occupant, a black schoolteacher, Nathaniel Lafleur, was hospitalized and charged with battery and obstructing a police officer in the performance of his duties. Late in 1979, Hialeah police shot and killed a black who had stopped his car in a warehouse district to urinate. Finally, an eleven-year-old black girl walking home from school was picked up by a Florida highway patrolman who fondled her and asked her to remove her panties. Then in February 1980, the black school superintendent, Johnny Jones, was charged with attempting to steal nearly $9,000 in gold-plated plumbing fixtures for his vacation home.

The most dramatic incident, however, was the 1980 riot: "McDuffie," as the case is known locally. It lasted three days, Saturday through Monday, left 18 dead, $804 million in property damage, and 1,100 arrested. McDuffie's antecedents occurred in December 1979. A thirty-three-year-old black insurance agent named Arthur McDuffie died in Miami's Jackson Memorial Hospital from injuries sustained after being chased by city and county police units. The chase ensued because McDuffie made a rolling stop at a red light plus an obscene gesture toward a nearby officer. Police claimed that McDuffie died as the result of accidental injuries during the chase. Black Miami knew better. On March 31, 1980, four white officers of the Dade County Public Safety Department were charged with playing some role in the beating of McDuffie and the subsequent attempt at covering up the causes of his death. Sensing the mood of tension in the city, a local judge granted a change of venue to Tampa. In his prophetic words, the case was "a time bomb" (Porter and Dunn 1984:37).

Similar uprisings in other cities have brought black leaders into the streets to calm down the masses. Older black citizens have generally tried to rein in ghetto youth. There were such attempts in Liberty City and other black areas of Miami, but they were countermanded by the opposite trend. A peaceful rally called by the local branch of the NAACP the day the McDuffie verdict was announced turned into a full-scale riot during which the seat of Dade County's justice system was broken into and torched. Black professionals along with shirtless teenagers took part in this event.

On ghetto street corners, adult blacks were observed egging on youths as they stopped and attacked cars driven by whites. The local head of the Urban League refused to go into the streets and calm the crowds, noting that "anyone who had any understandings of the ramifications of de-humanization and social isolation could understand the riots. . . . [W]hites thought . . . it was irresponsible . . . because they assumed that black leaders were there to protect them and not to lead black folks" (Stepick and Fernandez-Kelly 1987).

While the 1980 McDuffie riot was the most extensive, there have been other riots since then. In 1982, Overtown erupted after a Latino police officer, Luis Alvarez, fatally shot a black man, Nevell Johnson, at a video parlor. As mentioned in chapter 8, the mayor of Miami joined forces with two Cuban members of the city commission in 1984 to fire the popular black city manager, Howard Gary, raising the fears of another riot. While no riot occurred that time, the firing did spark a recall petition aimed at the mayor.

The 1980s closed with another police shooting of a black, an incident that trenchantly captures the changing Miami. In January 1989, William Lozano, a Colombian immigrant on the City of Miami police force, was writing up a routine traffic violation in the heart of Overtown, the former Colored Town at the edge of downtown Miami and only a few blocks away from the hotels in which the teams and press were staying for the Super Bowl that was slated for that weekend. Lozano was standing in the street as he wrote the ticket. He looked up and saw a motorcycle speeding down the street, a police car in pursuit. He claimed the motorcycle was threatening to hit him, and to protect himself he had to draw his gun and fire. Witnesses said that he deliberately stepped into the street. Regardless, his aim was good. The bullet ripped through Clement Lloyd, a Caribbean black immigrant, and the motorcycle careened out of control, crashed, and killed the driver. His passenger died the next day (Clary 1989). A crowd quickly gathered. After the ambulance arrived and covered the corpse, the crowd began to throw sticks, bottles, and stones. A few hours later, police cordoned off the area. Rioters burned and looted within sight of the national press covering the Super Bowl.

The white Anglo elite did what it could to divert attention from the plight of the native blacks. At the end of the year, a jury found Lozano guilty of manslaughter, the first guilty verdict against a police officer.[3] The Latin community, especially the Colombian component, protested. A little over a year later, an appeals court overturned the conviction, claiming that the jurors were unduly influenced by the fear of rioting if they had found Lozano not guilty.

As the 1990s dawned, Miami's black community continued the same trajectory. First, in July 1990, Haitians protesting alleged abuse at a Latin store were beaten indiscriminately by Miami police. The incident prompted a review board investigation and became a benchmark for what many Haitians consider police insensitivity (Clary 1991b). Then at the end of the same year, Miami's Puerto Rican community, which is primarily black, erupted after the acquittal of six police officers accused of beating to death a small-time crack dealer (Clary 1990). In short, Miami's black community has a long history of police harassment punctuated by black outbursts.

Economic Status

Miami's blacks were the original economic backbone of the city. When Henry Flagler extended his East Coast Railroad south to Miami in 1896, many of the laborers were black. Blacks also provided the work force when winter vegetable farmers and northern tourists followed the railroad. They tilled the fields and harvested the vegetables. They dug the ditches that defined the streets, then cleaned the streets, drove the cars of whites, hauled their garbage away, were nannies to their children, maids in their homes, and washerwomen for their clothes.

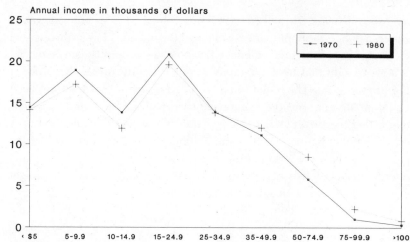

Annual income in thousands of dollars

Fig. 3.1. Distribution of black income, Dade County, 1970 and 1980. *Sources*: U.S. Census 1970, 1980.

Nearly a century later, Miami's blacks are getting both poorer and richer. During the 1970s, the number of blacks with incomes over $35,000 grew from 1,400 in 1970 to 4,600 in 1980. Dade County's affluent black families accounted for one-third of the total affluent black families in the entire state of Florida. Within Dade County, blacks increased their median income between 1970 and 1980 by 7 percent. Dade's blacks thus narrowed the income gap during the 1970s, contrary to the national trend of that decade, in which the income gap increased. Miami black median income was 68 percent of the national average, whereas U.S. blacks as a whole earned only 59 percent of the national average. Florida blacks fared comparatively worse, earning only 88 percent of Dade's blacks.

For some blacks the 1970s produced other gains, too. Blacks filled more new jobs in the professional, specialty, and technical occupations, registering a growth from 7 percent of blacks in this category in 1970 to 13 percent by 1980 (see fig. 3.1).

But not all blacks shared these gains. Black males had more difficulty remaining in the labor force during the 1970s. Their labor force participation rate declined from 76 to 74 percent during the decade while unemployment reached new highs, peaking in 1975 at the end of the 1973–75 recession. While the unemployment rate gradually improved through the last half of the 1970s, blacks were hit harder than anyone else by the recession of the early 1980s. In 1983 black unemployment achieved a new postwar high.

Latins and black Americans comprise the work force picking winter vegetables in southern Dade County.

Throughout this period, black unemployment increased more rapidly than did that of either whites or Hispanics. By 1980 blacks consti-tuted 24 percent of Dade's unemployment rolls, compared to only 17 percent in 1970. While the proportion of poor black families dropped from 31.6 percent in 1970 to 29.8 percent in 1980, the rate remained more than triple that of whites (8.3 percent) and almost double that of Hispanics (16.9 percent). Overall, in spite of narrowing the income gap during the 1970s, blacks still lagged far behind both whites and His-panics, earning only 63 percent of white and 80 percent of Hispanic family income.

Moreover, following a national trend (see, e.g., Staples 1991), the number of female-headed households grew rapidly, and these households were especially likely to be poor. Fatherless black families constituted about 30 percent (almost 19,000) of all black families in 1980, up from 23 percent in 1970. Blacks accounted for 42 percent of all such families in Dade County in 1980, a level almost three times higher than the black share of all families (15 percent). The poverty rate for female-headed households in 1980 was three times the rate for all families, accounting for about 40 percent of all black families with children and for 67 percent of all poor black families with children. More than 50 percent of these poor families had young children (under six years of age).

The 1990 census revealed a trend of both higher overall incomes and increasing inequality within the black community. The number of low-income blacks declined slightly, while the number of blacks at the high end of the income scale increased proportionately more (see fig. 3.1).

Education

Corresponding to an increase in income and occupational status for some, blacks in Dade, like blacks nationwide, made dramatic progress in educational attainment in the last two decades. Between 1970 and 1980 the median years of schooling completed by blacks increased from 9.5 to 11.9 years, leaving blacks only half a year behind whites. By 1980 the percent of black high school graduates was up from 28 to 50 percent; the number of blacks with one or more years of college more than doubled, from 9 to 20 percent; and the percent of the black population between 25 to 34 years of age enrolled in school doubled from 5 to 10 percent (Castro and Yaney 1989). College enrollment quadrupled from 3,500 in 1970 to 14,000 in 1980. More importantly, black college students as a percentage of all college students increased from 9 percent in 1970 to 15 percent in 1980 (Metro-Dade 1984).

Yet Dade County schools remained the most segregated schools in Florida and some of the most segregated in the South, with the number of all-black schools doubling between 1970 and 1987 (Shaw 1987). Moreover, blacks' test scores continued to be below those of Anglos, and the gap has not been narrowing (Grant 1989). Large numbers of blacks also still failed to complete high school. The 1980 census reported that 21 percent of the adult black population (25,000 persons) had failed to complete high school. This was only a modest improvement from the 1970 level of 25 percent and was still substantially higher than the 12 percent drop-out rate reported for whites.

Demographics

At the same time that the black population has become more stratified in terms of income and education, it has also become more diverse in terms of background. As mentioned above, the first blacks to settle and work in Miami came from the Bahamas at the turn of the century (Mohl 1987a).

Thousands

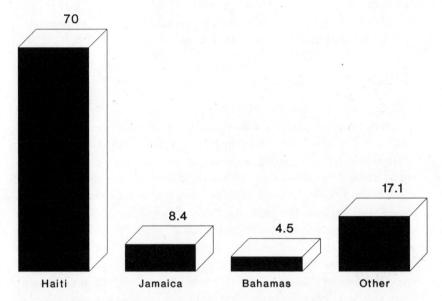

Fig. 3.2. Birthplaces of foreign blacks, Dade County, 1980. *Source*: Metro–Dade County Planning Department 1984:22.

Soon after, U.S. blacks also relocated in Miami, primarily from northern Florida, southern Georgia, and Alabama (George 1978:433). Still, many of the original Bahamians never lost their self-identity, and even today Bahamian black Miamians distinguish themselves from black Americans.

During the 1980s, the picture became considerably more complex as blacks from other Caribbean islands also began settling in Miami (Mohl 1983:67). Other than the early-arriving Bahamians, most Caribbean blacks coming to the United States up until the late 1970s had bypassed Miami and the rest of the South, fearing the legacy of segregation and attracted by the greater opportunities and openness of the Northeast, particularly New York City. Black Cubans, for example, were more visible in New York and New Jersey than in Miami. Similarly, when the Duvalier-inspired Haitian diaspora began in the late 1950s and 1960s, the primary destination was New York (see chapter 4). But the civil rights victories of the 1960s and 1970s made Miami more attractive to Caribbean blacks. Communities of Haitians, Jamaicans, and Dominicans soon became visible, while smaller groups of other Caribbean blacks also existed. By 1980, about 20 percent of Miami's black population was foreign-born (see fig.

3.2). By the early 1980s, Greater Miami became one of only sixteen metropolitan areas in the United States with more than 300,000 blacks. Between 1970 and 1980, Dade's black population grew by 47 percent, a growth rate exceeded only by that of Atlanta.

Housing and Integration

Before the incorporation of Miami, most blacks settled in the city's Coconut Grove section, a few miles south of the city center (Mohl 1983:68). The original deeds to the land that now forms Miami, however, contained restrictive clauses reserving for whites all land bordering Biscayne Bay and the Miami River and limiting blacks to a segregated quarter north of town, Colored Town, later to become known as Overtown. From the 1900s through its heyday in the 1950s, Colored Town was the business and cultural heart of the black population (George 1978). By 1930 there were about 30,000 black residents in Dade County. As the Colored Town population grew, row upon row of crowded, ramshackle houses sprang up along the district's dusty, unpaved streets. There was little or no running water and no indoor plumbing. Electricity, fast becoming commonplace in white residential areas, was practically unknown in Colored Town. Children and young adults died of tuberculosis and other contagious diseases at a high rate. Crime, primarily bootlegging, prostitution, and gambling, thrived. These worsening conditions, combined with white resistance to expansion of the city's black population into white residential areas to the east and south, led to the creation of a new black district to the north and west that later became known as Liberty City.

As the barriers of legal segregation disappeared, blacks became less segregated. In the 1990s blacks in Dade County still lived in highly segregated neighborhoods, primarily in Overtown and Liberty City. Some census tracts have few or no blacks, while other tracts indicate black population concentration greater than 95 percent. Not all blacks live in inner-city neighborhoods, as a number of small black communities have arisen on the urban periphery (Mohl 1983:68–69). These communities tend to be more middle class, and they also tend to remain segregated.

Nevertheless, there is a notable trend toward desegregation of housing in Dade County. In fact according to the 1990 census, the process of housing desegregation is moving more quickly in Dade County than it is in other parts of the state and nation (Holley 1991). The apparent desegregation of Dade neighborhoods, however, may reflect a tendency of Caribbean blacks and Hispanics to integrate more than black Americans moving into formerly all-white neighborhoods. Thus, despite some relative improvement in housing desegregation, in 1990 the vast majority of the black population of Dade County continued to reside in the northwest sections of the county with heavy concentrations of blacks in the Overtown, Allapattah, Liberty City, Brownsville, West Little River, and Opa-Locka areas (Holley 1991).

Responses

While Liberty City was still burning during the 1980 riot, white Miami business leaders were already formulating a plan to help Miami's black community. Congruent with the early 1980s emphasis on business and the private sector, the plan focused on assisting black entrepreneurs—as have most of the initiatives of Miami's white power structure. The Greater Miami Chamber of Commerce created a $5.4 million program, all of it from private money, to create jobs and businesses in Liberty City. The effort spawned the Business Assistance Center, which raised $8.3 million in capital by 1989 (Birger 1989). In 1981 community developers, the county, and the city tried to attract firms to a business park in the heart of Liberty City. In 1984 the city of Miami tried to develop a shopping center in Overtown, seeking to fill it with black-owned businesses. A black-controlled community business development organization opened a shopping center in 1985 on the border between Liberty City and Little Haiti (Reveron 1989).

The task for all these organizations was daunting. In the early 1980s there were only 3,885 black-owned businesses in Dade County that generated $110 million annually in sales and receipts. Only 11 percent of the black-owned businesses had employees, who totaled 2,323 in 1982 (Hartley and Martinez 1990). Not surprisingly, the efforts encountered difficulties. The Liberty City park had no firms in 1989, and the Overtown shopping center had only two stores in its nine spaces. The shopping center on the border of Liberty City and Little Haiti, however, was a success, providing more than 130 jobs (Reveron 1989). Its developer, Otis Pitts, was awarded a MacArthur Foundation "genius" award in 1990 (Viglucci 1990).

The Metro Miami Action Plan (MMAP) was created in the aftermath of the 1983 Overtown riot. It sought to tap the power of business and government and to become a powerhouse lobbyist for Dade County's black community. In the beginning MMAP had top local corporate involvement and pressured for positive changes, including sensitivity training for police officers; seminars for minorities on starting a business; and funding of the Enterprise Foundation and the Local Initiatives Support Corporation, which aided community organizations that build low-income housing. But by the late 1980s MMAP had lost its punch as the white community leaders who participated in it dropped out (Dugger 1987).

Just as important as private programs have been public sector minority set-asides for contracting and affirmative action in hiring. Blacks, however, have had to compete with Cuban immigrants for these set-asides. When Martin Luther King visited Miami in 1966, he noted Miami's racial hostility and warned against pitting Cuban refugees against blacks in competition for jobs (Porter and Dunn 1984:13).

While competition for jobs is difficult to document, in the area of governmental contracts with minorities Cubans clearly prevailed over blacks. In 1968 the Small Business Administration (SBA) distributed $1,078,950 in loans to Hispanics and $82,600 to blacks in Dade County. Between 1968 and 1980, the SBA cumulatively dispersed 46.6 percent ($47.7 million) of its Dade County loans to Hispanics and 6 percent ($6.5 million) to blacks. Following the 1980 McDuffie riots, nearly 90 percent of $22 million in SBA loans went to Hispanics or whites. Similarly the late 1970s construction of the county's rapid rail transit system, Metrorail, had only 12 percent black contractors compared to 53 percent Hispanics (Porter and Dunn 1984).

In response to these apparent inequities, the city and county made special efforts in the 1980s to induce black contractors to incorporate. The county's minority participation program was established in 1982. It sought to award $44 million annually (or 3.8 percent of the county's work) to black firms. The City of Miami's Minority and Women Business Affairs and Procurement Program took effect in January 1986; the city awarded 5.4 percent of its expenditures to black firms.

However by the late 1980s, black participation in business was declining. In 1988, 3.2 percent of the city's purchases went to black-owned firms. Black participation in the construction industry plummeted from 6.9 percent in 1985 to 1.5 percent in 1988 (City of Miami 1987). In 1988, after the U.S. Supreme Court ruled that local governments must show identified discrimination in establishing minority set-aside programs, Dade County abandoned its set-aside program, stating, "Metro will have to discontinue the program until it can better prove in court that the county needs one" (Petchel 1990).

Not surprisingly at the end of the 1980s, there were still few black businesses in Dade County. Only 1.4 percent of Dade's black population owned businesses in 1988, and only one black Miami business was among 300 firms on six separate lists of top firms in *Black Enterprise* magazine in June 1988 (Castro and Yaney 1989; Miami-Dade Chamber of Commerce and Greater Miami Chamber of Commerce 1990). In 1991 black businesses in Dade County numbered about 5,400 with an average revenue of $248,000 per firm. The total of all persons employed in those businesses (including the entrepreneurs) was 6,208, or 4 percent of the black population.

While many blacks have endorsed and participated in white initiatives for the black community, there have also been a separate set of projects launched within the black community. When Nelson Mandela made his 1990 tour of the United States, Miami was the only city not to roll out the red carpet for him. Mandela offended Cuban exile politicians with his kind words for Fidel Castro, who had supported the African National Congress since it was banned in South Africa in 1960 (Kraft and Bearak 1990).

In response to the snub, Miami's black community, led by the Black Lawyers Association, organized a convention boycott of Miami that succeeded in convincing at least thirteen national organizations to cancel Miami conventions (Clary 1990). In the fall 1990 election black leaders convinced thousands of blacks to stay home. When Dade County schools selected a Latin school superintendent, Octavio Visiedo, over a black, Tee S. Greer, with more experience, black leaders organized a school and work boycott.

While political leaders refused to apologize for their snub of Mandela, they did respond positively in other ways. The Greater Miami Convention and Visitors Bureau awarded twenty-one scholarships for blacks seeking hotel management degrees at Florida International University. Several blacks were appointed to management positions in area hotels. Single-member voting districts were put on the local ballot (Crockett and Kidwell 1991).

Conclusion

What, then, can be said of the status of blacks in Miami? Overall, blacks are the most frustrated residents of the city. Cubans have prospered

economically and have gained political control over much of local government. A good portion of the working-class Anglo community has simply
left, but most blacks have no place to which to flee. While some blacks
have truly become economically better off since the arrival of Cuban
immigrants in the 1960s and a few blacks hold important public positions, most blacks have seen Cuban immigrants leap past them. One-
third of the black population remains locked in poverty and for many,
conditions are getting worse. The extent of teenage childbirth out of
wedlock, the abandonment of the black family by many black men, the
vulnerability of inner-city blacks to criminal assault, and the scourge of
illegal drugs all make for a significant decline in the quality of life in the
inner city.

The black population will continue to become more ethnically diverse
as immigrants from the black Caribbean continue to arrive. The continued
self-identification of Bahamian-descended blacks as different from black
Americans indicates that a united black American population will probably not easily emerge. Yet, black Americans' lobbying for Haitian issues
via the convention boycott indicates that alliances and progress are
possible even if black Americans do not have direct political power.

Notes

1. Much of this history of Miami's black community is drawn from Porter and
Dunn 1984.

2. The one exception was the predominantly poor black suburb of Opa-Locka,
which did have mainly black-elected and -appointed officials.

3. *William Lozano v. State of Florida*, 90–127 Court of Appeal Fla. 3d District 584
So.2d 19.

References

Birger, Larry. 1989. "Minority Lending Agency Picks Up Speed." *Miami Herald*,
     April 17: BM7.
Castro, Max, and Timothy Yaney. 1989. *Ethnic Audit: Documenting Dade's Diversity.*
     Miami: Greater Miami United.
City of Miami. 1988. Minority Business Enterprise Annual Report.
————. 1987. Minority and Women Procurement Advisory Committee. Annual Re-
     port.
Clary, Mike. 1989. "Miami Jury Gets Case; City on Edge." *Los Angeles Times*,
     December 6: A4.

————. 1990. "Miami Boycott Leads to 'Quiet Riot.'" *Los Angeles Times*, December 9: A18, A20.

————. 1991a. "Miami Haitians Link Murders to Hated Macoutes." *Los Angeles Times*, May 13: A1, A14.

————. 1991b. "Order Restored to Riot-Torn Miami Streets." *Los Angeles Times*, December 5: A24.

Crockett, Kimberly, and David Kidwell. 1991. "Boycott Miami Debate Takes on Softer Tone." *Miami Herald*, August 18: 1B, 2B.

Dugger, Celia. 1987. "MMAP Losing Punch, Leaders Say." *Miami Herald*, July 17: 5C.

George, Paul S. 1978. "Colored Town: Miami's Black Community, 1896–1930." *Florida Historical Quarterly* 56 (April): 432–47.

Grant, Charisse L. 1989. "Ethnic Gap in Test Scores Still Plagues Dade Schools." *Miami Herald*, November 15: 1B, 2B.

Hartley, Kenny, and M. Martinez. 1990. "Black Businesses in Dade County." Unpublished paper, Florida International University, April 24.

Holley, Dan. 1991. "Racial Isolation Declining in Miami." *Miami Herald*, April 9: 1B.

Kraft, Scott, and Barry Bearak. 1990. "After Miami, Mandela Finds Hero's Welcome in Detroit." *Los Angeles Times*, June 29: A18, A19.

Metro–Dade County Planning Department. 1984. "Profile of the Black Population." Miami.

Miami-Dade Chamber of Commerce and Greater Miami Chamber of Commerce. 1990. "Tools for Change." Unpublished study, June.

Mohl, Raymond A. 1983. "Miami: The Ethnic Cauldron." In *Sunbelt Cities: Politics and Growth since World War II*, edited by R.M. Bernard and B.R. Rice, 58–99. Austin: University of Texas Press.

————. 1987a. "Black Immigrants: Bahamians in Early Twentieth-Century Miami." *Florida Historical Quarterly* 65 (January): 271–97.

————. 1987b. "Trouble in Paradise: Race and Housing in Miami during the New Deal Era." *Prologue: The Journal of the National Archives* 19 (Spring): 7–21.

————. 1989. "Ethnic Politics in Miami, 1960–1986." In *Shades of the Sunbelt: Essays on Ethnicity, Race, and the Urban South*, edited by R.M. Miller and G.E. Pozzetta, 143–60. Boca Raton: Florida Atlantic University Press.

Petchel, Jacquee. 1990. "Blacks Lose Metro Business Program." *Miami Herald*, April 18: 1B, 2B.

Porter, Bruce, and Marvin Dunn. 1984. *The Miami Riot of 1980: Crossing the Bounds*. Lexington, Mass.: D.C. Heath.

Reveron, Derek. 1989. "Violence, Delays Hurt Renewal in Black Dade." *Miami Herald*, February 13: 1A, 6A.

Shaw, Cathy. 1987. "System is Most Segregated in State; Busing Shunned." *Miami Herald*, April 19: 1A, 12A.

Staples, Robert, ed. 1991. *The Black Family: Essays and Studies*. 4th ed. Belmont, Calif.: Wadsworth Publishing Company.

Stepick, Alex, and Maria P. Fernandez-Kelly. 1987. Unpublished notes from inter-
    views in Miami.
U.S. Bureau of the Census. 1973. *Characteristics of the Population, Florida*. Part II,
    section 2. Washington: U.S. Government Printing Office.
———. 1984. *Detailed Population Characteristics, Florida*. Series PC80 = 1-D1-A.
    Washington: U.S. Government Printing Office.
Viglucci, Andres. 1990. "Liberty City Rises Like the Phoenix." *Miami Herald*, July
    22: 1B, 7B.

4

The Refugees Nobody Wants: Haitians in Miami

Alex Stepick III

Between 1977 and 1981, 50,000 to 70,000 Haitians arrived by boat in south Florida. The apparently desperately poor Haitians who made it to shore and the scenes of bloated bodies that did not make it provided dramatic images for the nation's media. "America's boat people" and the publicity surrounding them focused profound attention on Haitians in Florida.

In this chapter I examine the underlying causes and consequences of the Haitian presence in Miami and find (1) a consistent U.S. federal policy designed to repress the flow of Haitian refugees to Miami that was impeded by its own illegality, by political support from black Americans and national church, civil, and human rights organizations, and by the coincidental arrival and initial welcome of Mariel Cuban refugees; (2) a contrast between negative stereotypes of the Haitians and the reality of a diverse Haitian population, with some having comfortable middle-class life-styles and others being among the country's most suffering immigrants; and (3) their difficulties, afflicting even those relatively well-off Haitians. These difficulties do not occur because of Haitians' own attitudes, behaviors, or skills. Rather, the majority of the Miamians have discriminated against Haitians.

Recent Haitian Immigrants: The "Black Boat People"

Haitians have a long history of migration and temporary sojourns in other countries. For example, working-class Haitians have served as contract laborers harvesting sugarcane in the Dominican Republic for most of this century, while the children of Haiti's small middle and upper classes have traditionally attended schools in France. Political opponents of new Haitian presidents have also always tended to leave Haiti after power changes. After François Duvalier ("Papa Doc") assumed power in 1957, all levels of Haitian society joined the exodus. The first people to leave were the upper class, who directly threatened his regime. Around 1964 in response to the increasingly indiscriminate brutality of Duvalier's regime and economic insecurity, the black middle class began to leave. In the next wave of the late 1960s and 1970s, many of the urban lower classes departed. The primary destination of these groups was New York City, where an estimated 300,000 Haitians reside.[1] While many are legal migrants, others are not; nevertheless, illegal migrants are seldom pursued by the Immigration and Naturalization Service (INS) authorities in New York.

These previous migrating classes differ from the image of Haitians in Miami, the Haitian boat people who cram themselves twenty or thirty at a time into small, barely seaworthy vessels for the perilous 720-mile trip to southern Florida (for a more detailed overall view on Haitian migration to Miami, see Stepick 1982c, 1986). The first detected Haitian boat of refugees arrived in September 1963. They requested political asylum. The INS rejected their claims and dispatched the boatload back to Haiti. The second boat did not appear until 1973, and it was not until 1977 that Haitians began arriving regularly. From 1977 to 1981, between 50,000 and 70,000 Haitians arrived by boat in Miami. Another 5,000 to 10,000 came by airplane from Haiti, and a smaller number resettled in Miami after living in New York, Montreal, or some other northern metropolitan area (see fig. 4.1).

During the period of greatest influx at the end of the 1970s, a hysterical scare swept through south Florida that tuberculosis was endemic among Haitians and was likely to spread through the general population. Those businesses most likely to employ low-skilled Haitians, hotels and restaurants, were the most concerned that their employees might harbor a communicable disease. The fear proved unfounded, and the hysteria gradually subsided. But the damage had been done. Many Haitians lost their jobs, and negative stereotypes and fears of Haitians became firmly embedded in the general south Florida population. Haitians were perceived by many to be not only disease-ridden, but also uneducated, unskilled peasants who could only prove a burden to the community.

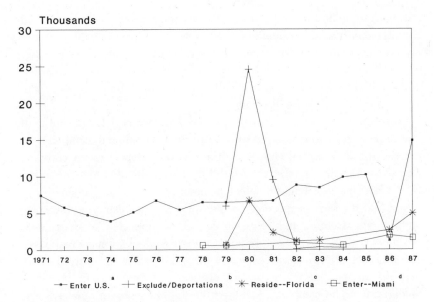

Fig. 4.1. Haitian immigration, 1971–87. *Source*: Immigration and Naturalization Service 1975.

a. "Enter U.S." refers to the total number of Haitians who entered as permanent immigrants according to the INS.

b. "Exclude/deportations" refers to the number of Haitians the U.S. Immigration Court had in either exclusion or deportation processing.

c. "Reside-Florida" refers to the number of Haitian permanent immigrants who indicated at the time of entry that they would reside in Florida.

d. "Enter-Miami" refers to the number of Haitian permanent immigrants who entered through the port of Miami.

These negative stereotypes, however, were misleading. First, not all recent Haitian immigrants who came directly to Miami from Haiti were boat people. A survey compiled in 1983 and 1984 revealed that 20 percent arrived by airplane, reflecting a higher socioeconomic background than the stereotype (see BSRI 1983; Stepick 1984; Stepick and Portes 1986).[2] This does not even include the earlier immigrants from the 1960s who have subsequently resettled in Miami. Even the arriving Haitians who did come by boat were much like immigrants from other countries, slightly better off than their compatriots left behind. The refugees tended to be semiskilled, had some education, and had lived in urban areas in Haiti.

Yet, because Haiti is the least developed nation in the Western Hemisphere, to be semiskilled and have some education and urban experience still leaves one at a disadvantage in the United States. The refugees had completed only an average of four to six years of formal education prior to arrival, and fewer than 5 percent had graduated from high school (see fig. 4.2). Although extremely low by U.S. standards, these levels of education still are higher than those of the Haitian adult population, 80 percent of which is estimated to be illiterate.

Nevertheless, the negative stereotypes prevailed. Local political groups goaded national authorities into an unparalleled campaign to repress the flow of Haitians into Miami and to deport those Haitians already in Florida. Members of south Florida's political elite—including Democratic party members, elected officials, and some Cubans—believed that the boat people were a disruptive force, destroying the community and draining public resources. They appealed to their local members of Congress, who apparently pressured the INS into a response. The INS thereafter began to expend a far greater effort in controlling the flow of Haitians than was expended on nearly any other group of illegal immigrants.[3] The campaign included the imprisonment of new arrivals, the denial of work permits to those who were allowed out of jail, the wholesale rejection of Haitian claims for political asylum, and since 1981 the permanent deployment of a U.S. Coast Guard cutter in Haitian waters to intercept potential refugees and return them to Haiti before they neared the United States.

These efforts failed primarily because of opposition from civil and human rights groups, church organizations, and black Americans; illegal implementation of much of the anti-Haitian refugee policy, denying equal protection and due process to Haitian political asylum claims; and the coincidental arrival of Cubans from Mariel in 1980 who, in the beginning, were favored by the U.S. government. An association of black Baptist churches in Miami, moved by an appeal from a local Haitian assistant pastor, cared for the first refugees who landed in 1972. But as the number of migrants grew, the Baptist churches felt that they would soon be unable to afford the cost of caring for the Haitians. In concert with other local Protestant denominations in 1973, they appealed to the National Council of Churches (NCC). The response was positive, and the NCC funded what would become the Haitian Refugee Center (HRC).

After HRC attained autonomy and a primarily Haitian staff, support from the local black community diminished and was limited to expressions of solidarity and appeals for equal treatment of the "black boat people." The struggle for the rights of Haitian boat people periodically

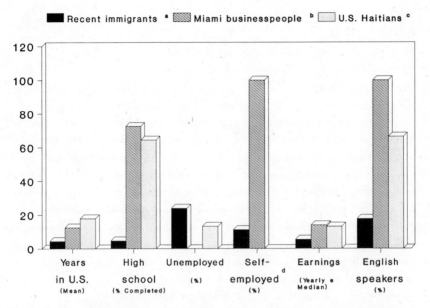

Fig. 4.2. Recent Haitian immigrants to Miami, Miami businesspeople, and U.S. Haitians: years in residence, schooling, employment, earnings, and language.

a. Data on recent Haitian immigrants are based upon survey data collected by methods described in Stepick and Stepick 1990. See Portes and Stepick 1985; Stepick and Portes 1986; and Portes, Stepick, and Truelove 1986 for further discussion of the results.

b. Data on Haitian businesspeople are based upon survey data collected in a 1985 survey of Haitian businesses in Miami's Little Haiti area.

c. Data on U.S. Haitians who were foreign born and who arrived between 1970 and 1980 as reported in U.S. Bureau of the Census 1984.

d. Data on percent of self-employed persons refers to employed respondents only.

e. Data on mean yearly earnings included wage earners only. The figure for Miami Haitian businesspeople was estimated upon the basis of the firm's reported sales and expenses.

crested around dramatic and usually tragic events, such as the drowning of refugees who almost made it to Florida's shores. The welcoming of Cubans in 1980 (and then Nicaraguans in 1989, when the city of Miami offered them temporary headquarters in a baseball stadium) was juxtaposed with the deportation of Haitians.

During these periods, black American community leaders publicly supported the Haitian cause. In 1990, in the week immediately after Miami political leaders snubbed Nelson Mandela, a confrontation occurred in Little Haiti between a Cuban-American shopkeeper and a

Haitian customer. Each accused the other of having initiated the dispute that came to physical violence. The following day, nearly one thousand Haitians collected in front of the store to protest. At a rally a few days later, one hundred police officers wearing helmets and carrying shields surrounded approximately fifty protesters and began closing in with their nightsticks flailing. While local television stations broadcast the melee, police knocked protestors to the ground and continued to hit many of them while they were down. The showdown polarized Miami's Haitian and black American communities and the city's Cuban-American population. As one Haitian asserted at a press conference that included Haitian and black American leaders, "We have a history of abuse, especially by police officers. I think blacks and Haitians realize they are in the same boat. The color of our skin all looks the same" (San Martin, Viglucci, and Hancock 1990). A black American added that the police would not attack Cubans the way they attacked "his brothers" and that, instead of being an international city, Miami seemed more like Selma, Alabama, Jackson, Mississippi, and South Africa (Santiago and Roman 1990).

The following year Haitians received continued support from the black American community after Haiti's overwhelmingly popular president, Jean Bertrand Aristide, was ousted in a military coup. The coup produced an immediate flow of refugees. The U.S. government attempted to return them to Haiti, but black American leaders joined Haitians in demanding that this policy not be implemented (Alvarez 1991).

Yet, in spite of the common experiences of prejudice and discrimination, black Americans and Haitians remain ambivalent toward each other. Rather than considering Haitians as brothers and sisters in solidarity fighting against racism and seeking equality with whites, many black Americans regarded Haitians as unwanted, immigrant competitors for jobs, just like the Cubans and more recent Nicaraguans. Some black Americans also thought that Haitians were unaware and unappreciative of the peculiar plight of black Americans. Haitians, in their view, came from a horrible society and should be glad for what little they received in Miami. As one black American high school girl put it when discussing the 1989 civil disturbances in Miami's Overtown and Liberty City black communities, "Y'all don't understand, y'all come from a country that's strugglin' already and when y'all get over here, y'all so happy, you know. We've been oppressed since we've been knee-high, but now y'all got better freedom [than in Haiti] but we still in the same position, see" (Nolan 1988).

Some Haitian female adolescents in Little Haiti, despite differences between Haitian refugees and black Americans, have adopted the "do's" (hair styles) and clothes of young black American women.

For their part, Haitians accept black American support in their trials against racism, but Haitians do not wish to be identified with what they view as the most downtrodden group in the United States. Haitians intend to advance beyond the bottom rung. A Haitian-American community leader claimed, "Haitians rarely cross 7th Avenue or I-95 [the locally agreed limits of Liberty City]. They call the area beyond 'Black Power' and do not want to live close to it. Haitians will not melt into the larger black community. There is just too much animosity between the groups—both in school and at work" (Stepick 1983).

As the numbers of Haitians in Miami continued to grow, local government became increasingly concerned about their impact on public services. A 1978 Dade County task force on Haitians called for the federal government to grant Haitians refugee status, which would trigger federal benefits for services provided to them. The county, however, did not claim that the Haitians deserved political asylum, only that the county deserved federal resources to take care of them.

More critical in the long run than either the local black American community or county government was the involvement of national church, civil, and human rights groups. The NCC hired lawyers to assist Haitians in their asylum claims, and it underwrote the services of other lawyers in the preparation of major class action suits against the federal government's policies aimed at Haitians. In time interest spread as other groups became involved, such as Amnesty International and the Lawyers Committee for International Human Rights, along with pro bono lawyers from top-notch firms in Washington and New York. A series of court victories for the Haitians began in 1977, each of which demanded due process for Haitian asylum claims and usually contained relief for some Haitians.[4] The federal courts, however, never accorded the Haitians a legal immigration status. The courts only forced the federal government to reprocess Haitian asylum claims and follow its own rules and regulations.

Simultaneously, the Congressional Black Caucus, led by Shirley Chisholm and Walter Fauntroy, pressured the federal government, branding its policies as racist. During the early years of the Carter administration, these forces induced a short-term policy change that released imprisoned Haitians and granted them work permits. After a near revolt by local Miami INS employees, the policy reverted to one of mass denial of Haitian asylum claims.

In the first days of the Mariel Cuban boatlift in the spring of 1980, the U.S. government attempted to admit these Cubans as political refugees, despite many of their statements that they were coming to the United States for economic reasons. The transparent and politically insupportable inconsistencies between the early policy toward Mariel Cubans and the efforts to repatriate Haitians because they were allegedly economic refugees produced a temporary legal immigration status, "Cuban-Haitian Entrant Status Pending," for approximately 25,000 Haitians. Cubans subsequently could adjust after one year under the 1966 Cuban Adjustment Act. Haitians had to wait for the 1986 Immigration Reform and Control Act (IRCA).

In 1981 the Reagan administration began to incarcerate newly arrived Haitians who illegally entered the United States, at the same time that it stationed a U.S. Coast Guard cutter in Haitian waters to intercept potential Haitian refugees before they reached the United States. The newly arrived Haitians were imprisoned in Krome detention center, described by many as a concentration camp in the middle of the Everglades swamps. At one point more than 2,000 Haitians were locked up, some for more than a year. Many became profoundly depressed and a few attempted suicide (Nachman 1983). The federal court ultimately ordered the release of the detained Haitians, but the federal administration still refused to provide a firm immigration status either to the recently released or to earlier arriving Haitians who had made claims for political asylum.

At about the same time, the Centers for Disease Control (CDC) announced that Haitians (along with homosexuals, HIV drug abusers, and hemophiliacs) were one of the prime at-risk groups for Acquired Immune Deficiency Syndrome (AIDS). The general response was just as it had been a few years earlier when Haitians were accused of spreading tuberculosis. Many Haitians lost their jobs. The primary employment agency for Haitians suddenly found it nearly impossible to place any of its clients, and the widespread negative stereotypes of Haitians stretched even more broadly and deeply. Subsequently, the CDC removed Haitians from the list of at-risk groups, but again it was too late. The damage had already been done. In the public mind, all Haitians were black boat people who were disease-ridden, desperately poor, and pathetic.

The political and legal controversy surrounding Haitians made their immigration status extraordinarily complex and confusing. Frequently neither the Haitian nor the INS knew precisely what a particular individual's status was nor what rights and benefits he or she had. Some Haitians had the right to work, and others did not. Some had rights to welfare benefits, and others did not. Some were subject to immediate deportation, and others had a right to a hearing, while still others could legally remain in the United States. Many in the United States, including government officials, simply treated all Haitians as if they were illegals, even though the majority had a claim to remain legally here. The INS frequently attempted to deport those who still enjoyed rights to hearings and state agencies often denied benefits to those who qualified for them.

After many legal battles and much public pressure, most of the Haitian boat people qualified for a legal permanent immigration status under the Immigration Reform and Control Act of 1986, and approximately 17,000 have begun the legal adjustment process. Haitian farm workers, along with other farm workers, were also supposed to be eligible. The INS District Office, however, suspected massive fraud in farm work applications and rejected the vast majority of them. In spite of these difficulties, by the mid-1980s there were approximately 80,000 Haitians in Florida, about half of whom lived in the Greater Miami area, Dade County. This number represents less than 1 percent of the total immigration to the United States in the past ten years. Moreover the number in the Miami area is less than one-fifth the number of Haitians in New York.

Street corner in Little Haiti where Haitian Creole is not as dominant as Spanish is in Little Havana. The beauty supply business across the street has one phrase in Creole (Vente en Gros & Details), but everything else is in English.

The vast majority of Haitians in Miami, and especially the recent immigrants, live in Little Haiti, which lies about three miles north of Miami's downtown and encompasses a rectangular area approximately fifty blocks by ten blocks. To the east, toward Biscayne Bay, is a narrow residential strip that remains primarily Anglo, some of it gentrified and one part a walled enclave containing some of Miami's most economically and politically powerful individuals. To the west lies Liberty City, Miami's largest black community. In between, what is now Little Haiti is one of Miami's oldest neighborhoods, which emerged before the turn of the century. Until the 1960s, it was primarily Anglo and blue-collar. In the 1960s, Cubans began to settle there at the same time that black Americans began to move east from Liberty City. In the 1970s it became predominantly black: 80 percent at the time of the 1980 census. The racial and ethnic changes lowered real estate values and made the area affordable to the Haitian refugees. In 1982 a city- and county-financed study revealed that Haitians were far short of a majority in the neighborhood but were a plurality at about 40 percent.

Recent Haitian immigrants have translated their negative experiences into perceptions of discrimination. Haitians believe all major ethnic groups in south Florida discriminate against them. Moreover, these perceptions seem to be on the rise. In the survey conducted from 1983 to 1984, 62 percent of recent immigrants believed that Anglos discriminated against Haitians, and 67 percent reported that Anglos regarded themselves as superior (see Stepick and Portes 1986). Two years later, the figures had increased to 67 and 94 percent, respectively. By the time of the survey conducted from 1985 to 1986, almost all recent Haitian immigrants perceived at least some form of Anglo discrimination, despite the much lower number who admitted to having suffered directly one or more such experiences (18 percent) (see Portes and Stepick 1987). Things are not much better with respect to other groups. Fifty-three percent of Haitians reported that American blacks discriminated against them in 1985. The number increased by almost twenty points (to 72 percent) in 1986. In 1986 a still higher proportion (77 percent) indicated that Cubans also discriminated against Haitians.

Given these perceptions it is not surprising that Haitians limit their social interactions to other Haitians. Three-fourths (78 percent) did not have a single Anglo friend, and only a third reported at least some opportunity to interact socially with Anglos. More significant is that the same pattern of social isolation also applies to black Americans, with whom Haitians share a common race and frequently the same urban neighborhoods. Fully 77 percent of the respondents did not have a single black American friend. At the other extreme, almost the entire sample (97 percent) reported that their socializing took place mostly with other Haitians.

The policy of persecution, legal confusion, and social isolation have all contributed to Haitians' dismal socioeconomic conditions in the United States. Their employment situation compares unfavorably to any other immigrant population in the country. In 1985 involuntary unemployment was 24 percent (see fig. 4.2). For those who were working, their places of employment were overwhelmingly apparel and furniture factories, restaurants, and hotels, where they were hired to perform the most menial tasks. Median earnings were $680 per month, and the proportion receiving food stamps or other welfare support was just below 25 percent. As is illustrated in figure 4.2, the recent Haitian immigrants fare worse than Haitian businesspersons in Miami or Haitians arriving earlier in the United States. While figures for other undocumented immigrant groups are less representative and not always directly comparable, Haitians also appear to be faring worse than Mariel Cubans who arrived at approximately the same time (Portes, Stepick, and Truelove 1986), Dominicans in New York City (Grasmuck 1984), undocumented aliens in northern New Jersey (Papademetriou and DiMarzio 1985), and documented Vietnamese refugees in southern California (Montero 1979). Moreover, statistical analysis indicates that increased education or skills do little to improve Haitians' chances of either getting a job or earning more money. Indeed, the only thing that seems to make a significant difference is gender—women have a much worse time finding a job or earning money than do men (Stepick and Portes 1986).

Haitian refugees are seldom employed by their compatriots. This contrasts sharply with the situation of recent Cuban refugees. For example, in a large sample of Mariel refugees interviewed at the same time as the recent Haitian immigrants, 45 percent of all wage earners were employed by other Cubans from 1985 to 1986. In contrast, less than 1 percent of Haitian refugees were employed by other Haitians in 1983; two years later, the figure remained unchanged. The lack of an ethnic economy that can provide jobs for recent arrivals and support their subsequent entrepreneurial initiatives represents a major handicap for Haitian refugees. It accounts, to a large extent, for the major differences found in employment and economic situation between post-1980 Cuban and Haitian arrivals after five years of U.S. residence (Portes and Stepick 1987).

One response to employment difficulties has been the creation of small and informal Haitian businesses.[5] Most Haitian self-employed, informal entrepreneurs become full-time informal sector entrepreneurs usually when they have no choice or when they lose or cannot obtain wage labor employment. The most common activities are dressmaking and tailoring; petty commerce; food preparation; child care; transportation; and the provision of semiskilled services such as construction work, automobile repair, and electronic repair. These activities clearly are survival strategies that produce goods and services consumed exclusively within the Haitian community. These activities also provide an income close to the poverty threshold. As figure 4.3 illustrates, Haitian informal-sector workers earn approximately the same as other recent Haitian immigrants and considerably less than either Haitian businesspersons who own formal businesses or Haitians nationally.

A consistent finding in past surveys of immigrant groups was the high number of immigrants who voiced satisfaction with their current lives in the United States, and the tendency of this figure to increase over time (cf. Portes and Bach 1985: chap. 8). The same was true even of Mariel

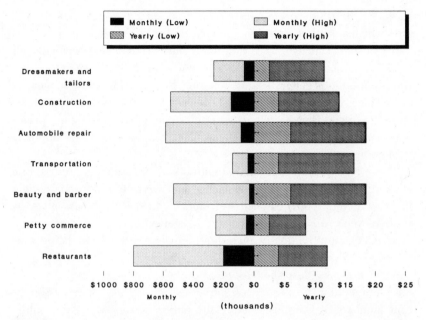

Fig. 4.3. Estimated income among informally self-employed Haitians. *Source*: Data gathered by Alex Stepick 1985–86.

Note: Estimates of monthly income refer only to the particular informal sector activity. Estimates of yearly income, however, refer to the individuals' total income, including other employment or receipt of government benefits.

refugees, surveyed in conjunction with the Haitians. From 1985 to 1986 over four-fifths (85 percent) of Mariel Cubans declared themselves satisfied with their present lives. In contrast, only 32 percent of the Haitians did so. More significant, this last figure represented a 5 percent decline from the number expressing at least some satisfaction two years earlier. Other results pointed in the same direction: Almost half of the persons in the Haitian sample believed that there was discrimination in economic opportunities in the United States, and a similar number (47 percent) complained that the American way of life weakened the family; fewer than a fourth of those in the survey indicated satisfaction with their present economic situation (Portes and Stepick 1987).

Middle Classes

In spite of the image of Miami Haitians as being "boat people" the Haitian community is actually quite diverse, with a significant middle class. As the Haitian community grew in Miami, it attracted other Haitians who had settled earlier in other North American cities, such as New York, Boston, Chicago, and Montreal. These Haitians are virtually all legal immigrants from the 1960s. Those who were adults when they left Haiti in the 1960s generally state that they bypassed Miami then because of the legacy of southern segregation. Virtually all Haitians who have moved to Miami from more northern cities claim that anti-Haitian prejudice is greater in Miami, although antiblack prejudice (i.e., racism) may be no different.

These Haitians are thoroughly familiar with American culture. While Haitian Creole is their native language and virtually all are also fluent in French, they know English well and might describe themselves as Haitian-Americans. Those under forty received a significant portion of their education, frequently including college, in the United States or Canada.

They are best described as middle class, although they are quite diverse, including every profession from secretary to psychiatrist. Significant numbers of Haitians work in the public sector, where the public schools have made a concerted effort to recruit Haitian educators. Most social service agencies also have at least one Haitian who, among his or her regular duties, provides translation services. Residentially the Haitian middle class is dispersed throughout the community, and middle-class families do not necessarily live in predominantly black neighborhoods. It is impossible to know how many middle-class Haitians Miami has, but a rough estimate, based on interviews with Haitian community leaders, would be 15,000 to 20,000.

Among this Haitian middle class in Miami are "invisible Haitians": those who do not proclaim a Haitian identity. They live outside Little Haiti and usually outside black neighborhoods, speak good English, and may be light-skinned enough to pass for whites to North Americans. They submerge their Haitian identity because of the intense and widespread anti-Haitian prejudice in south Florida. If they do admit that they are Haitians, they carefully distinguish themselves from the "boat people," who are presumably lower class, less educated, and the basis for south Florida's anti-Haitian prejudice. While admitting to being Haitian, Haitians afraid of discrimination may deny speaking Creole, claiming to speak only French. In middle- and upper-class households in Haiti it is common for parents to speak to their children in French. But children still learn Creole from servants, on the playground, and even from their parents when they are more relaxed. French becomes the polite, formal, and prestigious language and Creole the intimate, informal one.

In the wake of arrivals of Haitian boat people in the late 1970s, numerous organizations arose to provide services to the new immigrants. In 1981 there were nearly forty such organizations in Miami, although in the wake of the Reagan era in the late 1980s only about one-third of that number remained. New positions in these agencies increased the flow of educated Haitians relocating from northern cities. Those that have the most evident presence in Little Haiti include the Haitian Refugee Center (HRC), the Haitian American Community Agency of Dade (HACAD), the Haitian-American Chamber of Commerce (HACC), the Haitian Task Force (HTF), and the Haitian-American Democratic Club (HADC).

In the mid-1970s the Haitian Refugee Center began offering legal assistance, hosting Saturday night meetings to brief refugees on legal developments, and occasionally organizing local demonstrations. At the end of 1975 it received a significant boost when the National Council of Churches established Haitian Refugee Concerns, the original intent of which was explicitly political: to organize Haitian migrants and community support groups. The two soon merged, and by the middle of 1978 a solely Haitian-led group, Combité Liberté (rechristened "veye yo" [watch them] in the wake of Duvalier's 1986 demise, i.e., don't trust the new government), emerged and became the primary political voice of Miami's Haitian refugees.

Reverend Gérard Jean-Juste was the executive director of the Haitian Refugee Center and the leader of Combité Liberté from the time he arrived in Miami from Boston in 1977 until 1990. He left Haiti as a young man and attended a seminary in Puerto Rico. In 1971 an exiled Haitian bishop in New York ordained him. Jean-Juste then taught English to Haitians in Boston. Upon arriving in Miami he criticized the local archbishop, Edward McCarthy, for his inactivity on behalf of Haitian refugees. The local Catholic hierarchy soon ostracized Jean-Juste, barring him from giving mass locally. He relishes his role as a constant thorn in the side of the local establishment concerning Haitians, and he is by far the most outspoken and frequently quoted Haitian spokesperson. His vocal opposition to the status quo eventually resulted in Combité Liberté losing its support from the National Council of Churches. The Ford Foundation stepped into the breach for nearly ten years until the implementation of the Immigration Reform and Control Act of 1986 provided legal status to the majority of Haitians in Miami.

While Jean-Juste's political activities were highly visible, the legal services rendered by HRC were more critical to the formation of Miami's Haitian community. Most of HRC's work has been the representation of Haitians in asylum hearings and has been carried out by non-Haitian lawyers and Haitian legal aides. The most significant work, however, has been class-action suits on behalf of Haitian asylum claims. The legal victories frustrated the U.S. government's efforts to stop the flow of Haitians to south Florida. Without those legal victories, it is likely that the U.S. government would have succeeded in its efforts, and a critical nucleus of Miami's Haitian community never would have formed.

HACAD, the Haitian American Community Agency of Dade, is the only Haitian-run organization that provides social services to the Haitian community. It was chartered in the fall of 1974 by three Haitian businesspersons from New York. It had only two staff people on salary and offered no social services itself until Dade County government began to patronize it as a politically acceptable alternative to HRC. By 1979 its budget had swelled sufficiently to open a small health clinic. In the wake of funding for Haitian refugees occasioned by President Carter's creation of the Cuban-Haitian Entrant Status, HACAD burgeoned dramatically. Its budget increased 472 percent between 1981 and 1982. It has provided job counseling, training, and referral; legal services focusing on housing and employment problems; a host of classes ranging from English to ones that teach women how to operate day-care centers; and most recently AIDS education.

HACAD's executive director during this period of growth was Roger Biamby. He left Haiti in 1963, lived for a year in the Dominican Republic and then seventeen years in New York, where he obtained a master's degree in political science. He came to Miami in 1981 to assume the directorship of HACAD. Like HRC, HACAD also provides an institutional basis for its director's political activities. Biamby, however, has been somewhat more low-key than Jean-Juste and is not generally considered by outsiders as the spokesperson for the Haitian refugee community. Nevertheless his political activities have subjected him to considerable attention within the Haitian community, and in 1989 he was ousted as executive director.

Jean-Juste and Biamby are frequently seen as political competitors. The approximately twenty Haitian radio talk shows in south Florida frequently snipe at them with accusations of mismanagement, distribution of benefits only to their supporters, and similar practices that are commonly assumed to be the norm for organizations in Haiti. NCC withdrew its support from HRC ostensibly for these reasons, although most insiders agree that the real reason was Jean-Juste's political positions. He was more ideological than most Haitian political leaders, who tend to rely on charisma more than a coherent platform. He also worked closely with the Socialist Workers party, and a few of the party's members worked in his organization. His attacks on U.S. policy toward Haiti frequently labeled the United States as "imperialist." Biamby's politics, on the other hand, were far more to the right. A few years before Duvalier's fall, he supported an invasion that was depicted in the *Miami Herald* more as a tragicomedy than a serious military maneuver. In the period of hoped-for elections after Duvalier's demise, Biamby championed Marc Bazin, known as the "American candidate."

One Haitian organization assiduously avoids politics back in Haiti. The Haitian-American Democratic Club (HADC) is devoted solely to the task of speeding Haitian assimilation into U.S. culture and society. Its founder, Jacques Despinosse, left Haiti in the early 1970s and, like so many other members of the local Haitian middle class, came to Miami. He became a citizen in 1979 and founded HADC in 1980, after having been involved in the 1980 Democratic presidential race. By the mid-1980s the club had over 400 members, but Despinosse remained the dominant figure. In 1984 he sponsored a block party to celebrate the Fourth of July that was attacked by some Haitians, particularly those affiliated with HRC's Combité Liberté, as both unfaithful to Haitian heritage and unworthy given the U.S. government's mistreatment of Haitian refugees. Nevertheless, Despinosse forges on. He hosts a radio show that tends to have guests from outside the Haitian community and on which local and U.S. politics, rather than Haitian politics, tend to be discussed.

While these organizations are the most well-known Haitian organizations outside the Haitian community, the most popular organizations within it are undoubtedly religious. Compared to other recent immigrant groups to the United States, Haitians are exceptionally religious. Nearly 75 percent of recent Haitian immigrants reported in 1985 that they attended church at least weekly. Nearly 40 percent of the recent refugees are Protestants, substantially more than the estimated 15 to 20 percent in Haiti. Store-front Protestant churches abound in Little Haiti. Most have small congregations numbering under fifty, and what few services they have beyond religious rituals reach only their own members.

By far the most visible and important religious institution is the Haitian

Catholic Center. Its Sunday masses overflow with people. Ironically the Catholic Center is headed by a Polish-American priest, Father Tom Wenski. He, however, speaks fluent Haitian Creole and has sought to serve his parish at every turn. All services are conducted in Haitian Creole, and the center is staffed primarily by nuns and priests "on loan" from Catholic religious orders in Haiti. The center, which is housed in a former girls' Catholic high school, has provided room and support for night school English classes, day care, Catholic community charity services to Haitians, and numerous organizations and initiatives for the Haitian community. Satellite centers have also been established throughout south Florida wherever there is a significant Haitian community.

Two organizations were created by and serve the Haitian business community: the Haitian-American Chamber of Commerce (HACC) and the Haitian Task Force (HTF). HACC was founded in 1982 by a small group of Haitian businesspersons, most of whose businesses were within the Little Haiti area. HACC has never been very active and has never had any paid staff. Rather, it shares office space with HTF, which also was incorporated in 1982.

HTF was created by Yves Savain, another Haitian who came to the United States in the early 1960s and obtained most of his schooling, including a graduate degree, in the United States. The executive director for most of the 1980s, Henri-Robert Lamothe, grew up in Brooklyn and obtained a master's degree in public administration from Baruch College in New York. He came to Miami from New York originally to work for HACAD, operated a marketing consulting firm, and then assumed the directorship of HTF. HTF is a community development corporation recognized by the City of Miami, and it receives partial funding from the city. The bulk of its funding, however, comes from the Ford Foundation. Its primary program is a revolving loan fund for Haitian businesses, but it also promotes cultural events, particularly shows of Haitian paintings, and built a "Caribbean Market" in Little Haiti modeled after Port-au-Prince's Iron Market. HTF hopes that the market can become an anchor for Haitian businesses and a draw for tourists and others who live outside Little Haiti.

Perhaps even more visible to outsiders than Haitian organizations is the Little Haiti business community. Concurrent with the growth in Haitian population has been an ever-expanding Haitian business community. The first Haitian businesses in Miami opened downtown in 1974 before there was a focused Haitian community. The business community grew slowly at first, with only one or two new businesses opening up each year. First,

Caribbean Market in Little Haiti, created by the Haitian Task Force with support from the Ford Foundation, City of Miami, and Dade County, is modeled on the Iron Market in Port-au-Prince, Haiti.

there was a record shop, then a beauty salon, dry cleaners, automobile repair shops, a restaurant, and a grocery store. In 1976 there were probably fewer than ten Haitian businesses in Miami. As Haitian arrivals increased in the late 1970s, they and the Haitian business community focused on the Edison–Little River area that became known as Little Haiti.

By then the Haitian market had increased to such a size that it served many small entrepreneurs' needs. New Haitian businesses opened up in the area, and Haitian businesses that were outside this area relocated to it. Haitians in the northeastern United States began relocating to Miami specifically because of business opportunities. By the mid-1980s on some blocks in the area it appeared as if virtually every business was Haitian, sporting brightly painted walls and murals. In 1985 there were approximately 120 Haitian businesses in Little Haiti; by the late 1980s perhaps nearly 200.

Some black Americans see the highly visible Haitian business community and ignoring the much larger community of recent immigrants with its extreme economic problems, draw the conclusion that Haitians have already economically outpaced black Americans. However, the owners of these Haitian businesses, just like the leaders of Haitian organizations, are not recent immigrants. They are middle-class Haitians who left Haiti in the 1960s and lived in northern cities before coming to Miami. Haitian businesspersons interviewed in 1985 had been in the United States over ten years, and more than 70 percent had graduated from high school (see fig. 4.2). All spoke English. Moreover, their income was much closer to the overall average Haitian income in the United States than to that of the recent immigrants in Miami.

Yet it would be misleading to describe this business community as a robust recreation of the Miami Cuban success. In 1985 there were neither Haitian manufacturers nor wholesalers in Little Haiti. There were some importers and exporters, but they either did not focus on Little Haiti or if they did, they were strikingly small. Indeed all of the Little Haiti Haitian businesses are modest. Little grocery stores, auto repair shops, and various other service-oriented businesses predominate. In 1985 Haitian businesses had on average 1.5 employees, over half had other family members working in the business, and over a third had either the owner or someone else in the family holding down another job (see table 4.1). Nearly 80 percent had a predominantly Haitian clientele, and nearly 60 percent had total sales of less than $2,000 in the month before the survey and less than $50,000 for the previous year.

The transformation of Little Haiti has been obviously neither complete nor entirely successful. While Haitian businesses have constantly increased and added distinctive character to the neighborhood, there still remain significant numbers of non-Haitian businesses. In 1983, in the Little Haiti area, 60 percent of the businesses were still non-Haitian, although by the late 1980s they had apparently declined below 50 percent.

Moreover, there are still storefronts with old and peeling exteriors; vacant lots with trash and weeds; and streets without sidewalks, which force strollers onto the roadway. But the Haitian business community has been eager and willing to fill these gaps. These business leaders are filled with energy and optimism. They envision Little Haiti becoming another Little Havana or San Francisco Chinatown. They see the only Little Haiti in the United States as becoming a cultural and tourist attraction based upon Haitians' drive, enthusiasm, and unique cultural attributes: world-renowned painting, woodcraft, music, French-inspired cuisine, and numerous skilled trades.

Table 4.1. Formal Sector Haitian Businesses

	%[a]
Types of businesses	
Grocery	9.1
Restaurants	8.3
Automobile repair	12.4
Beauty and barber	11.7
Dressmakers and tailors	5.9
Miscellaneous services	21.5
Professional	2.5
Retail	35.0
Average number of employees	1.5
Percent with 50% or more Haitian clientele	87.5
Total sales in month before survey less than $2,000	60.0
Total sales in year before survey less than $25,000	65.8

Source: Data on Haitian businesspeople are based upon survey data collected in a 1985 survey of Haitian businesses in Miami's Little Haiti area. Percent of total surveyed.
a. Percent of total surveyed.

The origins of the now highly successful Cuban business community, as briefly discussed in chapters 1 and 5, contrast with the origins of the Haitian community in a number of ways. First, a much higher proportion of the initial wave of Cuban migrants was middle- and upper-class, since these persons were the most likely to have been displaced by a socialist revolution. Second, the U.S. government assisted the Cubans in a number of ways that totaled nearly an estimated $1 billion between 1961 and 1974. Not only were various kinds of general assistance programs available, but also Cubans were encouraged to take advantage of loans from the Small Business Administration. Third, many business owners were already closely linked with the U.S. economy. Some Cuban manufacturers had had contracts with U.S. firms before the revolution, and they simply moved their factory from Cuba to Miami and continued in the same business (Stepick and Fernandez-Kelly 1987). Others benefited from the millions of dollars poured into Miami by the CIA and established front organizations that gradually became legitimate and successful businesses. The Haitians have none of these advantages.

Prospects for the Future

The mere existence of the Haitian community in Miami is testimony to the perseverance and struggle to survive of its members. The U.S. government has done virtually everything possible to stop the flow of

Haitian boat people to south Florida. The federal government, however, has been thwarted by its own ineptitude and a coalition of church and civil rights organizations. With great difficulty a Haitian community has emerged in Miami. We cannot say, however, that it has flourished and prospered as has the Cuban community.

Recent Haitian immigrants in Miami (i.e., the black boat people) undoubtedly number among America's most suffering contemporary immigrant communities. Economically they lag behind every other major group in the region and behind their own compatriots who arrived in the United States earlier. Their condition has led the Haitians to perceive widespread discrimination against them. The Haitians also experience lower levels of subjective satisfaction than do other immigrant minorities.

Yet, this is not the full picture of Miami's Haitian community. A significant middle class also exists. These persons are secondary migrants who came to the United States primarily in the 1960s but bypassed Miami then because it was a southern, segregated city. Instead they settled in northern cities, where they attended school and learned English. They returned to Miami only after a substantial Haitian community was created by the flow of more recent migrants. Some within the Miami Haitian middle class, because of anti-Haitian prejudice, are invisible, masking their Haitian heritage. But others remain committed to the Haitian community. They head major Haitian organizations and run small businesses.

While unlikely to become as politically or economically successful as Miami's Cuban community, Haitians are a permanent and significant force, the most visible black immigrant group in Miami. In the wake of Duvalier's departure and the regularization of immigration status in 1987, Haitians did not massively return home. Quite a few returned for brief visits and to assess their prospects back home. The vast majority decided to remain in the United States. In spite of the enormous prejudice and discrimination they have encountered, they remain resolved to carve out a new life in their adopted country.

Notes

1. See especially Glick 1975; Buchanan 1979, 1980, 1983; Fouron 1984; Laguerre 1984; Glick-Schiller and Fouron 1990. For other concentrations see Dejean 1980 and Woldemikael 1985. For reviews of the literature on Haitians in the United States, see Mohl 1985 and Lawless 1986. See also Anderson 1975; Pie 1975; Elwell et al. 1977; Keely et al. 1978; Laguerre 1979, 1980.

2. There are numerous other short reports based on secondary data, including Bogre 1979, Walsh 1980, and Boswell 1983.

3. See Stepick 1982a, Zucker 1983, Loescher and Scanlan 1984, and Miller 1984 for discussions of the U.S. government's actions toward Haitian boat people. See also Powers 1976; Gollobin 1979; Colbert 1980; Walsh 1980; Wortham 1980; Schey 1981; Ryan 1982; Jean-Barte 1983; and Kurzban 1983.

4. See *National Council of Churches v. Egan* (1979), *Haitian Refugee Center v. Civiletti* (1980), *Haitian Refugee Center v. Smith* (1982), and *Sannon v. United States* (1978).

5. For a fuller description of the Miami Haitian informal sector, see Stepick 1990. For a comparison with the Miami Cuban informal sector see Stepick 1989.

References

Alvarez, Lizette. 1991. "Celebrities, Miami Leaders Bring Hope, Aid to Tent City." *Miami Herald*, December 8: 1A, 30A.

Anderson, Jervis. 1975. "The Haitians of New York." *New Yorker* 51, no. 6: 50, 52–54, 58–60, 62–75.

Behavioral Science Research Institute (BSRI). 1983. "Demography, Social Status, Housing and Social Needs of the Haitian Population of Edison-Little River." Paper, February 24.

Bogre, Michelle. 1979. "Haitian Refugees: (Haiti's) Missing Persons." *Migration Today* 7 (September): 9–11.

Boswell, Thomas D. 1983. "In the Eye of the Storm: The Context of Haitian Migration to Miami, Florida." *Southeastern Geographer* 23 (November): 57–77.

Buchanan, Susan. 1979. "Haitian Women in New York City." *Migration Today* 7, no. 4: 19–25, 39.

———. 1980. "Scattered Seeds: The Meaning of Migration for Haitians in New York City." Ph.D. diss., New York University.

———. 1983. "The Cultural Meaning of Social Class for Haitians in New York City." *Ethnic Groups* 5: 7–30.

Colbert, Lois. 1980. "Haitian Aliens—A People in Limbo." *The Crisis* 87 (August–September): 235–38.

Dejean, Paul. 1980. *The Haitians in Quebec*. Ottawa: Tecumseh Press.

Elwell, Patricia J., Charles B. Keely, Austin T. Fragomen, Jr., and Silvano M. Tomasi. 1977. "Haitian and Dominican Undocumented Aliens in New York City: A Preliminary Report." *Migration Today* 5, no. 5: 5–9.

Fouron, George. 1984. "Patterns of Adaptation of Haitian Immigrants of the 1970s in New York City." Ph.D. diss., Columbia University.

Glick, N. 1975. "The Formation of a Haitian Ethnic Group." Ph.D. diss., Columbia University.

Glick-Schiller, Nina, and George Fouron. 1990. "'Everywhere we go we are in danger': Ti Manno and the Emergence of Haitian Transnational Identity." *American Ethnologist* 17, no. 2 (May): 329–47.

Gollobin, Ira. 1979. "Haitian 'Boat People' and Equal Justice under Law: Background and Perspective." *Migration Today* 7, no. 4: 40–41.

Grasmuck, Sherri. 1984. "Immigration, Ethnic Stratification, and Native Working Class Discipline: Comparison of Documented and Undocumented Dominicans." *International Migration Review* 18, no. 3 (Fall): 692–713.

Haitian Refugee Center v. Civiletti. 1980. 503 F. Supp. 442, 522, 525, Southern District Florida.

Immigration and Naturalization Service. 1975. *Annual Report and Statistical Yearbook.* Washington: U.S. Department of Justice.

Jean-Barte, Rulx. 1983. "Afe Refijye yo Se Batay Pep Ayisyen an" [The Refugee Affair: The Struggle of the Haitian People]. *Sel* 54/55: 27–31.

Keely, Charles B., Patricia J. Elwell, Austin T. Fragomen, Jr., and Silvano M. Tomasi. 1978. "Profiles of Undocumented Aliens in New York City: Haitians and Dominicans." Occasional Paper no. 5. Staten Island, N.Y.: Center for Migration Studies.

Kurzban, Ira. 1983. "Long and Perilous Journey: The Nelson Decision." *Human Rights* 11, no. 2 (Summer): 41–44.

Laguerre, Michel S. 1979. "The Haitian Niche in New York City." *Migration Today* 7, no. 4: 12–18.

———. 1980. "Haitians in the United States." In *Harvard Encyclopedia of American Ethnic Groups*, edited by S. Thernstrom, 446–49. Cambridge, Mass.: Harvard University Press.

———. 1984. *Haitians in the United States.* Ithaca, N.Y.: Cornell University Press.

Lawless, Robert. 1986. "Haitian Migrants and Haitian-Americans: From Invisibility into the Spotlight." *Journal of Ethnic Studies* 14, no. 2: 29–70.

Loescher, Gilbert, and John Scanlan. 1984. "Human Rights, U.S. Foreign Policy, and Haitian Refugees." *Journal of Interamerican Studies and World Affairs* 26: 313–56.

———. 1986. *Calculated Kindness: Refugees and the Half-Open Door, 1945 to the Present.* New York: Free Press.

Metro–Dade County Planning Department. 1984. *Profile of the Black Population.* Miami: Research Division, Metro–Dade County Planning Department.

Miller, Jake C. 1984. *The Plight of Haitian Refugees.* New York: Praeger.

Mohl, Raymond A. 1985. "The New Haitian Immigration: A Preliminary Bibliography." *Immigration History Newsletter* 17, no. 1 (May): 1–8.

Montero, Darrel. 1979. "The Vietnamese Refugees in America: Patterns of Socioeconomic Adaptation and Assimilation." *International Migration Review* 13, no. 4 (Winter): 624–48.

Nachman, Steven. 1983. "Wasted Lives: Tuberculosis and Other Health Risks of

Being Haitian in a U.S. Detention Camp." Paper presented at meeting of the Southern Anthropological Society, April 15–16, University of South Florida, Tampa.

National Council of Churches v. Egan. 1979. No. 79–2959 Civ.-WMH, Southern District Florida (July).

Nolan, Peggy. 1988. Unpublished fieldnotes from "Changing Relations between Newcomers and Established Residents: The Case of Miami."

Papademetriou, Demetrios G., and Nicholas DiMarzio. 1985. "A Preliminary Profile of Unapprehended Undocumented Aliens in Northern New Jersey: A Research Note." *International Migration Review* 19, no. 4 (Winter): 746–59.

Pie, Rolan. 1975. "Kouman Yo Leve Ayisyin Nouyok" [How Haitians in New York Are Rising Up]. *Sel* 23/24: 9–18.

Portes, Alejandro, and Robert Bach. 1985. *Latin Journey: Cuban and Mexican Immigrants in the United States.* Berkeley: University of California Press.

Portes, Alejandro, and Alex Stepick. 1985. "Unwelcome Immigrants: The Labor Market Experiences of 1980 (Mariel) Cuban and Haitian Refugees in South Florida." *American Sociological Review* 50 (August): 493–514.

———. 1987. "Haitian Refugees in South Florida, 1983–1986." *Dialogue* no. 77, Occasional Papers Series, Latin American and Caribbean Center. Miami: Florida International University.

Portes, Alejandro, Alex Stepick, and Cynthia Truelove. 1986. "Three Years Later: The Adaptation Process of 1980 (Mariel) Cuban and Haitian Refugees in South Florida." *Population Research and Policy Review* (Summer).

Powers, Thomas. 1976. "The Scandal of U.S. Immigration: The Haitian Example." *Ms.* 4, no. 8: 62–66, 81–83.

Ryan, Michael C. P. 1982. "Political Asylum for the Haitians?" *Case Western Reserve Journal of International Law* 14: 155–76.

San Martin, Nancy, Andres Viglucci, and David Hancock. 1990. "Peaceful Rally Ends Days of Divisiveness." *Miami Herald*, July 8: 1B, 2B.

Santiago, Ana, and Ivan Roman. 1990. "Haitianos denuncian brutalidad policial." *El Nuevo Herald*, July 7: 1A, 6A.

Sannon v. United States. 1980. No. 74–428 Civ-JLK Southern District Florida (January).

Schey, Peter A. 1981. "The Black Boat People Founder on the Shoals of U.S. Policy." *Migration Today* 9, nos. 4/5: 7–10.

Stepick, Alex. 1982a. "Root Causes of Haitian Migration." *Immigration Reform* no. 30, part 1, House Committee of the Judiciary, U.S. Congress.

———. 1982b. "The Haitian Exodus: The Flight from Terror and Poverty." *Caribbean Review* 11, no. 1.

———. 1982c. "Haitian Boat People: A Study in the Conflicting Forces Shaping U.S. Refugee Policy." *Law and Contemporary Problems* 45, no. 2.

———. 1983. Unpublished field interviews conducted as part of the Cuban/Haitian project funded by the National Science Foundation, Alejandro Portes, principal investigator, Department of Sociology, Johns Hopkins University.

———. 1984. "Haitians Released from Krome: Their Prospects for Adaptation and Integration in South Florida." *Dialogue* no. 24, Occasional Papers Series, Latin American and Caribbean Center. Miami: Florida International University.

———. 1986. *Haitian Refugees in the United States.* 2d ed. London and New York: Minority Rights Group.

———. 1988. "Miami's Two Informal Sectors." In *The Informal Sector in Developing and Developed Countries*, edited by A. Portes, M. Castells, and L. Benton. Baltimore, Md.: Johns Hopkins University Press.

———. 1989. "The Haitian Informal Sector in Miami." In *The Informal Economy: Studies in Advanced and Less Developed Countries*, ed. A. Portes, M. Castells, and L. Benton, 111–31. Baltimore, Md.: Johns Hopkins University Press.

———. 1990. "Community Growth versus Simply Surviving: The Informal Sectors of Cubans and Haitians in Miami." In *Perspectives on the Informal Economy*, ed. M.E. Smith, 183–205. Washington: University Press of America.

Stepick, Alex, and Carol Dutton Stepick. 1990. "People in the Shadows: Survey Research among Haitians in Miami." *Human Organization* 49, no. 1 (Spring): 64–77.

Stepick, Alex, and Maria Patricia Fernandez-Kelly. 1987. Unpublished fieldnotes from interviews on informal sector in Miami.

Stepick, Alex, and Alejandro Portes. 1986. "Flight into Despair: A Profile of Recent Haitian Refugees in South Florida." *International Migration Review* 20, no. 2 (Summer): 329–50.

U.S. Bureau of the Census. 1984. *Detailed Population Characteristics, United States Summary.* Series PC80 = 1-D1-A. Washington: U.S. Government Printing Office.

Walsh, Bryan O. 1980. "The Boat People of South Florida." *America* 142: 420–21.

Woldemikael, Tekle M. 1985. "Opportunity versus Constraint: Haitian Immigrants and Racial Ascription." *Migration Today* 13, no. 4: 7–12.

———. 1989. *Becoming Black American: Haitians and American Institutions in Evanston, Illinois.* New York: AMS Press.

Wortham, Jacob. 1980. "The Black Boat People." *Black Enterprise* 10, no. 9: 34–35.

Zucker, Naomi F. 1983. "The Haitians versus the United States: The Courts as Last Resort." *Annals of the American Academy of Political and Social Science* 467 (May): 151–62.

Zucker, Norman L., and Naomi F. Zucker. 1987. *The Guarded Gate: The Reality of American Refugee Policy.* San Diego, Calif.: Harcourt Brace Jovanovich.

5

Cuban Miami

Lisandro Pérez

Persons born in Cuba or who are of Cuban descent represent Miami's largest ethnic group. Cubans account for 56 percent of Greater Miami's foreign-born population, and persons of Cuban origin constitute the bulk—nearly 70 percent—of all Hispanics in the area. About 30 percent of Dade County's population is of Cuban birth or descent (Miami-Dade 1985:13–31).

The demographic importance of the Cuban presence in Miami is evident in a myriad of ways. The "Cubanness" of the area is manifested not only in demonstrable terms, such as economic activities and cultural events, but also in a more intangible manner, such as "ambience" (Rieff 1987b:71). Rieff, a New Yorker who has written on Miami, has noted that Cubans have largely taken control of the "atmosphere" of the city. There is little point, therefore, in attempting to understand the Miami of today without a detailed analysis of the characteristics and development of its Cuban community.

The Cuban Migration to Miami

The large Cuban presence in Miami dates from 1959, the year that the rebel movement headed by Fidel Castro overthrew the government of Fulgencio Batista. Castro initiated a process of revolutionary change that, in its rapidity and pervasiveness, alienated large sectors of the Cuban population (Fagen, Brody, and O'Leary 1968:100–101). An exodus from the island was underway by 1960, and the principal destination was Miami.

Although by far most of Miami's Cubans arrived in the city in the three decades since 1960, the history of the Cuban presence in Miami does not, of course, start in 1959. Geographic proximity determined that Cuba and Miami would have interwoven histories, and that the island and its residents would play a role in the development during this century of a fledgling Miami.

Pre-Castro Cuban Miami

It was not until early in the 1960s that Miami emerged as the premier Cuban community in the United States. Throughout the history of the Cuban presence in this country, Miami, largely because of its youth and economic structure, was never the principal destination of Cuban immigrants.

In the nineteenth century, sizable Cuban communities thrived in New York, Key West, New Orleans, and in Ybor City on the outskirts of Tampa. New York, which contained one of the earliest Cuban-American communities in the nineteenth century, was still the premier destination for migrants from the island in the period between World War II and the rise of the Castro government.

Miami, in the 1940s and 1950s, did not have the employment opportunities that the Cuban immigrants of that time were seeking. Many were laborers who were attracted to New York by the factories and service industries of the region.

Despite not having a sizable and stable community of migrants from Cuba prior to 1959, Miami had nevertheless been greatly influenced by the considerable flow of people and goods across the Florida Straits throughout the twentieth century. The creation of rail and highway links between Miami and Key West and their extensions to Havana by way of regular ferry service established important connections between Miami and the Cuban capital. Air service between Miami, Key West, and Havana dated back to the 1920s and represented a pioneering effort in the history of passenger aviation.

The establishment of these transportation links served to accommodate a considerable flow of tourists and businesspeople who were the human barometer of the increasing integration of Cuba into the U.S. economic system throughout the first half of the twentieth century. Miami became a staging area for the increasingly close relationship between Cuba and the Florida peninsula. In 1948, for example, Cuba led all countries in the world in the volume of passengers exchanged with the United States (U.S. Immigration and Naturalization Service 1948).

Although during the first half of the twentieth century Cuban immigrants tended to go to New York, Miami did receive those seeking refuge from the shifting fortunes of the island's turbulent political history. Two deposed Cuban presidents—Gerardo Machado and Carlos Prío Socarrás—made their home in Miami. José Manuel Alemán, a prominent Cuban politician of the 1940s, built Miami's baseball stadium. Even Fidel Castro spent time in Miami in the 1950s, visiting Cubans to ask for their support.

The Cuban Exodus to the United States

With the start of the 1990s, the Cuban community of Miami entered its fourth decade. The rise of Cuban Miami as the largest concentration of Cubans in the United States—and the third largest Hispanic community in this country, after New York and Los Angeles—effectively started in 1959 with the massive exodus from the island.

The pattern of Cuban emigration since 1959 reflects primarily the availability of the means to leave Cuba. Until the Missile Crisis of October 1962 (and despite the severing of diplomatic relations in January 1961), there was regular commercial air traffic between the United States and Cuba. During that period, some 200,000 persons left Cuba (Pérez 1986a: 129). The U.S. government facilitated their entry by granting them refugee status, allowing them to enter without the restrictions imposed on most other nationality groups. This favored treatment continued until shortly after the termination of the 1980 boatlift.

The Missile Crisis ended all contact between the two countries, slowing down considerably the pace of Cuban immigration in 1964 and 1965. Persons leaving Cuba during those years were doing so clandestinely, often in small boats, or through third countries, usually Spain or Mexico.

In the fall of 1965, in a move that responded to internal pressures for emigration and that was to be repeated fifteen years later, the Cuban government opened a port and allowed persons from the United States to go to Cuba to pick up relatives who wanted to leave the country. Some 5,000 Cubans left from the port of Camarioca before the United States and Cuba halted the boatlift and agreed to an orderly airlift.

The airlift, also called the "freedom flights," started in December 1965 and lasted until 1973. The twice-daily flights brought 260,500 persons during those years. The termination of the airlift brought another period, during the mid- to late 1970s, of relatively low migration from Cuba. By 1980 however, the pressures for emigration once again caused the Cuban government to open a port for unrestricted emigration. The port was Mariel, giving the name to the boatlift that lasted for six months and that brought, in a manner uncontrolled by the United States, more than 125,000 Cubans into the country (Pérez 1986a:130).

The end of the boatlift and the onset of restrictions on Cuban immigration brought about a lull in the exodus during the 1980s. The activation of an immigration agreement between the United States and Cuba in November 1987 provided for the admission into the United States of about 20,000 persons from Cuba each year. Priority has been given to those who would qualify for political asylum. Most of the persons who have arrived since that date have been former political prisoners and their families. The actual number arriving has fallen considerably below the projected figure of 20,000.

Concentration and Settlement in Miami

Miami is the capital and mecca of U.S. Cubans. They now represent one of Miami's most "established" groups, despite the fact that, as usually happens with immigrants, they are still largely regarded—by others and by themselves—as newcomers. Cubans have a sense of "rootedness" in Miami. As David Rieff expressed it (1987a:224), "Cubans are probably the only people who really do feel comfortable in Dade County these days. . . . Miami is their town now . . ."

The importance of Miami for the Cuban population of the United States has been translated into a demonstrable demographic concentration in the south Florida region. This process of concentration was preceded by an intentional dispersion throughout the United States engineered by the Cuban Refugee Program (CRP).

The Cuban Refugee Program was established in February 1961 as a federal effort to provide assistance in handling the large influx from Cuba. Silvia Pedraza-Bailey (1985) argues that the assistance and encouragement given to Cuban immigration by the U.S. government were linked to the political functions of that immigration for the United States. The exodus ostensibly provided evidence that the Castro government was increasingly unpopular and therefore seemingly justified the maintenance of hostile relations with Cuba.

One of the stated purposes of the federal authorities in establishing the Cuban Refugee Program was to ease the demographic and economic pressures that the influx was exerting on south Florida. A resettlement program was established through which families arriving from Cuba were given assistance if they immediately relocated away from Miami. The assistance included transportation costs to the new destination, help in finding housing and employment, and financial assistance until such time as employment was secured.

According to a Cuban Refugee Program fact sheet (U.S. Department of Health, Education, and Welfare 1978), 300,232 persons were resettled away from Miami between February 1961 and August 1978. This figure represented 64 percent of all Cubans arriving in the United States and registering with the Cuban Refugee Program during that period. It was also equivalent to 37 percent of all persons of Cuban origin in the United States in 1980. The bulk of the resettled Cubans went to New York, New Jersey, California, and Illinois. The figures presented by Rafael J. Prohías and Lourdes Casal (1973:109) show that the height of the resettlement process actually occurred between 1965 and 1973, the period when a daily airlift between the United States and Cuba was in operation.

Prohías and Casal (1973:110), after analyzing both resettlement data and the results of the 1970 census, conclude that "the CRP resettlement program has been a determining factor in the geographic distribution of the Cuban population of the United States." Their conclusion is confirmed by the data on the "Cuban alien" population obtained by the Immigration and Naturalization Service through address report forms, which all aliens were required to file every year. Those data showed that in 1965, 42 percent of the Cuban population in the United States lived in Dade County.[1] Five years later, the 1970 census found that 40 percent of all persons of Cuban origin in the United States lived in the county. The resettlement process reached its peak precisely in the late 1960s. Contrary to the experience of most immigrant groups for which concentration in a city or region formed part of the process of adjustment to the United States, early in their recent history of immigration the Cubans underwent a process of intentional dispersion.

But as early as 1972, Prohías and Casal (1973:117–20) noted that there was increasing evidence that a "trickle-back" phenomenon to Miami had begun. The concentration in south Florida has been at the expense of precisely those states and cities that received large numbers of resettled Cubans in the late 1960s. By 1980 the U.S. Census found slightly more than 52 percent of U.S. Cubans living in Greater Miami (Pérez 1985:3). This trend was contrary to the patterns of geographic distribution among the two other major Hispanic groups in the United States: Mexicans and Puerto Ricans. These two populations in recent years have exhibited a tendency to disperse from their traditional regions of concentration.

The concentration of Cubans in south Florida increased during the 1980s. The Mariel entrants, who arrived after the 1980 census was taken, have undoubtedly contributed to raising the percentage of U.S. Cubans living in Miami. Most settled in Miami, where they could find employment within a familiar cultural environment and use their native language.

It is likely that the process of concentration in Miami will continue in the 1990s. The principal factor in sustaining that trend will be entry into the retirement age of the large middle-aged cohort of the Cuban-origin population. Many of these people were the young heads of households who were resettled away from Miami in the 1960s. Many who have not yet returned to Miami will undoubtedly do so when they retire in the years ahead.

Since Cubans represent nearly 70 percent of the Hispanic population of Greater Miami, an approximate measure of their spatial distribution within the metropolitan area can be obtained by looking at the percentage of the population of each census tract that was categorized as "Spanish-origin" in the 1990 census.

Generally, the heaviest concentrations of Hispanics within the county are found along a belt running west from downtown (which is located east on Biscayne Bay) all the way to the western edges of the metropolitan area. This belt includes the southern half of the city of Miami as well as the incorporated areas of West Miami and Sweetwater, the northern part of the city of Coral Gables, and unincorporated portions of the county in the west. Its rough boundaries are the 836 (Dolphin) Expressway on the north and Southwest 40th Street on the south. The belt's principal east-west arteries, on which the commercial activities of the Cuban population are most evident, are Northwest 7th Street, Flagler Street, Southwest 8th Street (the traditional Calle Ocho), Southwest 24th Street (Coral Way), and the western portion of 40th Street (Bird Road). Since the 1960s the settlement of Cubans along this belt has proceeded from east to west, emanating largely from the area known as Little Havana, which is located

Domino Park on Calle Ocho (8th Street) in the heart of Little Havana is frequented by older Cuban refugees who, in between considering their next play in the domino game, talk constantly about the horrors of Fidel and the glories of Cuba before the revolution.

within the city of Miami, some twelve to fifteen city blocks directly west of downtown and stretching west along Calle Ocho for about fifteen city blocks.

Middle-income Cubans, and especially professionals, are now hard to find in Little Havana. Their upward mobility has taken them to more suburban areas to the west. The current residents of Little Havana are likely to be blue-collar and service workers, the elderly, the poor, and the recent immigrants, including non-Cuban Hispanics (Longbrake and Nichols 1976:42).

As one moves north or south of the "Hispanic belt" the proportion of Hispanics declines, so that the northern and southern edges of the county contain some of the lowest concentrations of Hispanics. One exception is the city of Hialeah, located in the northwestern portion of Greater Miami. About two-thirds of its population is now Hispanic. Hialeah contains many of the region's manufacturing plants. During the late 1960s and the 1970s, its predominantly white, non-Hispanic, blue-collar population was rapidly replaced with Cuban blue-collar families (Longbrake and Nichols 1976:39–40).

The large unincorporated suburban area of Kendall, located to the southwest of the Hispanic belt, experienced a very rapid settlement during the 1980s. Hispanics—especially young professionals—contributed greatly to the area's booming growth.

Although there are evident concentrations of Cubans within the county, their presence is not strictly confined to one geographic area. Because of the sheer size of its population, Cubans can be found throughout most of Greater Miami, including predominantly white, non-Hispanic neighborhoods. Hispanic-Anglo segregation is not as high as one would expect.

That is not the case for Hispanic-black segregation. The two populations exhibit considerable spatial distance. Blacks in Miami tend to live in fairly confined areas, segregated from both Hispanics and Anglos. Those areas are located primarily—although not exclusively—in the northern half of the city of Miami, in unincorporated zones in northern Dade County, and in the city of Opa-Locka (also in the north). There are pockets of black settlements in the southern half of the county, in Coconut Grove, and in the Richmond Heights and Perrine area in southern Dade. These are all zones and neighborhoods with few Hispanics.

The Enclave

Miami's Cuban community is regarded as the foremost example in the United States of a true ethnic enclave. Alejandro Portes and Robert L. Bach (1985:203) define an ethnic enclave as "a distinctive economic formation, characterized by the spatial concentration of immigrants who organize a variety of enterprises to serve their own ethnic market and the general population."

Few immigrant neighborhoods are true enclaves because they usually "lack the extensive division of labor of the enclave and especially, its highly differentiated entrepreneurial class" (Portes and Bach 1985:205). Besides the Cuban community in Miami, the two most prominent examples of ethnic enclaves in the history of U.S. immigration are Manhattan's Eastern European Jews at the turn of the century and Japanese immigrants in California (Portes and Bach 1985:38).

A great deal of recent scholarly work on Miami has focused precisely on articulating the characteristics and implications of Miami's Cuban enclave. The presence of such an enclave is one of the reasons Cubans are concentrating in south Florida.

The basis of the enclave is highly differentiated entrepreneurial activity. Miami is the metropolitan area in the United States with the highest per capita number of Hispanic-owned businesses (O'Hare 1987:33). The community's entrepreneurial base was established largely by Cuban immigrants, especially those who arrived in the first wave in the early 1960s, who possessed the complex of skills and attitudes that eventually made possible their entry into a wide range of self-employment (Portes 1987). This is the process Portes and Bach (1985:203) call "the successful transplantation of an entrepreneurial class from origin to destination during the first waves of the migration."

Strong and diversified entrepreneurial activity is responsible for the enclave's most important overall feature: institutional completeness. Cubans in Miami can, if they wish, literally live out their lives within the ethnic community. The wide range of sales and services, including professional services, available within the community makes possible its completeness.

To understand Cuban Miami, it is important to trace the implications of the structural organization of the enclave. Foremost among them is the influence on the process of economic adjustment, but the enclave also affects such important areas as acculturation, interethnic relations, and female employment.

Most of the research by Portes and his associates on the Miami enclave deals precisely with its relationship to the relatively successful economic position of Cuban immigrants. The enclave insulates the immigrant somewhat against the usual processes of the segmented labor market. In contrast to Mexican immigrants, who must join the open labor market in peripheral sectors of the economy throughout the country, many recent Cuban immigrants enter the U.S. labor market largely through the large number of businesses in Miami that are owned or operated by members of their own group who arrived earlier. Compensation may not be higher in the enclave. However, ethnic bonds provide for informal networks of support that facilitate the learning of new skills and the overall process of economic adjustment, thereby blurring the usual differences between the primary and secondary labor markets. The enclave's positive implications for economic adjustment are seen as a factor that has maintained the Cubans' socioeconomic position, which is relatively high when compared with that of many other immigrant groups (Portes 1981:290–95; Portes 1982:106–9).

The enclave is also instrumental in determining the relatively high rates of labor force participation exhibited by Cuban-origin women. As Pérez

(1986b) has shown, female employment is critical in explaining the relatively high levels of family income found among Cubans in the United States.

Important in understanding the nature of female employment in the Cuban community is that such employment is not typically the result of transformations in the role of women, but rather a product of high aspirations regarding family income and social mobility (Ferree 1979; Prieto 1987). Among Cubans in the United States, therefore, a fairly traditional sex-role orientation coexists with high rates of female labor force participation. This situation occurs largely because the enclave provides culturally acceptable opportunities for female employment. The principal characteristics of enclave employment delineated by Portes and Bach (1985:200–239), although based on a sample composed exclusively of males, can be readily applied to an understanding of the manner in which the enclave facilitates traditional female employment.

One such characteristic, for example, is the high degree of entrepreneurship and the proliferation of relatively small immigrant enterprises within the enclave. Such enterprises, epitomized by—but not limited to—family-operated firms, utilize particularistic hiring criteria, providing women with the culturally acceptable opportunity of working with family and friends.

Another feature of the enclave is that immigrant entrepreneurs frequently invoke the idea of ethnic solidarity in order to have exclusive access to new arrivals, who represent sources of low-wage labor and expanding consumer markets. Invoking ethnic solidarity also facilitates greater control of the work force, minimizing worker opposition and unionization (Portes and Bach 1985:203). Given the fairly traditional sex-role orientation among Cubans and their view of female employment as purely instrumental in assisting and furthering the family's economic status, it is not difficult to see how women are particularly susceptible to employers' use of the principle of ethnic solidarity to attract a low-wage work force that is willing to be exploited. It is likely, therefore, that the work force of many firms in the enclave is predominantly female and ethnically homogeneous, characteristics that also tend to make such firms culturally acceptable as work settings for women.

In south Florida the enclave has largely created the conditions that make possible high rates of female employment, despite the persistence of relatively traditional sex-role orientations. The extent to which women work outside the home in the Cuban community is crucial to understanding the large number of workers in the Cuban household and the relatively high median family income of that population.

Acculturation

The existence of the enclave also has evident implications for the process of acculturation. The completeness of the enclave has the effect of slowing down that process, for it tends to insulate the immigrant from the "dominant" society and culture, allowing for the retention of the culture of origin.

Using language as one indicator of the degree of acculturation, one study found that most Cubans use only Spanish at home and in many of their daily activities (Díaz 1980:48–50). In 1980 the U.S. Bureau of the Census (1983b:163) found that 43 percent of the residents of Dade County spoke a language other than English at home. Of those who spoke a foreign language at home, one-third indicated that they spoke English "not well or not at all."

The institutional completeness of the enclave has made Spanish a public language in Miami, a language that is not confined to the intimacy of the family or the peer group. It is the lingua franca for conducting a wide range of business and personal matters beyond one's primary groups. Cubans in Miami can purchase a home or automobile, obtain specialized medical treatment, or consult with a lawyer or accountant, all using only Spanish. This extensive use of Spanish is one reason why language use is such a critical—and often explosive—issue in Miami, one that is the frequent battleground for interethnic conflicts. It is not a coincidence that the "English Only" movement was born in Miami.

The retention of the language and cultural patterns of the country of origin cannot, of course, be attributed exclusively to the presence of a strong enclave. Most Cubans in Miami are immigrants, with an overrepresentation of the middle-aged and elderly. Most of the population has arrived in this country only within the past three decades. In relative terms, it is a fairly recent immigrant group. Another factor that retards the process of acculturation among Cubans in Miami, especially important in the early stages of the exodus, is the perception many U.S. Cubans have of themselves as reluctant migrants, compelled to leave their country, but expecting to return. They consequently have little desire or motivation to assimilate into this society.

It is also important to remember that there have been periodic waves of

Beauty salon in Little Havana is typical of small Latin businesses in Miami. The phrase "beauty salon" is the only English on the front window and door. The rest is all in Spanish. The front door has decal flags of the United States, Peru, and Cuba.

massive arrivals from Cuba, of which the largest and most recent was the Mariel boatlift. The new arrivals are fresh from the culture of origin and they renew and reinforce that culture within the immigrant community.

A third major consequence of the enclave is in the arena of interethnic relations in Miami. The insulation of the immigrant within the enclave, while it may have positive implications for the initial process of economic adjustment, poorly serves interethnic communications and understanding in Miami. In a metropolitan area in which the various ethnic groups—especially blacks—are spatially segregated, the existence of an institutionally complete community among Cubans makes it even less likely that Hispanics and blacks will create the basis for better understanding and a common agenda. There are, of course, many causes for this social distance, but the ability of the Cubans to live largely within their own community is undoubtedly one of them.

The Exile Ideology

No aspect of Cuban Miami attracts more national and international attention than its politics. This is so largely because even after thirty years, Cuban Miami remains a community of exiles largely preoccupied with the political status of the homeland. At the same time, however, it has demonstrated at a relatively early point in its development a strong participation in the U.S. political system at the local and state levels. The political culture of Miami's Cubans is therefore a fundamental and complex topic.

The "exile" ideology among Cubans in Miami has four principal and interrelated characteristics.

1. *The primacy of issues and concerns that deal with the political status of the homeland.* Although the past few years have witnessed a rise of concerns that can perhaps be regarded as "immigrant" issues (Grenier 1990), that is, issues regarding adjustment to life in the United States and local political questions, the principal focus of political discourse and mobilization in the Cuban-American community is still Cuba. Issues such as TV Martí, U.S. policy toward Cuba, and the internal situation on the island continue to predominate and are causes for the mobilization of resources. In contrast a certain apathy reigns over more domestic issues, such as the adoption of English as the official language of Florida.

2. *Uncompromising struggle against and hostility toward the current Cuban government.* The goal of the Cuban exile is the overthrow of Fidel Castro and the establishment in Cuba of a democratic government. This is to be accomplished through hostility and isolation, not rapprochement. Such an ideology has, in general terms, been consistent with U.S. policy toward Cuba over the past twenty-eight years.

3. *Lack of debate allowed about the "exile" ideology within the community.* The Cuban-American community has been formed by a particular set of political circumstances. Those circumstances have had a great personal impact on members of the community. Cuban-Americans—as with exiles everywhere—are therefore not likely to be objective about the situation that has so intrinsically altered their lives and compelled them to live outside their native country. Anticommunism and anti-Castroism are "givens" in the community. Any debate proceeds from that basis.

The less favorable side of this lack of objectivity is the presence of an obvious intolerance to views that do not conform to the predominant "exile" ideology of an uncompromising hostility toward the Castro regime. Those inside or outside the community who voice views that are "soft" or conciliatory with respect to Castro or who take a less than militant stance in opposition to Cuba's regime are usually subjected to criticism and scorn, their position belittled, and their motivations questioned. Liberals, the "liberal press," most Democrats, pacifists, leftists, academics, intellectuals, "dialoguers," and socialists are favorite targets. Any dissent within the community is especially difficult, since greater pressures could be brought to bear on the individual or group than on entities outside the community. Intolerance of opposing views has frequently been a source of friction between Cubans and other groups and institutions in Miami. The exiles' inflexible anti-Castroism has frequently been criticized—and even ridiculed—by non-Cubans in Miami.

One example of the conflicts and tensions that this political culture has engendered is the running battle between more than a few Cubans and the *Miami Herald*, Miami's major daily newspaper. The exiles frequently take exception to the paper's coverage and editorials, and the *Herald* is routinely accused of being antagonistic to the cause of a liberated Cuba and to the Cuban community. In October 1987 the Cuban American National Foundation, a prominent exile organization, took out a full-page ad in the *Herald* to accuse the paper of "ignoring [the] political and civic well-being of the Cuban-American community."

4. Overwhelming support for the Republican party among Cubans in Miami. Registered Republicans far outnumber registered Democrats among Cubans in Miami. Loyalty to the Republicans demonstrates the importance of international issues (especially anticommunism, support for the Contras in Nicaragua, and hostility toward Castro) in the political agenda of Cubans. If a substantial number of that community did not agree with the elements of the exile ideology, or if there were a greater balance in that agenda, with importance given to purely domestic issues, the Democratic party would have made greater inroads.

In fact if Cuban-Americans viewed themselves as immigrants in this country rather than as political exiles, and if they made judgments about political parties based upon their needs and aspirations as immigrants in the United States, they would be Democrats in overwhelming numbers, as is the case with other immigrants in the United States and with other Hispanics. This would be true not only because of the general social agenda of the Democrats, but also specifically because of the experience of Cuban migration. The measures that have greatly facilitated Cuban immigration and the adjustment of Cuban-Americans in the United States have all been enacted by Democratic administrations: the Cuban Refugee Program and its resettlement efforts, the assistance given to the Cuban elderly and the dependent, the establishment of the airlift or freedom flights, and permission for the Mariel boatlift to take place, among others. In contrast, it was under a Republican administration that the special "refugee" status for Cuban entrants was eliminated and that the first restrictions ever on Cuban immigration were instituted. Only under a Republican Justice Department have Cubans been deported back to the island.

The fact that Cubans are overwhelmingly Republicans is therefore a testimony to the predominance of the "exile" ideology. That ideology is apparently one that has greater common ground with the Republicans, especially with the administrations of Ronald Reagan and George Bush. Reagan's candidacy in 1980 gave a major impetus to citizenship and voter registration efforts among Cubans in Miami, who apparently found a substantial ideological affinity with the Republican candidate.

The essential elements of the "exile" ideology have predominated, presently predominate, and will likely continue to predominate in the near future. The primacy and durability of that ideology in the political culture of Cubans in Miami is being sustained and reinforced by three important forces.

1. Demographics. At least 70 percent of all Cuban-origin persons currently residing in Greater Miami were actually born on the island. In other words, most Cuban-Americans are persons who lived through the experience of exile. It is a population that overall is not far removed in time from the Cuban revolutionary process. This is still not a community of second- or third-generation Cubans.

Furthermore, the age composition shows a continued predominance of the age groups that left Cuba as adults (see fig. 5.1). The older age structure of the Cuban-origin population has clear origins: (a) the priority given by the Cuban government to the emigration of the elderly, especially during the airlift (1965 to 1973); (b) restrictions on the emigration of persons in productive ages and particularly on males eligible for military service; and (c) the very low birth rate among Cuban-Americans (lower even than the fertility of the white, non-Hispanic metropolitan population of the United States).

Clearly those whose ages would make them adult émigrés from Cuba's revolution have had a relatively large numerical representation among Cuban-Americans. In other words, exiles still predominate. Furthermore, they will continue to predominate in the near future. The younger generation—those persons who arrived from Cuba as children or those actually born here—have been numerically underrepresented.

2. Political and economic predominance of exiles from the earlier waves. Separate from but related to the demographic importance of the exiles

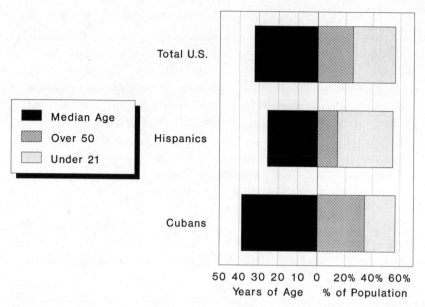

Fig. 5.1. Comparison of Hispanic, Cuban, and U.S. age distributions. *Source*: U.S. Census Bureau 1988:7.

among Cuban-Americans is the political and economic significance of those who arrived—either as children or adults—in the earlier waves of the exodus. The upper and upper-middle levels of the socioeconomic structure of Miami's Cuban community are disproportionately composed of those who arrived from Cuba in the 1960s: those who arrived in the "first wave" (from 1959 to the October 1962 Missile Crisis), those who arrived through third countries (primarily from 1962 to 1965), and those who arrived through the first half of the airlift (1965 to 1970).

Although one can overgeneralize on this point, it is probably valid to conclude that, in comparison with later arrivals (especially the Mariel entrants), the population that arrived in those earlier waves has a higher incidence of the following three characteristics: they do not have immediate family members in Cuba; they gained nothing by the process of revolutionary change—on the contrary, they lost property, livelihood, and a way of life; and they are likely to cast the struggle against the Castro regime in ideological terms.

Because of those characteristics, these earlier migrants are much more likely to argue for a total ideological incompatibility between the émigré community and the Castro government and to support a policy of hostility and especially isolation toward Cuba. They are overall the group that has the least interest, for example, in breaking Cuba's isolation for the purpose of family reunification. Since they have been here the longest amount of time, and since they were the group that came best equipped to socially and economically adjust to life in the United States, these earlier Cuban arrivals—and their ideology—tend to predominate in the political and economic hierarchy of the community.

3. *The enclave.* The enclave has implications for the persistence of an "exile" ideology. The most obvious one was noted earlier: the institutional completeness tends to insulate the members of the ethnic community, minimizing outside contact, and thereby reinforcing the culture (including ideology) of the group. It is likely, for example, that Cubans who have lived for considerable periods of time outside of Miami are more likely to hold views that vary somewhat from the traditional "exile" ideology than are those who have resided almost exclusively in Miami since arriving from Cuba.

The enclave also has its own media. The Spanish-language media in Miami are major factors in the persistence of an "exile" ideology. There are currently two television stations, two daily newspapers, and countless weekly tabloids that transmit or publish in Spanish. But of special importance in the reinforcement of the "exile" ideology are the four principal Spanish-language radio stations on the AM frequency. These stations are almost exclusively devoted to "talk" and news, much of their programming is devoted to Cuba, and their tone is usually combative and strident. Many—not all—of their announcers and commentators are important agents in the maintenance of a climate of intolerance in the public discourse regarding Cuba.

Deviations and Changes from the Exile Ideology

It has been argued that Miami's Cuban community is more heterogeneous with respect to its position on relations with Cuba than is frequently assumed. Indeed, it would be difficult for a community of three-quarters of a million people to be monolithic in its political ideology. At various times and for various reasons, individuals and groups have emerged that have espoused views inconsistent with the exile ideology as outlined above.

The presence of such groups and individuals became more noticeable during the period in which the Carter administration appeared to substantially relax U.S. hostilities toward Cuba (from 1978 to 1979). Fidel Castro announced the "dialogue" of November to December 1978 with the Cuban community in the United States and for the first time permitted visits of Cuban-Americans to the island. These events gave visibility to persons within the Cuban community who advocated a lifting of the embargo and a normalization of relations. Many of these persons traveled to Havana to form part of the dialogue convened by Castro.

While such groups and individuals attracted considerable attention at the time, they were probably considered fringe elements by the bulk of the Cuban community. The "dialoguers," as they became known, were scorned, threatened, and two were murdered (Maier and McColm 1981: 148). Furthermore, neither the ranks nor the leadership of such groups were composed of individuals who could claim legitimacy as leaders of the Cuban-American community. With the advent of the Reagan administration, the activities and visibility of these groups declined.

At present, a major driving force behind a measure of dissension from the predominant ideology is the need of many to have contact with family members in Cuba. Although family contact and reunification have long been issues in the Cuban community, they gained new relevance with the Mariel boatlift, which separated many close family members.

The limited avenues of contact between the United States and Cuba have long frustrated those who wish to communicate with or visit their families. The telephone lines are few and old; placing a call takes hours and even days. Sending packages to Cuba has been costly and chancy. Mail service takes weeks and sometimes months. The number of persons who may travel to Cuba is limited, and the flights to the island do not come close to meeting the demand.

Faced with all of these limitations, groups such as the Cuban American Coalition have surfaced that have argued for the rights of separated families. Evidently however, the goals of these groups imply some process of negotiation with Castro's government and an increase in contact between the United States and Cuba, both of which run counter to the prevailing ideology of hostility and isolation. This point, of course, has not been lost on many in the community, and the efforts of such groups are frequently criticized, especially on the radio.

Those seeking greater contact with Cuba are relatively powerless within the community. Returning to a point made earlier: those who have close family members still in Cuba are likely to be somewhat later arrivals and at a greater political and economic disadvantage when compared with those who arrived in the earlier waves and who probably do not have family members in Cuba. Nevertheless, it is clear that there is a distinct—and not insignificant—constituency among Cubans in Miami that favors greater ties with Cuba, at least for the purpose of increasing family contacts.

The changes initiated in the Soviet Union and that swept through Eastern Europe in 1989 and 1990 have brought about some changes in the political discourse of the exile community. Of special significance for Cuban exiles are some characteristics of those changes: (1) radical changes have come from within the system; (2) reforms have been spearheaded in most cases by card-carrying members of the Communist party, cadres who are products of the system; (3) the changes are the culmination of a developmental process that has included Western influence, not isolation, with the catalyst being the policy of a Soviet leader to open up even more to that influence; and (4) external economic and political pressures have played a secondary role, if any, in instigating reforms.

Those Cuban exiles who have long struggled to do what had never been done before—overthrow an entrenched communist regime—are now faced with an operational alternative model of how such a thing might be accomplished. The model runs counter to traditional Cuban-exile wisdom, for it says that overthrow is not an overnight process, but rather an evolution that may be led by elements from within the system. Hostility and isolation may not help, but openness does.

And so it is that some leaders of the Cuban exile community—even traditional hard-liners—are now talking about how the world is changing and how perhaps one has to engage in talks with Communists in Cuba. Political pragmatists will probably take that route. If Cuba were to follow the Eastern European model of change, an exile community that has no contacts with potential new centers of power inside the island would have no hope (if it ever had any) of being a player in the process.

Most Cuban exile leaders, however, favor staying the course. Since Castro will resist the Soviet-initiated reforms, it is argued, he will be increasingly isolated from his longtime patrons and allies. Isolation and external pressure, the argument goes, continue to be the key to the overthrow of Castro.

The changes in Europe have brought into question the traditional strategies of the exile community. The goal of a democratic Cuba is unaltered. But the means to that goal are now going to be subject to much more scrutiny and discussion, perhaps even redefinition. The scope of that discussion will probably reach a breadth and a level of subtlety that are unprecedented in the exile community.

The intergenerational transition that lies ahead may well signal the advent of substantial changes in the ideology of the Cuban community of Miami. Many believe that it is with the transition from the "exile" generation to the "immigrant" generation that true changes will occur in political culture. No doubt changes will occur, but the forces of continuity are strong. As noted above, numerically there are fewer of the younger generation than of the generations that arrived as adults from Cuba. The insulation of the community has socialized that younger generation into anti-Castroism and most elements of the "exile" ideology. A great intergenerational change in the Cuban-Americans' view of the Cuban regime does not appear likely.

What will undoubtedly change, however, are those elements of the exile ideology that cannot be passed on to the younger generation: the personal passion with which many Cubans who experienced the process of exile approach the Cuba issue. In other words, although the position toward Cuba may remain one of hostility and isolation, it is not likely that newer generations, detached from the exile experience, will view the Cuba issue with the intolerance and vehemence of their predecessors. It is inevitable that the younger generation's political agendas will be balanced, reflecting "immigrant" domestic concerns, without the primacy their parents or grandparents gave to the situation in Cuba.

Participation in the U.S. Political System

Although participation in the political system of the United States at all levels has traditionally taken a backseat to concern with the politics of the homeland, the 1980s saw the rapid and massive entry of Miami's Cubans into the realm of electoral politics in the United States. That entry, however, was not entirely unrelated to and did not signal a departure from traditional exile politics. As noted earlier, one factor that encouraged Cubans in Miami to become citizens and register to vote was the candidacy of Ronald Reagan. The ideology of the Republican candidate on foreign policy was appealing to many Cubans, and this ideology caused Cuban exiles to register and vote in the United States. Participation in the U.S. political system, therefore, is not necessarily an abandonment of the concern with the political status of the homeland, but may actually be an extension of those exile concerns.

The size of the Cuban community in Greater Miami and its fairly high turnout rates during elections have produced a boom in the number of Cubans in elected positions at all levels of government (Viglucci 1986). Cubans are mayors of the incorporated areas of Miami (Xavier Suarez), Hialeah (Julio Martinez), Sweetwater, West Miami (Pedro Reboredo), and Hialeah Gardens, all within Greater Miami. Cubans form a majority on the commissions or councils of those cities.

At the beginning of the 1990s, there were already ten Cubans in the Florida legislature: seven in the house and three in the senate. In 1989 a Cuban reached an elective office at the federal level, when Ileana Ros-Lehtinen was elected to the U.S. Congress, succeeding longtime member of Congress Claude Pepper.

Acculturation and Social Change

Although, as noted previously, the enclave tends to favor the retention of the culture of the homeland, delaying the process of acculturation, it is unlikely that the Cuban community in the United States will be an exception to the usual intergenerational shift toward greater acculturation and assimilation. English is the principal language among Cubans who have lived all or most of their lives in the United States.

José Szapocznik, Mercedes A. Scopetta, and Wayne Tillman (1978) found sharp intergenerational differences in the level of acculturation among Cubans in Miami, with early adolescents demonstrating the highest scores of all age groups in measures of behavioral accultura-tion. Furthermore, males evidence greater acculturation than females. An exaggerated acculturational gap is a major source of intergenera-tional conflicts. Alienation between parents and children is usually found in Cuban families with interactional problems (Szapocznik, Scopetta, and Tillman 1978:42–44; Kurtines and Miranda 1980:181–82).

An important focus of intergenerational tensions is the conflicting value orientations with respect to dependence and independence (Bernal 1982:197). Cuban culture calls for the continued dependence of children on their parents, even into the teenage years and beyond. Children, however, are more likely to have internalized the norms of independence commonly found in U.S. society.

One adaptation that reduces intergenerational tension is "bicultural-ity," by which each generation adjusts to the other generation's cultural preferences. In the words of José Szapocznik and Roberto Hernandez (1988:168): "[P]arents learn how to remain loyal to their ethnic background while becoming skilled in interacting with their youngsters' Americanized values and behaviors, and vice versa."

Intergenerational shifts will be apparent not only in cultural terms, but also in the very structure of the enclave. Coming up rapidly behind that large cohort of first-generation entrepreneurs who have created the enclave are those Cuban-Americans born in the United States or who arrived as children from the island. Largely educated in this country, the influential persons in that group are less likely than the older generation to be entrepreneurs and more likely to be professionals.

Those younger professionals have the credentials to break away from the ethnic enclave and obtain employment in the larger firms and institutions outside the ethnic community. If this is the case, then it is obvious that a rapid change will take place in the years ahead in the very economic basis of the Cuban community. The community will change from one dominated by first-generation entrepreneurs to one of second-generation professionals. Such a shift will alter the Cuban community's relationship with the rest of the city.

The advent of that dramatic intergenerational shift is already evident in the participation of Cubans within the traditional Anglo institutions that hold true economic power in Miami: banks, law firms, insurance companies, real estate agencies, advertising, professional services, and public bureaucracies. At the upper levels there are few Cuban faces in these institutions, especially in the private sector. At the lower- and middle-management levels there is a critical mass of young Cuban professionals. Their training, as well as their bilingual and bicultural skills, have made them very attractive to these institutions, particularly as more and more firms strive to serve the growing Hispanic population of the area. Furthermore, Anglo flight from Dade County has removed the Cubans' Anglo contemporaries from the competition for these jobs.

Barring the possibility of discrimination in promotions, there should be more and more Cubans in the years ahead reaching the upper levels of Miami's major firms and bureaucracies. This will obviously serve to blur the boundaries of the Anglo and Cuban "establishments" of the city. Removed somewhat from their Cuban origins, the new generation of Miami Cubans will think like immigrants rather than exiles, will have a new agenda, and will easily find common ground and solidarity with other ethnic groups in the community, especially the growing number of non-Cuban Latins.

Cuban Miami in the 1990s

In the 1990s Cuban Miami will reach a crossroads. The 1990s will be the decade of a basic restructuring of that community.

In order to survive the 1990s, Castro will have to live to be nearly seventy-four. But with the changes sweeping the Communist world at the close of the 1980s, it is likely that his longevity may prove irrelevant, and that early in the decade change will come to Cuba—with or without him. If such changes in Cuba are positive (in the direction of democratization), they will produce a warming in U.S.-Cuban relations. The basic conditions that have created and shaped Miami's exile community will finally be meaningfully altered after more than three decades.

But not all the changes affecting Miami's Cuban community will begin in Cuba. Just as Castro will pass on in the 1990s, so too will his contemporaries here: the exile generation. In 1990, that large cohort of exiles was already between the ages of fifty and sixty-nine. These exiles will be in the twilight of their lives in the 1990s, and their economic and political (and ideological) influence will wane, rapidly making way for the new generation discussed earlier in this chapter.

It will be during the 1990s, then, that both Cuba and Cuban Miami will see fundamental changes. The traditional relationship between the two will be basically altered, but the directions and forms of that change remain to be seen, especially with respect to Cuba. It is likely that, one way or another, we will see the reestablishment of normal transportation, communication, and commercial links between Miami and Cuba. The far-reaching implications of such a situation for Cuban Miami are difficult to fathom at this time, especially with regard to a new generation of Cuban-Americans. We have little empirical basis for formulating generalizations about that generation, but the crossroads that Cuban Miami will reach in the 1990s leads to many possibilities.

Note

1. The 1965 data are found in U.S. Immigration and Naturalization Service 1965. Limited to Cuban aliens (non-citizens of the United States), these data are not strictly

comparable to the censuses. It should be kept in mind, however, that very few of the
Cuban refugees could have attained citizenship status as early as 1965.

References

Bernal, Guillermo. 1982. "Cuban Families," In *Ethnicity and Family Therapy*, ed. M.
    McGoldrick, J. Pearce, and J. Giordano, 187–207. New York: Guilford Press.
Boswell, Thomas D., and James R. Curtis. 1984. *The Cuban-American Experience:
    Culture, Images and Perspectives*. Totowa, N.J.: Rowman and Allanheld.
Díaz, Guarioné M., ed. 1980. *Evaluation and Identification of Policy Issues in the
    Cuban Community*. Miami: Cuban National Planning Council.
Fagen, Richard R., Richard A. Brody, and Thomas J. O'Leary. 1968. *Cubans in Exile:
    Disaffection and the Revolution*. Stanford, Calif.: Stanford University Press.
Ferree, Myra Marx. 1979. "Employment Without Liberation: Cuban Women in the
    United States." *Social Science Quarterly* 60 (June): 35–50.
Grenier, Guillermo. 1990. "Ethnic Solidarity and the Cuban-American Labor Move-
    ment in Dade County." *Cuban Studies/Estudios Cubanos* 20: 29–48.
Kurtines, William M., and Luke Miranda. 1980. "Differences in Self and Family Role
    Perception among Acculturating Cuban-American College Students: Implica-
    tions for the Etiology of Family Disruption among Migrant Groups." *International
    Journal of Intercultural Relations* 4: 167–84.
Longbrake, David B., and Woodrow W. Nichols, Jr. 1976. *Sunshine and Shadows in
    Metropolitan Miami*. Cambridge, Mass.: Ballinger Publishing Company.
Maier, Francis X., and R. Bruce McColm. 1981. "Nation in Our Midst: The Cuban
    Diaspora." *National Review* (February 20): 148–52, 184.
Metro–Dade County Planning Department Research Division. 1985. *Hispanic Profile,
    Dade County, Florida, 1985*. Miami: Metro–Dade County Planning Department.
Muir, Helen. 1953. *Miami, U.S.A.* Coconut Grove, Fla.: Hurricane House Pub-
    lishers.
O'Hare, William. 1987. "Best Metros for Hispanic Businesses." *American Demo-
    graphics* (November): 31–33.
Pedraza-Bailey, Silvia. 1985. *Political and Economic Migrants in America: Cubans
    and Mexicans*. Austin: University of Texas Press.
Pérez, Lisandro. 1985. "The Cuban Population of the United States: The Results of the
    1980 U.S. Census of Population." *Cuban Studies/Estudios Cubanos* 15: 1–18.
———. 1986a. "Cubans in the United States." *The Annals of the American Academy
    of Political and Social Science* 487: 126–37.
———. 1986b. "Immigrant Economic Adjustment and Family Organization: The
    Cuban Success Story Reexamined." *International Migration Review* 20: 4–20.
Portes, Alejandro. 1981. "Modes of Structural Incorporation and Present Theories of
    Labor Immigration." In *Global Trends in Migration: Theory and Research of*

International Population Movements, ed. M.M. Kritz, C.B. Keely, and S.M. Tomasi, 279–97. New York: Center for Migration Studies.

————. 1982. "Immigrants' Attainment: An Analysis of Occupation and Earnings among Cuban Exiles in the United States." In *Social Structure and Behavior: Essays in Honor of William Hamilton Sewell*, ed. R.M. Hauser et al., 91–111. New York: Academic Press.

————. 1987. "The Social Origins of the Cuban Enclave Economy of Miami." *Sociological Perspectives* 30 (October): 340–71.

Portes, Alejandro, and Robert L. Bach. 1985. *Latin Journey: Cuban and Mexican Immigrants in the United States*. Berkeley, Calif.: University of California Press.

Prieto, Yolanda. 1987. "Cuban Women in the U.S. Labor Force: Perspectives on the Nature of Change." *Cuban Studies/Estudios Cubanos* 17: 73–91.

Prohías, Rafael J., and Lourdes Casal. 1973. *The Cuban Minority in the U.S.: Preliminary Report on Need Identification and Program Evaluation*. Boca Raton, Fla.: Florida Atlantic University.

Rieff, David. 1987a. *Going to Miami: Exiles, Tourists, and Refugees in the New America*. Boston: Little, Brown.

————. 1987b. "A Reporter at Large: The Second Havana." *New Yorker* (May 18): 65–83.

Szapocznik, José, and Roberto Hernandez. 1988. "The Cuban American Family." In *Ethnic Families in America*, 3rd ed., ed. C.H. Mindel, R.W. Habenstein, and R. Wright, Jr., 160–72. New York: Elsevier.

Szapocznik, José, Mercedes A. Scopetta, and Wayne Tillman. 1978. "What Changes, What Remains the Same, and What Affects Acculturative Change in Cuban Immigrant Families." In *Cuban Americans: Acculturation, Adjustment and the Family*, ed. J. Szapocznik and M.C. Herrera, 35–49. Washington, D.C.: National Coalition of Hispanic Mental Health and Human Services Organizations.

United States Bureau of the Census. 1983a. *1980 Census of Population, General Population Characteristics, United States Summary*. Washington, D.C.: United States Government Printing Office.

————. 1983b. *1980 Census of Population, General Social and Economic Characteristics, United States Summary*. Washington, D.C.: United States Government Printing Office.

————. 1988. *The Hispanic Population in the United States: March 1988 (Advance Report)*. Washington, D.C.: United States Government Printing Office.

United States Department of Health, Education, and Welfare. 1978. "Cuban Refugee Program Fact Sheet." Washington, D.C.

United States Immigration and Naturalization Service. 1948. *Annual Report*. Washington, D.C.: United States Department of Justice.

————. 1965. *Aliens in the United States*. Washington, D.C.: United States Government Printing Office.

Viglucci, Andrés. 1986. "Hispanics Growing in Numbers, Clout." *Miami Herald* (March 26), 1B.

Wilson, Kenneth L., and W. Allen Martin. 1982. "Ethnic Enclaves: A Comparison of the Cuban and Black Economies in Miami." *American Journal of Sociology* 88: 135–60.

Wilson, Kenneth L., and Alejandro Portes. 1980. "Immigrant Enclaves: An Analysis of the Labor Market Experiences of Cubans in Miami." *American Journal of Sociology* 86: 295–319.

6

The Politics of Language
in Miami

Max J. Castro

The late twentieth century has witnessed the rapid growth of the Hispanic and the foreign-born population of the United States. The cultural, linguistic, political, and economic impact of Hispanic growth and of the "new immigration"—related but distinct phenomena—is already being felt acutely, especially in certain areas of the country. Increased cultural and linguistic diversity has been one obvious major consequence. Reactions to this diversity by the culturally dominant population have ranged from a celebration of pluralism and multiculturalism as the essence of American society to the rise of a new nativism.

The decade of 1970 to 1980 saw the reversal of a long trend toward the "Americanization" of the U.S. population. The antibilingualism/English Only movement made its appearance on the historical stage in 1980 in Miami, where the new trend was being manifested most dramatically. In the 1980s an Official English movement was organized on a national scale.

In this chapter I look at the consequences of immigration and Hispanic population growth in Miami, focusing on linguistic diversity and the range of reactions to it by different sectors of the resident population. In Miami the new immigration and Hispanic population growth have been virtually synonymous and especially dramatic processes. While the experience of Miami may not be uncritically generalized to other locales or to the nation as a whole, developments in Miami have often prefigured national trends. Miami had the first bilingual public school program in the modern period (1963) and the first English Only referendum (1980). In the 1990s Miami is certain to become the first metropolitan area in the United States of more than two million people with a Hispanic majority (Wallace 1991:1A).

I address several questions. (1) Why did Miami pioneer the national trend toward bilingualism and biculturalism *and* give birth to the backlash movement against it in the form of the 1980 antibilingualism campaign? (2) How did different segments of the resident population respond to the challenge of Hispanic immigration, and why? (3) What has been the net effect of these responses? (4) What are the implications of the experience of Miami?

The explanation for Miami's seemingly contradictory role as a harbinger first of pluralist and later of nativist trends in late twentieth-century American society lies in the radical, rapid, and profound nature of the ethnic transformation that has occurred since 1959. This transformation has posed an extraordinary challenge to the resident population of the city. The responses to that challenge have also been extraordinary and have varied across a wide spectrum, from an unusual level of accommodation to various forms of resistance and rejection. The nature of the response has been influenced by social and racial differences among the resident population as well as by the characteristics of the incoming population. Language has been a key issue through which battles over power and identity have been fought, feelings of displacement and alienation have been expressed, and xenophobic and ethnocentric sentiments have been politically organized. Below I discuss why the Hispanic challenge in Miami has been so formidable that the expectation of immigrant subordination has been violated, calling forth among other responses a movement to reclaim Anglo linguistic and cultural supremacy.

The Force of Numbers: A Lightning Latinization

The extent and speed of immigration and Latinization in Miami between 1960 and 1980 is exceptional. As is discussed in chapter 1, the Hispanic population grew from a small minority in the 1960s (5.3 percent in 1960) to a significant community (23.6 percent in 1970), overtaking the black American population (15 percent in 1970) to become the largest minority in the city (see fig. 1.2). Despite a slowdown in Cuban immigration during the next decade, in the 1970s the Hispanic minority continued to grow in absolute and relative size (to 35.7 percent of the area's population in 1980) (Metropolitan Dade County 1983:4). By 1980 the demographic trend was clear: Hispanics were fast becoming the predominant population in

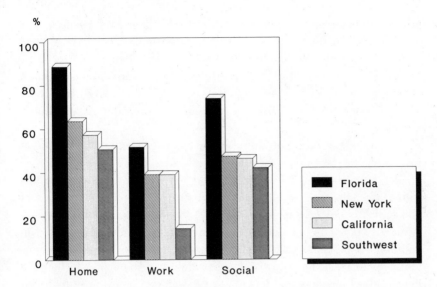

Fig. 6.1. Reported use of Spanish by Hispanics in selected states and regions, 1984. *Source*: Strategy Research Corporation 1984, 90–93.

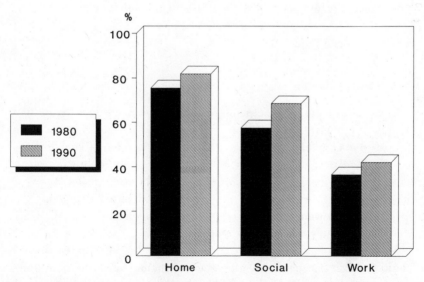

Fig. 6.2. Use of Spanish as most frequent language of Hispanics in south Florida, 1980 and 1990. *Source*: Strategy Research Corporation 1988, 40–41.

Miami. By that year the city of Miami, the largest of twenty-seven municipalities in the Miami metropolitan area, was one of only three cities in the United States of more than 250,000 with a Hispanic majority (U.S. Bureau of the Census 1984). Not only were there suddenly many more Hispanics in Miami, but most of them were recently arrived foreigners who maintained their customs, allegiances, and cultural traits, especially language.

The linguistic impact of Miami's new Hispanic immigrant population was dramatic. Obviously the number of native Spanish speakers rose greatly, but also Spanish was spoken more extensively than in other cities with a large Hispanic population and in more diverse settings (see figs. 6.1 and 6.2). A study by the Cuban National Planning Council found that in 1977, 91.9 percent of Cubans in Miami spoke only Spanish at home and an additional 4 percent spoke mostly Spanish (Díaz 1980:48). More importantly Spanish also became a language widely spoken outside the home in the worlds of business and leisure. A 1984 market research study found that Florida Hispanics were more likely to speak Spanish than English not only at home, but also at work and at social functions. In other markets, Spanish dominated only in the home environment (Strategy Research Corporation 1984). This meant that non-Hispanics encountered Spanish more frequently and pervasively in Miami than in other cities. In Miami, Spanish had become a public as well as a private language; the city had become de facto bilingual.

A Radical Break

The dramatic ethnic succession just described was especially radical because it represented a sharp break with Miami's previous history. As is discussed in chapter 1, despite its geographical location, Miami grew up as a decidedly Anglo-dominated city with a large and oppressed black population, a substantial Jewish minority, and an insignificant Hispanic presence (Porter and Dunn 1984). While the roots of the Hispanic presence in Florida were inscribed in the very name of the state, Hispanic Miami is definitely a post-1950s creation.

Miami was founded in 1896 long after the end of Spanish rule in Florida, and it became a city after the first major Cuban influx into the state in the latter half of the nineteenth century (this influx produced important settlements in Key West and Tampa) and before the second great Cuban influx in 1959. In the intervening years, Cuban immigrants to the

United States, like their Puerto Rican and Dominican counterparts, were more likely to be destined for New York City than Florida (Boswell and Curtis 1984). Consequently in 1950 Hispanics made up only about 4 percent (20,000) of greater Miami's population, a figure that increased only to about 5.3 percent (50,000) by 1960. Not only was Miami an overwhelmingly Anglo-dominated city in every way, but it was becoming even more so in the 1950s. While the Hispanic population increased by about 30,000 to a total of about 50,000 between 1950 and 1960, the non-Hispanic, white population increased by 337,548 to 747,748, or 80 percent of the total population (see fig. 1.2) (Metropolitan Dade County 1983:4).

Thus, unlike other cities where Hispanics currently make up a large proportion of the population (San Antonio, El Paso, and even Los Angeles), before the process of Latinization began in 1959 there was a scant Hispanic legacy or demographic presence in Miami. As a result of this history, the Latinization of Miami that occurred beginning in 1959 would not be experienced by much of the resident American population as a historical continuity with Florida's Hispanic past and Cuban connection. Rather, for a significant proportion of the resident population Latinization would be experienced as a traumatic rupture; an alien (and alienating) invasion; and ultimately as a "takeover," a transgression against the expected relation of domination/subordination between native and immigrant, newcomer and established resident, American and foreigner, Anglo and Hispanic. When the *Miami Herald* conducted a poll in November 1980 about the Hispanic influence in Dade County, most non-Hispanics did not see Latinization in a favorable light (see fig. 6.3).

An Empowered Community

What was so unusual about Spanish in Miami was not that it was so often spoken, but that it was so often heard. In Los Angeles, by contrast, Spanish remained a language only barely registered by the Anglo population, part of the ambient noise: the language spoken by the people who worked in the car wash, trimmed the trees, and cleared the tables in restaurants. In Miami, Spanish was spoken by the people who ate in the restaurants and owned the cars and the trees. On the socioauditory scale, this contrast made a considerable difference (Didion 1987:63).

What made the newcomers to Miami a special challenge to the natives

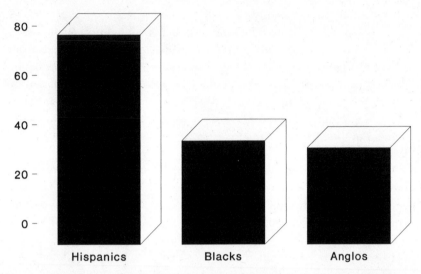

Fig. 6.3. Percentages of Dade County residents agreeing with "The Latin influence helped this county's economy and made it a more enjoyable place to live." *Source*: Browning 1980, 11A.

was not merely (or basically) the power of numbers. Unique among Latin American immigrant groups and established Hispanic minority communities in the United States, Hispanics in Miami (and particularly Cubans) were establishing not only a surpassing demographic and cultural presence, but also a strong economic base. The number of Hispanic-owned businesses in the area zoomed from 3,447 in 1969 to 24,898 in 1982 (Cuban American Policy Center 1988). More importantly some of these businesses were relatively large. They were not confined to typical ethnic retail businesses such as restaurants and small stores, but included manufacturing, construction, insurance, real estate, banking, advertising, and export-import firms (Portes and Bach 1985). The structure of this Latin economy in Miami was not only diverse but integrated, with forward and backward linkages among the individual enterprises (Wilson and Martin 1982).

The Hispanic enclave economy in Miami provided not only a source of employment and economic development for the community, but also a resource for political empowerment and a sphere of cultural and linguistic maintenance. While Cubans and other Hispanics did provide a source of labor and consumers for Anglo businesses, and Hispanic businesses traded with Anglo enterprises, the Hispanic enclave economy also competed with Anglo businesses, often successfully.

Speed, numbers, historical discontinuity, and economic empowerment meant radical change for Miami's resident population. How did it respond? In Miami the responses of some key educational, bureaucratic, political, business, and other institutions and the elites that controlled them have generally been characterized by an evolving accommodation to the new cultural and linguistic reality within the framework of Anglo dominance. I term this approach enlightened assimilationism. In contrast the response of a significant proportion of grass roots whites has more often been characterized by expressions of nonacceptance of the new reality, including flight and attempts to reestablish the expected hierarchy. The response of the black community has differed from the responses of both the elites and the white grass roots.

Enlightened Assimilationism

In the 1960s and 1970s, key institutions in Miami adopted significant policies in the area of language that represented a substantial departure from policies adopted at that time by their counterparts in other parts of the country in which large populations of Hispanic immigrants or native minorities lived. In general the policies adopted in Miami tended to be more accommodating of the linguistic and cultural background of the newcomers.

The three most significant policies in this regard were the institution of bilingual education in the Dade County public schools in 1963, the declaration of Metropolitan Dade County as officially bilingual and bicultural in 1973, and the creation of *El Herald* in 1976.

Despite the presence of larger and earlier established Hispanic concentrations in New York City, California, and the Southwest, it was in Dade County in 1963 that the first bilingual program in a U.S. public school in the modern period was founded. The pioneer program at the Coral Way elementary school, while clearly aimed mainly at teaching English to native Spanish speakers, also attempted to maintain Spanish-language skills among Spanish speakers and to teach Spanish to native English-speaking students. This concept of two-way maintenance bilingual education was subsequently implemented in some other schools in the Dade County system. The Dade County bilingual program, while

limited, was a harbinger and a model for programs that would be adopted
later in other parts of the country.

A decade later, in 1973, the Dade County Commission (which at the
time did not contain any Hispanic members) took the unprecedented step
of declaring the county officially bilingual and bicultural. The declaration
specifically identified Spanish as the second official language and created
a division of bilingual and bicultural affairs. The reasons cited for the
resolution included the fact that "a large and growing percentage of Dade
County is of Spanish origin . . . many of whom have retained the culture
and language of their native lands, [and therefore] encounter special
difficulties communicating with governmental agencies and officials." The
resolution also held, significantly, that "our Spanish-speaking population
has earned, through its ever increasing share of the tax burden, and active
participation in community affairs, the right to be serviced and heard at all
levels of government" (Metro–Dade County Board of County Commissioners 1973).

Another unprecedented concession to the new linguistic reality was
made by the *Miami Herald*, when it began publishing a daily Spanish-
language edition, *El Herald*, in 1976. The *Miami Herald* thus became the
only major metropolitan daily in the United States to publish a daily
edition in Spanish, despite the fact that Miami is only the third largest
Hispanic market in the United States, following Los Angeles and New
York (Strategy Research Corp. 1984:131). By creating *El Herald*, the
Miami Herald, a leading business institution, civic actor, and editorial
voice in Miami, made a decision based largely on business considerations, but which had important symbolic and political implications. For
whatever reasons, the Miami establishment had found it necessary not
only to listen to the newcomers, but also to speak to them in their native
language.

Thus, within the first two decades of massive Hispanic immigration,
three leading institutions in Miami—the public school system, the largest
governmental entity, and the leading communications media corporation—had made substantial commitments to some level of bilingualism
and biculturalism. Why did these institutions—and the political, bureaucratic, and business elites that controlled them—adopt the path of
enlightened assimilationism?

The genesis of each of the three instances of accommodation cited
above was specific to Miami and Dade County. The immigration of
thousands of Cuban teachers and of other professionals who could be

retrained as teachers was key in the early institution of bilingual education in Dade, as was the presence in Miami of Anglo educators who had experience with and sympathy for bilingual and foreign-language education. The looming prospect of a large Hispanic vote and growing Hispanic economic clout were undoubtedly factors in the decision to declare the county bilingual and bicultural. The consumer power of Dade Hispanics and the low rates of subscription to the *Miami Herald* among Hispanics were key to the creation of *El Herald*.

More generally the reason for enlightened assimilationism in Miami was that unlike most other Latin immigrant groups, Cubans came largely from urban, middle-class, relatively educated backgrounds. By the 1960s Cubans were swiftly acquiring the economic power that, in the language of the Dade County resolution, "earned them the right to be serviced and heard" by politicians and newspaper publishers. Cubans had more resources and power than most immigrant groups in bargaining with native elites to preserve their linguistic heritage, and as exiles planning to return to their country they had more motivation to do so. Also there was no essential class conflict or radical difference in worldview between the newcomers and native elites. Often the newcomers were drawn from the same class and from the same professions as native elites and could speak the same (class/professional) language. Elites often had sympathy for these mostly white, middle-class refugees from communism. The background of the newcomers sometimes made it relatively easy for the elites to adopt enlightened assimilation. The policy of providing education bilingually as a transition to English appeared rational and efficient because the immigrant group, drawn from the middle class, contained in its rank both the potential consumers of bilingual educational services (students) and the potential suppliers (teachers).

The "right to be serviced and heard" meant that businesses and politicians sought to obtain the newcomers as clients. Cubans provided a good labor force for many businesses and excellent consumers as they sought to rebuild their previous economic status. Although the growing number of Cuban enterprises brought unwelcome competition for some smaller Anglo entrepreneurs, many Anglo businesses, such as wholesalers, profited from the proliferation of small Cuban businesses. Many larger Anglo businesses and professional elites were not adversely affected by the competition (particularly during the early period) and when they were, they often sought to counter it by catering to the clientele in their own language. The *Miami Herald* created the Spanish edition because its market penetration—the proportion of households that subscribes to the paper in the market area—was lower in Miami than other cities in the Knight-Ridder market due to low rates of subscription among Hispanics.

In practice and by international standards, bilingualism in Miami's educational, governmental, and media institutions in the 1960s and 1970s was quite limited. True bilingual education as pioneered in the Coral Way elementary school was carried out on a very limited scale in the Dade County public school system as a whole. Bilingual education in Dade County mostly concentrated on transitional programs. Metro–Dade County's official bilingual/bicultural declaration clearly defined Spanish as a *second* official language. In practice Spanish did not function co-equally with English in local government. Rather, official bilingualism meant merely that certain county documents were translated into Spanish, and a limited range of services was provided bilingually. *El Herald* was an insert provided upon request at no cost to subscribers of the *Miami Herald*, had only a fraction of the staff and budget of the English-language paper, and had no editorial independence. It was consciously and explicitly conceived as a Spanish-language *American* newspaper, and it largely consisted of translations from the English paper. Yet in contrast with the undiluted assimilationist policies just then coming under challenge throughout the United States, key institutions in Miami in the 1960s and 1970s responded to the huge and growing Cuban presence and emergent economic power with substantial concessions to the linguistic and cultural characteristics of the immigrant population.

The enlightened assimilationist policies adopted by the elites appeared to many rank-and-file whites to deepen and extend the process of Latinization by reducing the cost of nonassimilation, institutionalizing Spanish in key institutions, and providing vehicles (media, schools, and government) for maintaining and socially reproducing the immigrant language and culture. Practically and symbolically the official recognition of bilingualism and biculturalism further upset expectations among large sectors of the Anglo population about immigrant/Hispanic cultural and linguistic subordination and assimilation to the dominant culture. It seemed that rather than assimilating promptly, these newcomers from Cuba and other parts of Latin America were "taking over." In the face of this perceived "takeover," some Anglos who did not identify with the accommodationist path chose to abandon the field, and others attempted to reclaim the turf.

The Antibilingual Referendum: The Language of Resentment

"The presence of so many clever, industrious, and frugal aliens, capable of competing successfully . . . with the native whites constitutes a political and economic problem of the greatest importance." So read, in part, a 1927 study of Japanese and Chinese schoolchildren in Vancouver, Canada (Portes and Rumbaut 1990:210). These same fears surfaced in Miami much later in the century.

If key Miami institutions and elites adapted to the Hispanic challenge through accommodationist policies, some other sectors of the population responded decidedly differently. Flight has been probably the most common manifestation of rejection of the growing Hispanic influence. It is clear from much anecdotal evidence that the Hispanic phenomenon has been one reason that the Anglo population of Dade County has been declining since 1970. In 1990 there were 161,748 (21 percent) fewer non-Hispanic whites in Dade County than in 1960. During this period the total population of the area more than doubled, the black population tripled, and the Hispanic population increased nineteen times (see fig. 1.2) (Metropolitan Dade County 1983; Wallace 1991).

The paradigm of a more organized and active resistance was the antibilingualism movement. That movement arose in Miami in 1980 as a response to growing Hispanic numbers and empowerment. The antibilingualism movement aimed specifically at rolling back official bilingualism/biculturalism in Metropolitan Dade County and substituting English as the only language of government.

Miami thus became the birthplace of the contemporary English Only movement in the United States. It happened in November 1980, when voters in Dade County (Greater Miami) approved a landmark ordinance that reversed the policy of official bilingualism and biculturalism established by the Board of County Commissioners in 1973. The measure, passed overwhelmingly, prohibited "the expenditure of any county funds for the purpose of utilizing any language other than English or any culture other than that of the United States" (Section 1) and provided that "all county governmental meetings, hearings, and publications shall be *in the English language only*" (Section 2; emphasis added) (Metro–Dade County, Board of County Commissioners, 1980).

Arising as it did not only against the Hispanic upsurge but also against the elite policy of accommodation, the antibilingualism campaign did not emerge from any established interest group. Rather, it seemed to spring spontaneously from mass sentiments. The account that appeared in the *Miami Herald* on the day after the election suggests an instance of collective behavior, akin to a panic or craze: "It began as an idea batted around on a late-night talk show last July, and that swiftly gathered irresistible momentum. . . . Marion Plunske heard Emmy Shafer on a WNWS radio talk show on July 8. The two women started their campaign the next day and the Citizens of Dade United registered as a political action group on July 21. From the start, the campaign seemed to run itself. In just over four weeks the group had gathered 44,166 signatures, nearly twice as many as they needed. Exulting in their strength, they brought another 25,767 signatures to the supervisor of elections on Sept. 16" (Browning 1980:11A).

The antibilingualism movement, led by nonelite whites, was actively opposed by the city's white corporate and civic elite, signaling the differences between the elite accommodationist approach and the rejectionist implications of the movement. According to the *Miami Herald*, "by late October, Shafer reported she had received only about $10,000 in campaign contributions from about 1,100 people, an average of $8.06 per contributor." In contrast, the Greater Miami Chamber of Commerce alone spent $50,000 on newspaper and television advertisements in its campaign against the ordinance, called "Together for Dade's Future" (Browning 1980:11A).

In spite of the active opposition of the white elite, support for the antibilingualism ordinance was widespread among virtually all subgroups of the white population, with 71 percent of non-Hispanic whites supporting the referendum. A *Miami Herald* study concluded that "little else besides ethnic group—not age, nor sex, nor education, nor choice of presidential candidate made much difference in how people voted on the ordinance."

If the ethnically dominant population was solidly behind the referendum, the minorities—both Hispanic and black—did not share the enthusiasm. Among blacks only 44 percent supported the antibilingual referendum (Browning 1980:11A); among Hispanics a mere 15 percent favored it.

What explains the massive white rejection of the elite accommodationist policy and the lack of black support? The explanation involves both material interests and symbolic issues. An economist has remarked that the higher one goes in the elevator in a particular major bank in Miami that occupies a downtown skyscraper, the less Spanish is heard.[1] While white elites often were relatively secure from Hispanic competition and often shared similar class interests, this was not necessarily the case for other sectors of the population. Smaller Anglo businesses were no doubt more vulnerable to competition than national and multinational corporations. In the labor market, studies have shown that bilingual requirements for employment—which affect a substantial number of jobs in Miami—are concentrated in entry-level positions.[2] The fact of having to know a "foreign language" in order to qualify for a job in "our own country" was particularly galling to many Anglos, symbolizing a reversal of roles.

In contrast to whites' massive support, blacks, despite what the *Miami Herald* at the time described as "their history of cool relations with Latins in Dade" (Browning, 1980:11A), did not join in support for the anti-bilingualism ordinance. The split black vote was no doubt the result of several contradictory factors. It is generally argued that blacks have suffered most from Hispanic/immigrant economic competition in Miami (Porter and Dunn 1984). If this were the case, and if economic interests were the only factor, one would expect blacks to have supported the referendum massively. On the other hand, if the referendum was seen as an expression of white racism against a minority group, one might expect massive black opposition. In fact, blacks were divided on the issue, with a majority opposing the antibilingualism ordinance (56 percent) and a substantial minority supporting it (44 percent) (Browning 1980:11A).

What explains the pattern? Black workers, overrepresented in entry-level positions, might be expected to have faced disproportionate Cuban/Hispanic competition. Yet several indicators suggest that from 1970 to 1980, demographic and economic displacement related to the Hispanic presence was felt more keenly by whites than by blacks. The black population of Dade County rose by 52,367 between 1970 and 1980, while the white population dropped by 3,792 (U.S. Bureau of the Census 1984). In the city of Miami, the number of black employees increased by 25 percent between 1977 and 1985, while the number of Anglo employees dropped by 36 percent. The number of black employees classified as officials, administrators, and professionals more than tripled in the same period (City of Miami 1985:24, 28).

Ideologically one might expect that blacks did not identify as closely as whites with the Anglo cultural dominance that was being threatened. One might also expect that some blacks did see a component of racism, prejudice, or discrimination in the antibilingualism movement. The *Miami Herald* survey of voters found that "nearly half the blacks who voted against the ordinance said they believed it to be an insult to Spanish speakers that would hurt relations between Latins and non-Latins." In contrast "only about one non-Latin white voter in four said he or she thought the vote was an insult." (At the other end of the spectrum, more than 65 percent of Latin voters saw the ordinance as an insult.) (Browning 1980:11A).

The antibilingualism movement was a vehicle for the expression of mass native white resistance to Latinization and was a political project aimed at symbolically reestablishing Anglo dominance. The *Miami Herald* reported that over half of the non-Latin, white voters who supported the antibilingualism ordinance would be pleased if it "would make Miami a less attractive place to live for Cubans and other Spanish-speaking people." Over 75 percent of the persons in this same group of voters said they would like to leave Miami if it were practical (Browning 1980:11A).

The level of alienation of Anglo voters in Miami and the intensity of their anti-Hispanic sentiments is interesting in light of the nature of the Hispanic population of Miami. Miami Cubans, who in 1980 made up 70 percent of all Hispanics in Miami, were mostly middle income, conservative, and Caucasian; they had low rates of crime and dependence on public assistance, high rates of labor force participation, and growing rates of naturalization and political participation (Llanes 1982; Boswell and Curtis 1984; Pedraza-Bailey 1985; Portes and Bach 1985; Portes and Mozo 1985; Metro-Dade Planning Department 1986; Pérez 1986; Masud-Piloto 1988). Media coverage of the sudden arrival in Miami in the spring of 1980 of tens of thousands of Cubans (some of them with criminal backgrounds or mental health problems) as a result of the Mariel boatlift undoubtedly tarnished the public image of what might otherwise have been considered a "model minority" (Portes, Stepick, and Truelove 1986). But it was the very success of the Cubans and not the presence of some social deviants among them that produced a backlash. The backlash against bilingualism in the United States began in Miami specifically because Miami had been a pioneer in bilingualism and because Hispanics in Miami were an increasingly large and successful group.

The antibilingualism campaign elevated language to preeminence as an issue of open interethnic struggle in Miami. The vote also marked the beginning of a backlash against the trend toward linguistic pluralism in the United States. In the 1980s this backlash crystallized around the English Only/Official English movement.

Language became a key issue in a battle that was essentially about ethnic dominance and cultural hegemony because language choices reflect relations of power and because language is a key constituent of culture, identity, and nationality. Opinion polls have shown that Americans overwhelmingly believe that to be a true American, one must know English (Citrin 1988). That the government itself accepts bilingualism is seen by many Americans as a surrender of a key constituent element of nationality to an alien influence. For these reasons, language proved to be an issue upon which xenophobic and ethnocentric campaigns could be built, even in the post–civil rights era. In Miami beginning in 1980, language would serve as a symbolic battlefield upon which battles over power, culture, and identity would be waged. In a short time, other states and cities across the nation would follow.

Implications: The Limits of Success

As an electoral campaign, antibilingualism was wildly successful. Emmy Shafer and her Citizens of Dade United proved that an English Only campaign hastily organized by a political novice could triumph in the face of opposition by the established Anglo civic leadership, the English-language press, the majority of black voters, and one of the largest and most powerful Hispanic communities in the United States.

What were the direct and indirect local and national implications? Were the narrow and overt objectives accomplished? Was the larger (and latent) agenda of the movement (that antibilingualism would make Miami a less attractive place for Cubans and other Spanish speakers) fulfilled? Did antibilingualism work as a solution to the Hispanic problem?

The vote did succeed in reversing the institutionalization of Spanish in county government and forestalling the potential institutionalization of other languages, such as Haitian Creole. The most direct effect of the vote was the elimination of translations of public documents and the elimination of a range of bilingual services provided by the county. Clearly the clients affected by these changes were among the most vulnerable in the immigrant population: the elderly; the poor, who had to make use of now monolingual county services, such as the public hospital; the newly arrived; and the uneducated.

The vote also had some consequences regarding the county's ability to support certain cultural activities because the antibilingualism ordinance encompassed both language and culture. The ordinance prohibited "the expenditure of any county funds for the purpose of utilizing any language other than English or promoting any culture other than that of the United States."

More indirectly the vote also likely had a chilling effect on the development of bilingualism in other public institutions, notably the public school system. Although the referendum had no legal effect on the Dade County public schools, and bilingual education is mandated by federal laws and regulations, the school board is elected by the same countywide constituency that voted decisively for the antibilingualism ordinance in 1980. Since that time and up to the present, even school board members enthusiastically in favor of expanding bilingual education have been extremely reluctant to champion its expansion.[3]

The enduring political deterrence effect of the antibilingualism vote is suggested by what has happened to efforts to repeal the ordinance. On two occasions in the 1980s, George Valdes, then the only Hispanic commissioner on the board, declared his intention to present a motion to repeal the antibilingualism ordinance. Valdes was dissuaded each time by lack of support for repeal among fellow commissioners and on one occasion by an appeal to desist from Hispanic leaders worried about stirring up community strife for what, at that juncture, might still prove a losing battle.

Hispanic leaders were not mistaken in believing that repeal would be divisive. Following one of Valdes's announcements and at the urging of a radio talk show host, callers jammed the phone lines at the county commission. Valdes himself received bomb threats. In 1984 Valdes did manage to secure commission approval to amend the ordinance to exempt medical services at the county hospital and other medical facilities; essential services to the elderly and handicapped; the promotion of worldwide tourism; and emergency police, fire, ambulance, medical, rescue, and hurricane-preparedness services. But in order to secure the agreement of the English Only forces not to oppose the changes, Valdes had to include in the ordinance a declaration that English is the official language of Dade County as well as make provision for a program for English-language training for county employees. The cumulative effect of political deterrence, Hispanic caution, and the elimination of some of the worst aspects of the ordinance has been that repealing the antibilingualism ordinance has virtually disappeared from the Hispanic political agenda in Dade County since the mid-1980s.

One reason why Hispanic leaders may have been willing to give up (or postpone) the repeal fight is that, except for a limited number of county staff directly charged with administering bilingualism, upwardly mobile and younger Hispanics were hardly affected by the repeal of bilingualism. The impact for older Hispanics was cushioned by the existence of a strong set of parallel ethnic institutions. A more important reason is that, despite the consequences outlined above, the antibilingualism movement has failed in its broader agenda of stopping Hispanic growth and advancement. Demographically, politically, economically, and (arguably) culturally and linguistically, Latinization has accelerated since 1980.

In the 1980s, fueled by the Cuban Mariel boatlift, massive Nicaraguan immigration, and significant contingents of immigrants from other Latin American countries, Hispanics overtook whites as the largest population segment in Miami and were nearly a majority by the 1990 census (see fig. 1.2) (Wallace 1991). Clearly the antibilingualism referendum utterly failed to make Miami a less attractive place for Hispanics.

Hispanics also continued to advance economically in the 1980s. With about 5 percent of the country's Hispanic population, Miami has almost half of the largest Hispanic-owned businesses in the United States. The rate of business ownership among Miami Hispanics (43 per 1,000) far exceeds that in other large metropolitan areas, such as Los Angeles (14 per 1,000) (Boswell and Curtis 1984). Beyond the ethnic business enclave, Hispanics made important advances in private Anglo-owned corporations and particularly in top public sector positions. From the mid-1980s to the early 1990s, Cubans were appointed to top administrative posts in several key institutions, including Octavio Visiedo as superintendent of Dade County's public schools, Modesto Maidique as president of Florida International University, Marty Urra as president of the South Florida AFL-CIO, Xavier Suarez as mayor of the City of Miami, and Joaquín Aviño as manager of Metropolitan Dade County. Clearly antibilingualism failed to prevent continued Hispanic economic advancement.

If stemming the Hispanic tide in politics was a hope of the antibilingualism movement, the post-1980 era has brought very bad news. Building on demographics and economic development, the 1980s also saw major Hispanic advances in electoral politics and to a significant but somewhat lesser extent, into the higher spheres of the community power structure. Beginning in the early and mid-1980s, Cubans won an increasing number of elective offices in municipalities with large Hispanic populations, including the mayor's office in the two largest cities in the metropolitan area, Miami (Xavier Suarez) and Hialeah (Raul Martinez), and in newly created single member state legislative districts. While Hispanics currently occupy a single seat on both the Metro Commission (Alex Penelas) and the Dade County School Board (Rosa Castro Feinberg), the most important governmental bodies in Dade County, their votes are increasingly essential to the electoral prospects of any candidate. Finally in 1989, Republican Ileana Ros-Lehtinen became the first Cuban-American and the first Hispanic woman to be elected to the U.S. Congress (Malone 1988).

During this period Hispanics for the first time began to play a significant role on boards of directors of key civic organizations. Hispanics for the first time chaired such organizations as the Greater Miami Chamber of Commerce, the Dade Community Foundation, and the Dade Public Education Fund.

Even in the areas of culture and language directly addressed by the ordinance, antibilingualism failed to stop the trend. In the 1980s the Calle Ocho festival, a street festival in celebration of Latin culture, grew to become a huge event with national and international prominence. Also in the 1980s, a Cuban-American film enthusiast, Natalio Chediak, created the Miami Film Festival, which includes many Spanish-language films. In the world of popular music, the Miami Sound Machine put the city on the map to a distinctively Latin beat.

If legislating away or marginalizing the use of Spanish was a key intention of the antibilingualism effort, that hope was certainly dashed. A study by Strategy Research Corporation (1989) found that a higher percentage of Hispanics in Miami spoke Spanish at home, on the job, and on social occasions in 1989 than in 1980.

The ineffectiveness of antibilingualism to banish Spanish to the private sphere does not mean that Miami Hispanics eschew English or even that the place of Spanish is secure in Miami indefinitely. In 1980 fully 94.3 percent of Cuban-Americans born in the United States (more than half of whom live in Miami) reported they spoke English well (U.S. Bureau of the Census 1989). A study by David E. Lopez (1982) found that for 80 percent of U.S.-born Cubans, English was the main language. While these data are for Cubans in the United States, there is no doubt that even in Miami, English tends to replace Spanish as the dominant language intergenerationally. Continuing immigration to Miami masks this intergenerational process. It is an open question whether massive migration, Hispanic economic and political empowerment and other factors (such as Miami's

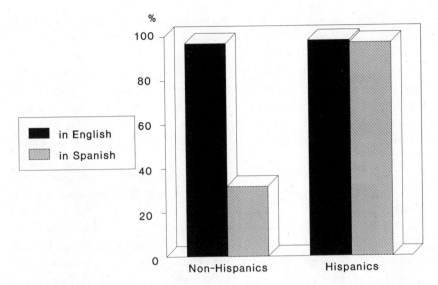

Fig. 6.4. "Very important" for children to read and write perfectly by language. *Source*: Strategy Research Corporation 1988, 42–43.

geographic location) may change the context so as to retard or reverse this shift.

A recent market study throws further light on the contrasting views of Anglos and Hispanics in Miami on the question of language. The data suggest that Hispanics almost unanimously prefer bilingualism over either Spanish or English monolingualism (see fig. 6.4). About one-third of Anglos also appears to favor or accept English/Spanish bilingualism. The battle over language in Miami is not about English versus Spanish but rather about English monolingualism versus bilingualism and about the eradication of Spanish or its survival.

National Implications

The 1980 antibilingualism campaign in Dade County was a spontaneous, local affair, but it had important national implications. It was the first reversal of the trend toward a measure of language pluralism in the United States and the first political battle over language in many decades. The 1980 Dade County vote showed for the first time the extent of voter support for language restrictionism and for the politics of anti-Hispanic and anti-immigrant backlash. The campaign also provided the method—

the referendum—that could and would later be used with tremendous success to institute English Only measures in other states and cities. The Dade County campaign foreshadowed both the ethnically polarized and bitter nature of language battles of the 1980s and the use by both sides of the theme of unity as a centerpiece in future campaigns. It showed the impotence of white leadership and elite groups to effectively oppose such a movement, a pattern that would later be repeated in California and virtually every other state and locality in which the issue has been put to the voter.

In the wake of the Miami vote, the prospects for a well-organized and -funded language restrictionist movement on a national scale must have seemed bright indeed. In 1981 a national English Only movement was launched with the introduction of the first Official English measure in Congress by Senator S. I. Hayakawa. Hayakawa would go on to found U.S. English, the flagship organization of the movement, in collaboration with John Tanton. In the 1980s, U.S. English would succeed in getting many states to pass Official English measures. The organization targeted mainly those states that have large Hispanic populations, seeking to symbolically reaffirm through the ballot Anglo political, cultural, and linguistic hege-mony. In California, Florida, Arizona, and Colorado, the organization used its resources to put state constitutional amendments on the ballot. U.S. English won four important victories, although the Arizona amend-ment subsequently has been declared unconstitutional.

Miami had been a leader in a limited form of bilingualism and bi-culturalism in the 1960s and 1970s; in 1980 it provided a blueprint for their undoing. The 1980 antibilingualism movement provided the form that a nativist, anti-immigrant, anti-Hispanic national movement might take in a post–civil rights America. In an America where avowed racism had become taboo, language provided a deniable vehicle for the expres-sion of ethnocentric fears and resentments. In Miami in 1980, two-thirds of Anglo voters thought antibilingualism would not hurt relations between Hispanics and non-Hispanics, while 65 percent of Hispanics said it would hurt relations (Browning 1980:11A).

The Miami case also has shown something about the successes and limitations of the type of politics embodied in the antibilingualism move-ment. Successful in reversing the trend toward bilingualism in govern-ment and slowing it down in the public schools, the movement was powerless to stem the larger demographic, economic, political, and cultural forces at work in Dade County. In the face of such forces and of the opposition of both significant white elites and minorities, the antibilingualism movement has been unable to legislate away Latin culture and language. The wish expressed by Anglo voters who supported anti-bilingualism that the ordinance make the area less attractive to Spanish speakers utterly failed to accomplish this end but did reveal the subtext of the movement (a subtext easily read by the victims).

The history of the national Official English movement so far has reflected much of the pattern observed in Dade County. After spectacular successes in referenda in several states with large Hispanic populations and in the legislatures of some states with small Hispanic populations (and in helping create a climate hostile to bilingual education throughout the 1980s), the Official English movement appears to have stalled. The efficacy of Official English measures has been far more limited than proponents had hoped. In California, courts have ruled that the constitutional amendment passed in 1986 is essentially symbolic. In Arizona, where a highly restrictive constitutional Official English amendment barely passed in 1988, a court has found the measure unconstitutional. In Florida, where an Official English amendment was passed in 1988, Cuban-American Republican legislators from Miami struck a deal with Democratic leaders that effectively blocked the enactment of any enforcement provisions (Castro, Haun, and Roca 1990). The end of the reign of William J. Bennett, an opponent of bilingual education, at the U.S. Department of Education meant the end of the period of greatest federal hostility to bilingual education.

More broadly the 1980s saw very rapid growth in the Hispanic population of the United States and substantial political gains (U.S. Bureau of the Census 1990). In light of growing Hispanic numbers and electoral strength concentrated in key states, neither political party has been willing to adopt Official English as a goal. In 1988 George Bush blocked the inclusion of Official English in the Republican party platform, and Michael Dukakis delivered part of his acceptance speech at the Democratic convention in Spanish. So far Official English measures have also stalled in Congress. In 1988 U.S. English was torn apart by the resignation of its president, Linda Chavez, and some prominent board members, including Walter Cronkite, after a memo with anti-Hispanic undertones written by U.S. English cofounder John Tanton was made public.

Conclusion

As in Miami, English Only/Official English advocates elsewhere have found that it is far easier to enact measures than to implement them. They have also found that the very Latinization that they seek to arrest makes it difficult to implement their broader agenda. Politicians and businesspersons nationally have been too intent on capturing the growing number of Hispanic votes and Hispanic dollars to heed the English Only message.

But the battle is far from over, in Miami or in the nation in general. Because English Only/Official English measures have proven insufficient to curb Latinization, the conflict has partially shifted to other arenas. Bilingual education in particular is likely to continue to be a focus of attack, for English Only advocates see it as an institution through which a U.S.-Hispanic culture and consciousness can be created and transmitted. Immigration policy is a second important arena insofar as it provides a steady stream of additional and unassimilated Hispanics. In frustration over the relative impotence of the antibilingualism ordinance, one English Only advocacy group in Miami reached the conclusion that the main problem is immigration and sought a moratorium on immigration.

Nationally less draconian measures in this direction have already been adopted. The Immigration Reform and Control Act had as it main objective the curbing of undocumented immigration, mostly from Latin America. More recently many bills to reform legal immigration have been proposed in Congress. These measures would reduce the weight of family reunification in the immigration preference system, with the effect of reducing Latin American immigration.

As we approach the end of the century, the growth and development of the Hispanic population continues in Miami and the nation despite these efforts. As the process continues, the battle over language in Miami is a harbinger of battles yet to come over what this trend will mean for the identity of a community and a nation.

Notes

1. Kenneth Lipner, economist, Florida International University, Miami, personal communication with author.

2. Findings are from the Equal Opportunity Board of Metropolitan Dade County, Marcos Regalado, director, which has conducted two unpublished studies of job advertisements appearing in the *Miami Herald*. Personal communication from the director.

3. Anonymous member, Dade County School Board, personal communication.

References

Boswell, Thomas D., and James R. Curtis. 1984. *The Cuban-American Experience: Culture, Images and Perspectives*. Totowa, N.J.: Rowman and Allanheld.

Browning, Michael. 1980. "Antibilingual Backers Celebrate Early." *Miami Herald.* November 5: 1A, 11A.

Castro, Max J., Margaret Haun, and Ana Roca. 1990. "The Official English Movement in Florida." In *Perspectives on Official English*, edited by K. L. Adams and D. T. Brink, 151–60. Berlin and New York: Mouton de Gruyte.

Citrin, Jack. 1988. "American Identity and the Politics of Ethnicity: Public Opinion in a Changing Society." Paper presented at the eleventh annual meeting of the International Society of Political Psychology, Secaucus, N.J., July 1–5.

City of Miami. 1985. *Affirmative Action Annual Report.* City of Miami: Department of Internal Audits and Reviews, Affirmative Action Division.

Cuban American Policy Center. 1988. *Miami's Latin Businesses.* Miami: Cuban American National Planning Council.

Díaz, Guarioné M., ed. 1980. *Evaluation and Identification of Policy Issues in the Cuban Community.* Miami: Cuban National Planning Council.

Didion, Joan. 1987. *Miami.* New York: Pocket Books.

Llanes, José R. 1982. *Cuban-Americans, Masters of Survival.* Cambridge, Mass.: ABT.

Lopez, David E. 1982. *Language Maintenance and Shift in the United States Today.* Los Alamitos, Calif.: National Center for Bilingual Research.

Malone, Joseph. 1988. *The Second Half of the 1980s: Voters and Votes: Emphasis on Hispanic Influence 1985–1987.* Metro-Dade Elections Department.

Masud-Piloto, Felix. 1988. *With Open Arms: Cuban Migration to the United States.* Totowa, N.J.: Rowman and Littlefield.

Metro–Dade County. 1983. *Dade County Characteristics.* Miami: Department of Human Resources.

———, Board of County Commissioners. 1973. Agenda Item no. 7(g)(3). Resolution no. R–502–73, Declaring Dade County a Bilingual and Bicultural County.

———. 1980. Ordinance no. 80–128, "Ordinance Prohibiting the Expenditure of County Funds for the Purpose of Utilizing Any Language Other than English or Promoting Any Culture Other than that of the United States; Providing for Governmental Meetings and Publications to Be in the English Language . . . Effective . . . November 4, 1980."

Metro–Dade County Planning Department. 1984. *Profile of the Black Population.* Miami: Research Division, Metro–Dade Planning Department.

———. 1986. *Hispanic Profile: Dade County's Hispanic Origin Population 1985.* Miami: Research Division, Metro–Dade Planning Department.

Miami Herald. 1980.

Pedraza-Bailey, Silvia. 1985. *Political and Economic Migrants in America: Cubans and Mexicans.* Austin: University of Texas Press.

Pérez, Lisandro. 1986. "Immigrant Economic Adjustment and Family Organization: The Cuban Success Story Reexamined." *International Migration Review* 20, no. 1 (Spring): 1–20.

Porter, Bruce, and Marvin Dunn. 1984. *The Miami Riot of 1980: Crossing the Bounds.* Lexington, Mass.: D.C. Heath and Company.

Portes, Alejandro, and Robert L. Bach. 1985. *Latin Journey: Cuban and Mexican Immigrants in the United States.* Berkeley: University of California Press.

Portes, Alejandro, and Rafael Mozo. 1985. "The Political Adaptation Process of Cubans and Other Ethnic Minorities in the United States." *International Migration Review* 19, no. 1 (Spring): 35–63.

Portes, Alejandro, and Rubén G. Rumbaut. 1990. *Immigrant America: A Portrait.* Berkeley: University of California Press.

Portes, Alejandro, Alex Stepick, and Cynthia Truelove. 1986. "Three Years Later: The Adaptation Process of 1980 (Mariel) Cuban and Haitian Refugees in South Florida." *Population Research and Policy Review* 5: 83–94.

Stepick, Alex, Max J. Castro, Marvin Dunn, and Guillermo Grenier. 1990. "Changing Relations among Newcomers and Established Residents: The Case of Miami." Final report (unpublished) to the board of the "Changing Relations Project." Miami.

Strategy Research Corporation. 1984. *The U.S. Hispanic Market.* Miami: Strategy Research Corporation.

———. 1988. *The 1989 South Florida Latin Market.* Miami: Strategy Research Corporation.

U.S. Bureau of the Census. 1984. *1980 Census: Detailed Population Characteristics.* Release PC–80–1–D1–A. Washington: U.S. Department of Commerce.

———. 1989. *The Hispanic Population of the United States: March 1989.* Current Reports, Series P–20, No. 444. Washington: United States Government Printing Office.

Wallace, Richard. 1991. "South Florida Grows to a Latin Beat." *Miami Herald*, March 6: 1A, 22A.

Wilson, Kenneth L., and W.A. Martin. 1982. "Ethnic Enclaves: A Comparison of the Cuban and Black Economies in Miami." *American Journal of Sociology* 88 (July): 135–60.

7

The Cuban-American Labor Movement in Dade County: An Emerging Immigrant Working Class

Guillermo J. Grenier

As throughout the country, the labor movement in Dade County has been in decline. Runaway shops, offshore production, and anti-union employer practices have cut into the manufacturing and construction sectors. Unions have been hesitant to mount major organizing drives in an area characterized by heavy immigrant labor and a growing service economy. In recent years, however, labor has shown signs of renewed vigor. Ironically a force that is invigorating the labor movement is one of those blamed for its decline: immigrant, specifically Cuban, labor.

The most recent census estimates place the population of Dade County at slightly over two million. Of these, just under 50 percent are of Latin origin. Cubans are by far the most numerous of this group, numbering approximately 600,000 (Strategy Research Corporation 1989). The American Federation of Labor–Congress of Industrial Organizations (AFL-CIO) estimates that there are approximately 361,982 union members in the state of Florida.[1] In Dade County union membership is approximately 59,746. Of these persons, 15,414, or 26 percent, are Latins, nearly all of whom are Cubans (see table 7.1).

For the last decade, analysts of various disciplines have generated a vast literature on the experiences of Cubans in the Miami area but have largely ignored this working-class group. Inspired by the analysis of the

Table 7.1. Dade County Union Membership, 1988 (by sector)

Dade County unions	Total members	No. Latins	% Latins
Building trades/construction[a]	9,882	2,276	23
Manufacturing[b]	1,888	1,187	62
Service/public[c]	48,038	11,951	25
Total Dade County Latin union members	59,808	15,414	26

Sources: National AFL-CIO Research Department, Committee on Political Education; author's research into Carpenters Union membership from original lists.
a. Includes Aluminum Workers, Asbestos Workers, Boilermakers, Bricklayers, Carpenters, IUE (electrical), IBEW (electrical), Elevator Constructors, Operating Engineers, Laborers, Longshoremen, IBPAT, Plumbers, Pipefitters, Roofers, Rubber Workers, and Sheet Metal Workers.
b. Includes Bakery Workers, ACTWU, IUE (Furniture Workers), ILGWU, Glass Bottle Blowers, Paperworkers, Steelworkers, and Upholsterers (Steelworkers).
c. Includes Barbers, Flight Attendants, Service Employees, CWA (communications), Fire Fighters, Oilers, Government Employees, Letter Carriers, Graphic Arts Workers, Machinists, Maintenance-of-Way Employees, Musicians, OPEIU, Chemical Workers, APWU, UTU, Transportation-Communication Workers, UFCW, RWDSU, IATSE, AFSCME, Printing Graphic Comm., AFT, ATU (transit), TWU, Utility Workers, Telegraph Workers (CWA), Typographical Workers, Hotel and Restaurant Workers, and Teamsters. Also includes two estimates totaling 7,000 members given by local leaders of major unions.

enclave community, many have focused attention on the modes of incorporation of the Cuban community into the U.S. social system. These analysts have examined the ways in which Cubans respond to labor market pressures; reorganize familial responsibilities; and assimilate into or resist the social, political, and cultural institutions of the host country (Wilson and Portes 1980; Wilson and Martin 1982; Portes and Bach 1985).

With few exceptions (Moncarz 1978; Jorge and Moncarz 1982; Pérez 1986), analysts studying the Cuban experience have been preoccupied primarily with how Cubans have "made it" in the United States in comparison with other minority groups (Portes 1981, 1982). Conceptually this has translated into the description and analysis of the entrepreneurial voice of the Cuban community in Dade County and a general emphasis on the development of the Cuban middle class. When the working experience of contemporary Cuban-Americans has been studied, the context has been the family or gender issues related to the work experience (Ferre 1979; Pérez 1986; Prieto 1987).

Meanwhile the Cuban working class, which for this purpose is defined as the nonmanagerial or nonprofessional wage-earning sector of the population, has continued to grow. As figure 7.1 shows, most Cuban workers

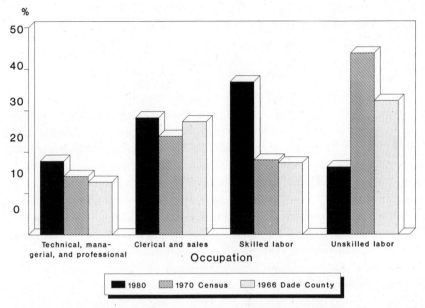

Fig. 7.1. Cuban occupations in Miami, 1966, 1970, and 1980. *Sources*: 1966, University of Miami; 1970, U.S. Bureau of the Census; 1980, U.S. Bureau of Labor Statistics.

have occupied nonmanagerial positions of wage earners employed as producers of goods and services since immigrating.

Too little has been done to analyze the process of incorporation of the Cuban-American working class into the United States. Have the Cubans really made it? How much of the success is due to the protections provided by the enclave community? How much is attributable to other means of incorporation, such as organized action in labor organizations within the primary and secondary labor markets? Can Cuban-Americans unite around domestic policy issues of interest to a broad cross section of North American workers? Can the labor movement in south Florida successfully incorporate immigrant workers into its unions? Answering these questions is difficult in the absence of a broader understanding of the Cuban-American working class in south Florida.

The voice of this working class has been monolithically classified as one that is preoccupied with an anti-Castro, foreign policy–oriented agenda to the exclusion of domestic concerns. The assumption implicit in this interpretation is that the major concerns of all Cubans are the return to Cuba and the opposition to Communist regimes everywhere. The massive exodus from the Democratic party in the 1960s and 1970s of the majority of Cubans further reinforces the vision of a dramatically right-wing working class dominated by a foreign policy agenda. This type of immigrant worker does not hold much promise for organizers.

Yet the recent surge in Cuban-American labor activity in south Florida, the most populous area of the fastest-growing state, shows evidence of promising diversity for the future of organizing Cuban immigrants. While maintaining a strong anti-Communist ideology, Cuban-Americans are tapping a rich, progressive labor tradition to gather support for the domestic labor agenda. It is this emerging working-class voice that interests organizers and analysts alike.

Any attempt to begin the process of analysis of the Cuban-American working class should describe how the voice of the working class is being expressed and how its expression is affecting the political, social, and economic dynamics of Dade County.

In this chapter I explore some of the dynamics involved in the contemporary development of a self-conscious Cuban working class in Dade County. Specifically I will discuss the emerging organization of this working class into class-based groups within the American labor movement and how this emergence is affecting the politics of the area and of the labor movement.

Since no baseline data exist for the incorporation of Cuban-Americans into the American labor movement in Dade County, I initiated this ongoing project by conducting open-ended interviews with fifteen labor leaders on the role of Cuban-Americans in the labor movement. This chapter contains a preliminary review of these interviews, original research into the membership history of the Carpenters Union of south Florida, and findings from participant observation during two years of work with the Cuban-American labor movement.[2] From the interviews and observations emerged the major themes around which the material is organized: the importance of understanding the working-class nature of the Cuban-American population in Dade County, the militant labor tradition of Cuban workers, the overcoming of initial barriers to entering North American working-class organizations, the overcoming of the myth of the unorganizable Cuban, the development of ethnic solidarity within American labor organizations, the apparent ethnic succession of leadership of the south Florida AFL-CIO, and the efforts to develop nonpartisan political coalitions on labor issues.[3]

The Enclave and the Cuban-American Working Class

The concept that has most influenced the analysis of the contemporary Cuban-American experience in Florida is the enclave community. While analysts are still developing the full dynamics and characteristics of the Cuban enclave in southern Florida, two related characteristics are of relevance to the present discussion: the size of the labor force employed in the enclave and the impermeability to unionization of the enclave.

A basic characteristic of the enclave, according to Portes (1981:291), is that "a significant proportion of the immigrant work force works in enterprises owned by other immigrants." This conceptualization has implications for the analysis of the Cuban working class in Dade County since it establishes limits to the incorporation of Cuban-American workers into the mainstream economy, where unions operate. The size of the enclave labor force thus serves as a delimiter to the potential growth of an organized Cuban labor force, especially since a second characteristic of the Cuban enclave is its exceedingly low level of unionization (Portes and Bach 1985). Simply put, the larger the enclave, the smaller the potential to incorporate Cuban-Americans into the labor movement.

While the enclave protects immigrant workers from discriminatory labor market dynamics (Portes, Clark, and Manning 1985), it also inhibits the establishment of working-class organizations that represent the interest of the workers in the face of management. Ethnic solidarity, in this case, is used as a vehicle for class subjugation.

How much of the Cuban working class is employed by Cuban entrepreneurial capitalists? According to the Bureau of the Census, Cubans have the highest rate of business ownership among Hispanic groups. The Census Bureau reports 47,725 Hispanic-owned businesses in Dade County in its most recent minority business report, which was issued in 1990. Of these, approximately 34,771 (73 percent) are Cuban (U.S. Department of Commerce 1990). While the entrepreneurial Cuban sector is the largest among Latins in Dade County, it comprises a small portion of the Cuban-American work force. At the time of the survey (1987), the work force of Dade County consisted of approximately 380,000 Cubans. This means that approximately 10 percent of Cubans owned their own businesses and could be structurally classified as "entrepreneurial" in economic activities.

Furthermore a large number of Cuban firms do not employ any paid employees. Only 2,643 Cuban enclave firms hire workers. The number of employees reported by these firms totals 12,618. Even assuming the untenable (that all of these employees are Cubans), these firms, the backbone of the Cuban enclave, only employ 4 percent of the Cuban labor force. That leaves the rest of the Cuban nonmanagerial labor force, approximately 96 percent of the total, working for wages outside the enclave. While a percentage of these wage workers occupies supervisory positions, most of these persons belong to the working class—the class of hourly, production, or service laborers that occupies a nonsupervisory role and earns a living by selling its labor power in the process of producing a product or a service.[4]

Studies show that Cuban workers in Dade County earn around 26 percent less than Anglo workers and about 5 percent less than black American workers, even after human capital differences are taken into consideration (Jorge, Moncarz, and Cruz 1983). In addition, Carlson and Swartz (1988), using national data, assert that Cuban women earn less than their male counterparts. While those working within the enclave are treated somewhat better (Portes 1982), the picture remains one of inequality. In this environment, the voice of the working class is being expressed through its organizations.

The Inheritance: Militancy and Ethnicity

The contemporary focus on Cuban entrepreneurs contrasts sharply with the historical literature on Cubans in the United States. These studies emphasize the militant nature of the Cuban-American working class in the cigar factories of Tampa, Key West, Jacksonville, and New York, as well as the intransigence of Cuban workers in joining North American labor organizations.

Relations with the Cuban and American labor movement have a long history. The activities of the American Federation of Labor were monitored by and to some degree influenced the development of the labor movement in Cuba. The Cuban labor movement was one of the first to celebrate May 1 as a workers' celebration. Labor papers extensively covered and condemned the Haymarket murders in Chicago (Instituto de Historia 1975). Similarly since its inception, the AFL cultivated an interest in Latin America and Cuba. In 1895 it endorsed the stand of the separatist Cubans. Samuel Gompers expressed his support at the AFL convention of 1896 for the Cuban proletariat and its attempts to organize in the face of the

Spanish occupation (Alba 1968). When strikes broke out on the island in 1917, Gompers traveled to Havana in an attempt to convince American strikebreakers to return to the United States. The AFL also took the lead in establishing inter-American labor organizations, which included Cuban labor federations. The first major organization through which the AFL exerted direct influence over Cuban labor was the Confederación Obrera PanAmericana (COPA), which was organized through the initiative of the Mexican labor movement and the AFL executive committee during the 1916 convention. Gompers was elected founding president of COPA.

The American labor movement, either through the AFL or the CIO, also worked closely with Cuban workers in other inter-American organizations such as the Confederación de Trabajadores de America Latina (CTAL), founded in 1938, and the Confederación Interamericana de Trabajadores (CIT), founded in 1948. During the regime of Gerardo Machado, the AFL sent an investigative mission to Cuba as a symbol of solidarity with the cane workers, who were experiencing a rash of "suicide" hangings throughout the island. As a result of the AFL report, New York longshore workers refused to unload Cuban sugar.

On the mainland, however, attitudes toward Cuban-American workers have not been as supportive. While the Cuban-American working class has played a significant role as a social and productive force in some regions of the United States for over a century, the American labor movement has had little success organizing the Cuban-American worker.

Paradoxically the tradition of the Cuban-American working class in this country is a militant one. The militancy of Cuban workers in New York, Key West, and Tampa has been well-documented by participants as well as by contemporary analysts (Instituto de Historia 1975; Poyo 1986). Yet this militancy directed itself toward the political struggles occurring on the island, rather than expressing its concern for the development of the American labor movement. As early as 1890, organizers from the International Union of Cigarmakers complained that Cuban workers were more interested in organizing along ethnic lines and mobilizing support for the separatist movement on the island than in joining American labor. Indeed, open conflict between independent Cuban unions and AFL affiliates was frequent in the Tampa area among the cigar workers (Long 1965). As a result, part of the reason why the AFL supported the separatist movement in Cuba was the opinion of the leadership that the unorganizable Cuban-American workers would return to the island if it were free from Spanish rule (Appel 1956).

After independence the Cuban labor movement had a prominent position of power on the island. Not only did it make or break presidencies but it also succeeded in passing some of the most progressive labor legislation in the western hemisphere. Paid maternity leave and vacations, job security, and pension benefits are but a few of the social guarantees institutionalized in the 1940 Constitution (Dominguez 1978). It is this tradition that the Cuban-American labor leaders of south Florida want to continue while overcoming the negative stereotypes inherited and developed during the last thirty years.

Overcoming "Redneckismo"

The national decline in unionism during the last two decades has been magnified in Dade County by the steady flow of immigrants. The Cubans, as the earliest of the immigrants, have been associated with that decline on two fronts. Some within the labor movement accuse the Cubans of being unorganizable because of their all-encompassing concern with foreign policy issues regarding communism and U.S. relations with Cuba. Other critics point to the exclusionary practices of some building trade unions during the early years of the immigration.

Academics and progressives within the movement have consistently criticized the building trades for erecting barriers to Cuban and other minority participation in unions. Race- and ethnicity-based exclusionary practices of craft unions were, in fact, the focus of intense national political and legal action in the late 1960s and 1970s (Marshall and Briggs 1967a; Hall 1969; Marshall et al. 1976; Gould 1977). In Dade County these barriers took the shape of referral systems, English-language examinations, and discriminatory hiring hall practices. These practices were particularly prevalent among the licensed trades, such as plumbers and electricians.

A current Cuban leader of the union recalled his first attempts at joining the Carpenters Union in 1969.

> What they gave me was a desk and a test, and they told me that the test would cost me 20 or 25 dollars. I . . . paid the 20 or 25 dollars, did not pass the test because number one: I did not read English, I had problems with the language; and number two, the type of test they can give you . . . are so that one will not pass it. Three weeks after . . . there were ads in the newspapers . . . looking for people. I returned. They gave me a little better

attention this time, did not give me the test, but they did not let me get in, either. I got in on the third time because my (Anglo) father-in-law was a member of a local and had become a friend of the local representative. I came in recommended by him and the business agent helped me to pass the test and I started working.

These are also the unions that suffered some of the most severe economic conditions of the last thirty years. Cubans who managed to join those unions were often the first to lose their jobs through last-hired-first-fired provisions and because of discrimination by the contractor, since in the trades the contractors, dominantly non-Latin, have exclusive control over the labor force. When they lost their jobs, Cubans, like other immigrants, used their human capital to find employment in the nonunion sectors of the trades. While the pay was lower, the jobs were growing.

A non-Latin leader of the Plumbers Union says of the first wave of Cubans: "We are a pretty red-neck union. . . . At first, we wanted to keep them out. That was OK with my members. I was one of the few that wanted them in anyway. Then, we decided we had to let them in . . . so we loosened up and set up some training. . . . So, then the contractors put them on but they are the first ones out when the job gets done. . . . The contractors are red-necks too. . . . To keep working, then they go work non-union. You can't blame them but that's our problem."

While the charges of exclusion are well-founded, they ignore the fact that other unions (in the service and public sectors, for example) did not erect such barriers. Even in craft unions, the legal and social pressures increased the rates of minority representation in unions.[5]

In Dade County some service and public-sector unions benefited from the economic cycles of the area and have provided much-needed job security for the Cuban immigrants. These unions grew in Cuban membership and today form the backbone of the Cuban-American labor movement in Dade County.

The Myth of the Unorganizable Cuban and Ethnic Solidarity

The intransigence of Cuban workers in joining American labor organizations has a tradition going back to the cigar workers of Tampa, Key West, Jacksonville, and New York. In spite of their radical ideological posture, these workers exercised ethnic rather than class solidarity in the American workplace.

The contemporary situation is different. While the nature of U.S./ Cuban relations still plays a dominant role in the Cuban-American policy agenda (Díaz 1980; Gallagher 1980), Cuban-American labor leaders recognize that they have to develop a broad-based domestic policy agenda combining the interests of class and ethnicity. Indeed there is a great deal of resentment expressed by labor leaders about the excessive discussion of foreign policy issues on Cuban radio talk shows. These talk shows are the dominant form of expression for the anti-Castro sentiments of the community and enjoy a wide listening audience. Labor leaders view the lack of domestic focus of these shows as an attempt to divide the Cuban-American community by those who benefit from the domestic results of such a division: the Latin and non-Latin power brokers of Dade County. To overcome this problem, Cuban labor leaders recognize that they have to redraw the playing field by focusing attention on a domestic labor agenda and becoming involved in community issues of importance to Cuban-American workers. As one labor leader explained: "They control the media. Everything you hear is the same thing every day, all day long. What we have to do is solve the local problems. If we join together with the community in solving the problems here, you will see that the unions grow . . . and the people that want to divide us will become silent."

The developing consensus among Cuban labor leaders is that the politics of Cuban-American labor should focus on domestic rather than foreign-policy issues. The domination of foreign-policy discourse within the Cuban community is viewed as a major obstacle to the potential growth of labor in south Florida.

While nationally Latin membership in unions as a percentage of total participation in the labor force has been decreasing over the past few years—from 21.1 percent in 1983 to 17.3 percent in 1987 (U.S. Department of Labor 1985, 1988)—all the labor leaders interviewed agree that Latin and Cuban-American membership in their particular unions has increased over the last decade. While the longitudinal data to verify this are still being gathered, respondents point to the growing numbers of Cuban-American labor leaders as evidence of growing membership power. Labor organizations must respond in some measure to the demands of the membership.

The opinion that Cubans not only are organizable but make good unionists is expressed by a cross section of union leaders. Cubans, according to one respondent, feel more "comfortable being union" because the cultural tradition supports collective action. A common theme is

The old guard: Members of the Amalgamated Clothing and Textile Workers Union (ACTWU) at work in a Hialeah plant. The mostly female work force is predominantly Cuban and has been since the 1970s.

that Cubans are more loyal to the unions than are non-Cubans. The usual evidence presented for this belief is that Cubans will turn out for union activities such as picketing and meetings. A leader of the Carpenters Union recognized the militancy of his Cuban workers in the late 1970s, and he decided to run for office: "I began to realize that this local has about 600 people. Only about 30 show up to the meetings. So with 15 people you can run the local. . . . You can always get 20 Cubans to show up to a meeting." He became the youngest member to win an officer election and the only one to do so on the first ballot.

Similarly a non-Cuban business agent of a major union in south Florida responded to a question about his Latin members as follows: "Man, are they radical. You can show them a contract and talk to them about language but if they think that an injustice has been done, they figure it's the union's job to undo it. They always want the union to step in and fight. They drive me crazy."

This opinion is not reserved for Cuban men. In the garment industry, gender and ethnic issues combine to create a unique climate for Cuban unionists. Each of the three major plants organized by the Amalgamated

New blood: A Haitian man is one of the few non-Cubans in the mostly female work force at a Hialeah garment factory organized by the Amalgamated Clothing and Textile Workers Union.

Clothing and Textile Workers Union have 100 percent of the workers as members of the union, a rare occurrence in a right-to-work state. Approximately 90 percent of the workers are Latin women.

This willingness to become involved in unionism has caused a steady increase in the percentage of Cuban unionists in major unions. In the hotel and restaurant sector, for example, Cuban union members have grown from a relative few in the early 1960s to become the major portion of the approximately 65 percent of Latin members out of a total membership of 4,000. In other unions, increases are associated with sporadic increased hiring in a company or an industry. For example, the Machinists Local, which represents Eastern Airlines maintenance crews, experienced binge hiring by the company in 1967, 1973, and 1980. During each of these hiring periods, approximately 1,000 new workers were added to the company. The president of the local estimates that during the last two hiring spurts, Cubans in Miami represented 75 percent of those hired. While membership in his union has suffered during the last few years, over 30 percent of the union is Latin, and most of these are Cubans. The Carpenters Union is another example of a union with a growing

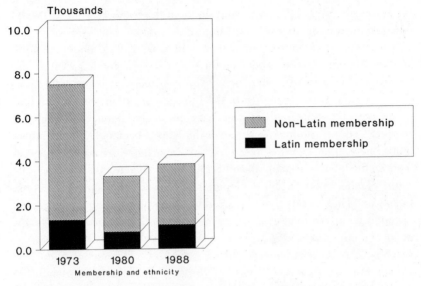

Fig. 7.2. Carpenters union membership, Dade County, 1973–88.

Latin/Cuban membership (see figure 7.2). While total membership has decreased considerably since the 1960s, the percentage of Cubans and Latins in the organization has increased steadily. This trend has intensified since 1979, when a major leadership position was won by a Cuban-American. Approximately 802 (44 percent) of the 1,828 carpenters hired between January 1979 and September 1988 are Latin, nearly all of whom are Cubans.[6]

Ethnic Succession of Leadership

Part of the reason that the perception of Cubans as unorganizable attained the currency of an axiom has do with the leadership of the South Florida AFL-CIO. The South Florida AFL-CIO has been controlled for many years by the building trade unions. The president since 1964 (who recently died) belonged to the International Brotherhood of Electrical Workers (IBEW). While his particular local was associated with the Florida Power and Light service sector, he was heavily influenced by the Building Trades Council of Dade County. (His father was a business manager for the Philadelphia Plumbers Union.) For decades the politics of the movement were expressed through the Building Trades Council. For the last twelve years, the political director of the South Florida AFL-CIO has also been a member of a building trades union.

The strength of the movement has shifted with the economy. As the service and public sectors become the engines of economic growth in the area, their unions, with their heavy Cuban-American membership, increase in power. In alliance with the Carpenters Union, the most immigrant-inclusive of the building trades, a coalition has been formed that has restructured the ethnic power base of the labor movement. The members of the "new labor" coalition recognize the importance of minority involvement in the labor movement of south Florida. As one leader reports, "The future of labor in South Florida depends on the enfranchisement of Latins, blacks and Haitians. Period." The old leadership and most unions are out of touch with this idea of minority involvement. The unions that know about the ethnic power base are the ones that will grow.

The efforts of the coalition resulted in the May 1988 election of the first Cuban-American in the history of the American labor movement as president of an AFL-CIO central labor council. The new president often emphasizes the potential for organizing Cubans by discussing the progressive labor legislation that was present in Cuba when he was born: "I was born under a law that allowed my mother to stay home, with her job secure and her paycheck still coming, for 45 days before my birth and 45 days after my birth. And my mother even applied for an extension and got it because that was the law. We should work for those same kinds of benefits here, in this country, and we can't do it, unless we organize."

The organizational driving force charged with focusing the new Cuban-American unionism on domestic labor issues is the Labor Council for Latin American Advancement (LCLAA) of Dade County, affiliated with the AFL-CIO. LCLAA has within its ranks twenty-seven Cuban labor leaders representing twenty-one local unions (see table 7.2). These labor leaders are officers in their major unions in Dade County. They represent a broad cross section of organized labor in the county, but the union membership reflects the growing importance of the service and public sectors. The building trades have eight representatives, manufacturing/industrial unions have three representatives, and service/public-sector unions have sixteen. As the self-conscious core of Cuban labor leadership in the South Florida AFL-CIO, the members of LCLAA actively encourage the Latin members in their industries to join unions. Within their own unions, they also push to increase the involvement of Cubans and Latins in the administration of the unions.

Table 7.2. Labor Council for Latin American Advancement,
Dade County Board Members, 1988

Sector	Number of board members	Members represented	% Latin members
Building/construction	8	4,532	26.7
Industrial/manufacturing	3	1,512	67.9
Service/public	16	32,821	20.7

Sources: National AFL-CIO Research Department, Committee on Political Education list; Dade County LCLAA Annual Report, 1988

While only one member of the organization is not Cuban-American, the leadership perceives the role of LCLAA to be the organizing force for all Latins. The organization is developing a role as a broker of Latin immigrant worker power. By reaching out to community groups and new arrivals, especially the growing Nicaraguan population, it hopes to become the representative of labor within the Latin community. It is not unusual for LCLAA to invite representatives of Nicaraguan unions in exile to address membership meetings or to sponsor activities in support of other immigrant worker groups. For example, during the recent revision of the immigration law, the group sponsored a meeting of Nicaraguan community members to inform them of the provisions and procedures of the law. [7]

Part of the organizational goal of LCLAA and of the new president of the South Florida AFL-CIO is to establish a link between the Cuban labor tradition before 1959 and the present and future Cuban-American labor tradition in the United States. During one organizational meeting, a top official of a building trades union announced to a room full of Cuban unionists at a Dade County meeting in 1987: "We should have the Cuban leaders join the movement here. I know the AFL-CIO and the American politics . . . but we are not leaders of the type there was in Cuba . . . that talk to the people and motivate them. . . . That's what we need in Miami."

Present in the room was the late Marcos Hirigoyen, a top labor leader in prerevolutionary Cuba and a member of a local AFL-CIO union. He, along with Angel Cofino, Oscar Salamea, and Conrado Rodrigues, among others, form the cadre of "lideres Cubanos," who serve as a basis for much of the discussion about the potential of Cuban labor in Dade County. [8]

Most of these activists are not incorporated into the American labor movement but serve as leaders of Miami-based working-class organizations from pre-1959 Cuba. The Federación de Trabajadores del Transporte de Cuba, the Federación de Trabajadores Telefonicos de Cuba en el Exilio, and the Plantas Eléctricas unions are three groups that have a patently working-class orientation. Of the three organizations, the Telefonicos have the closest ties with the American labor movement. The Communication Workers of America (CWA) logo is clearly visible on the regular publication of the federation's newsletter, *Unidad.*

There is a dual purpose in utilizing the traditions of the old guard: credibility within the Cuban community and political insurance. The Cuban-American leaders view the old guard as voices that can be used to reach the Cuban workers partly because of their experience in labor struggles in Cuba but also because their politics are beyond reproach. In an environment in which red-baiting is viewed as a real problem, those who were persecuted by the revolutionary government on the island for labor activity become ideal linkages for American labor: "Nobody can blame this people for being Communist because everybody knows that they suffered there."

It is also true that Cuban-American labor leaders are also anti-Communists. While there might be a varying strength of commitment to specific issues (such as support of the Contras), the Cuban-American labor leaders align themselves strongly as anti-Communists on foreign policy issues. During the Florida state AFL-CIO convention in 1987, one Cuban-American labor leader expressed his relief after a presentation by the American Institutes for Free Labor Development (AIFLD) on the situation in Nicaragua: "At last it seems that the AFL-CIO is taking a stand that we can support [about Nicaragua]. Before they have always been against the Contras and that is difficult to push with my members."

While strategically it is necessary to avoid being called a Communist, it is also true that Cuban-American labor leaders perceive the threat of being so labeled as the unique Cuban twist to anti-unionism in Dade County. The issue of anticommunism is never discussed during organizational meetings.

Effects of the Cuban Labor Voice

The increase in the importance of Latin labor in Dade County is having its effects in the political alliances of south Florida.[9] The Cuban-American labor leadership is predominantly Democratic in party affiliation, while the rank and file is considered to be overwhelmingly Republican. While there appears to be a shift toward the Democratic party within the

Hispanic community (in 1984, 29 percent of Hispanics were Democrats, while in 1988, the number increased to 35 percent, according to the Dade County Elections Department), the Hispanics in Dade County are still overwhelmingly Republican in registration. As a result, the local AFL-CIO and LCLAA have developed a practice of accommodation, which includes a practical policy of supporting candidates who advance labor's agenda regardless of party affiliation.

Similarly at the recommendation of the LCLAA, the national AFL-CIO cosponsored an award to a Republican state senator during the annual executive committee meeting in Bal Harbour in February 1989. This was the first time in AFL-CIO history that a Republican has been awarded such recognition in the state of Florida.

This representative belongs to what is commonly called the Cuban Caucus of the Republican party. From 1982 to 1987 the force of the caucus increased from three to eight representatives out of twenty-one in the Dade delegation (Malone 1985). Strongly influenced by the Cuban labor leadership, this group is viewed as a liberal force within the Republican party and often enters into coalition with Democrats to impede the domination of the state legislature by conservative Republicans or Democrats. In the recent jockeying for the speaker of the house seat, the Cuban Caucus is given credit for securing the position for a liberal Democrat from south Florida. The south Florida Cuban unionists, in turn, are given credit for delivering the Cuban Caucus. A top staffer for the new speaker admits the influence of Cuban unionists: "[He] owes these guys a lot. He knows who got him over the hump and he is going to listen to them now. He owes Cuban labor and he owes the Cubans."

Evidence of the Cuban labor influence on the Republican Cuban Caucus is seen in the labor voting record of these representatives. In 1989 members of the Cuban Caucus voted for labor-supported legislation 81 percent of the time, a voting record 5 percent better than that of Democrats statewide and 21 percent better than Republicans (Florida AFL-CIO 1987, 1988). Many Republican Latin representatives to the state legislature receive the support of labor because of the influence of the Cuban-controlled LCLAA. For example, during the 1989 political screening process, during which the AFL-CIO developed its endorsement list for candidates, the only Republicans from Dade County to receive the support of the labor federation were Cuban-Americans. All of the five Cubans endorsed won election. No other labor council in the state endorsed as many Republicans as did the South Florida AFL-CIO.

Cuban Republicans direct at least part of their campaign messages toward the Dade County labor community, something that other Republicans cannot do very efficiently. I have been present during various meetings at which the Cuban Caucus members have expressed their support of the agenda of the Cuban labor leaders. As a legislator said at one such meeting: "You know that you can always count on me to promote the agenda of Latin workers. . . . Party or no party."

In a recent election, this same legislator acknowledged the importance of labor in securing his successful bid for reelection (Dewar 1988). The Cuban-American labor movement is rapidly achieving recognition as a vital force in Dade County politics.

Equally significant effects of the Cuban voice are developing within the structures of the American labor movement. A primary source of problems is the fact that the rank-and-file Cuban is still perceived by the national labor organizations to be a right-wing zealot with very little concern with domestic issues. The fact that the Republican party is strong also increases the national AFL-CIO's distrust of the Cuban worker. The new leadership in south Florida has made it a priority to erase this distrust: "We have to prove to them that we are for real. That we can organize Cubans and that the future of labor in Florida depends on it."

From the perspective of the national labor organizations, resources targeting Hispanics in general are better used in the Mexican-American community, a community that not only votes Democratic and responds to labor issues but that also numbers 11 million persons. Thus, innovative programs to organize immigrants are developed in Los Angeles rather than in Miami.

The president of the LCLAA in Dade County, José "Pepe" Collado, is not content to see this status quo maintained. Along with the new president of the South Florida AFL-CIO, Marty Urra, he actively campaigns for the national AFL-CIO's commitment to organizing in south Florida and for Washington to increase services to the area.

There is evidence that this type of pressure is working. At the recent national meeting of the LCLAA, a floor battle over representation on the executive board was won by a delegate from Miami over a delegate from Los Angeles. This win gave the Cuban delegation two representatives on the forty-eight-person board. Similarly the national AFL-CIO has expressed interest in funding a full-time LCLAA position in Florida to assist in organizing Latin workers.

At the level of individual unions, the voice of the Cuban labor movement is also being heard. Already mentioned are the increasing numbers of Cubans in leadership positions in major labor organizations and the regional central labor council. A propensity to vote as a bloc for Cuban/ Latin officers has not only increased the number of leaders but has also caused concern among the most conservative union leaders. While most agree that unions must organize Latins, they also realize that this in all probability will mean an increase in Cuban and Latin representatives at the expense of Anglo positions. Yet, even representatives of the most conservative labor sector (the building trades) realize the need to change. A top official of a building trades union reports: "We simply have to get Latins in. We don't know how to do it because many of our contractors don't want them but if we don't do something, I might not be here to talk to you next year. Not because I'll be voted out, but because the union won't be here."

This realization does not diminish the fact that some unions are actively campaigning against the current Cuban leadership. Comments about how the Cubans are taking over are commonly heard at Anglo-dominated meetings. Strategy session discussions on how to defeat the current president began over a year before the election of September 1990.

Conclusion

Immigration has always posed a challenge for the American labor movement. While established immigrants often contribute to the development of unions and progressive movements, new immigrants clustering in low-skilled occupations and living in enclave communities promote a different result. The experience of the Cubans in Dade County supports this perspective. While the Cuban population becomes established, it is becoming more incorporated into the American labor movement. At the same time, the continued influx of immigrants, Haitians, Nicaraguans, and other Central American and Caribbean people poses a continued challenge to labor.

The issues discussed in exploring the experiences of Cuban-American workers in Dade County often form part of the general debate between assimilation and ethnic identification perspectives. The former and most commonly accepted position argues, in our specific case, that Cubans want to join the mainstream of society and that doing so is prevented by a series of obstacles that block the acceptance of the Cuban-American by the established groups in the host country.

The ethnic identification perspective presents the possibility that many immigrant groups might not be able to assimilate because of racial, geographic, or labor market segregation. They might also prefer to remain segregated as much as possible from the host country institutions, since segregation has its advantages. Analysts who developed the concept of the Cuban enclave argue that the segregation of the Cuban community in Dade County not only has resulted in a development of ethnic awareness and ethnic solidarity but has also facilitated the formation of an economic environment that reduces the economic disadvantages of segregation.

As is characteristic of preliminary studies, this one suggests a series of research trajectories. From the perspective of exploring the degree of ethnic group solidarity of the Cuban-American working class, this chapter supports the view that the occupational concentration of an immigrant cohort enhances the potential for maintaining group solidarity. Certainly in a case in which the concentration occurs in sectors formally organized into class-based organizations, the potential is expressed through explicit policies designed to increase the power of the ethnic group within the organization as well as within the community at large. This behavior in turn signals a significant commitment away from a "refugee" agenda, which is primarily concerned with return to the mother country, and toward an "immigrant" agenda, which is concerned with domestic policy issues (Portes 1984).

The study also suggests that while Cuban immigration might have had a negative impact on the power of organized labor in some sectors of the south Florida labor market, this was not a uniform effect. Indeed, some sectors of the organized work force, notably the public and service sectors, might have benefited from Cuban-American labor. The growth and stability of these sectors have contributed to the documented achievements of the Cuban-American population.

Thus, for Cuban-American unionists, the immigrant experience is one characterized by ethnic solidarity within the dynamics of organizational assimilation. Unions protect as well as segregate the Cuban-Americans from economic and social hardships. Not only are Cuban-American unionists in a structural position outside of the Cuban enclave, but they are also members of organizations that are explicitly class-based and nonethnic specific. Becoming American for these Cubans means, among other things, having to work within a national, class-based agenda of workers. Yet, to express an ethnic voice, the Cuban-American working class is developing an ethnic agenda that includes mobilization of Latin immigrants; organizing along ethnic lines; and developing a domestic, community focus for ethnic policy initiatives. Cuban-American labor activists have managed to convey the message that to a large extent the future of labor in Dade County depends on how well the concerns of the Cuban and Latin communities can be refocused away from foreign policy toward construction of a domestic, class-based policy agenda.

Cohesion and homogeneity have never been characteristics of the American working class. Immigrants and their children have consistently constituted a large portion of this working class and have always posed a challenge to the American labor movement. The AFL used the myth of the "unorganizable immigrant" to express its failure to meet this challenge with the Cubans during the last century and with the European immigrants of the early twentieth century (Dubofsky 1968; Greene 1968). In each case, labor had to contend with a "foreign" labor force clustering in unskilled occupations and living in tightly knit communities with relatively stable and long-lasting enclaves, which provided considerable interclass interaction and insular separation from American life.

Similarly, shortsighted policies of exclusion have been used for a number of reasons to exclude immigrants and minorities from craft unions. The conservatism of the craft unions, the belief that minorities lack the necessary skills to form stable unions, market pressures that encourage monopolistic union control, and nativist sentiments of the AFL-CIO are all reasons that rightly serve to criticize the failed policies of some labor organizations toward immigrants and minorities (Olson 1970; Gutman 1976).

Yet, it is also true that because of their structural position within the American class system, immigrants have used established American labor organizations as organizational vehicles for becoming American. In fact part of the traditional strengths of the American labor movement derives from the fact that while immigrants stamp the labor force in a region with "ethnic" characteristics, it is often the labor movement that "Americanizes" the immigrants. As the current immigrants "Latinize" the labor force, it is up to the labor movement to incorporate the immigrants into a class-based movement.

Organizing, in this context, becomes even more important since it is essential to take advantage of the cognitive shift that is taking place within the Cuban-American community at the present time. The willingness of a significant portion of the Cuban-American working class to join and actively participate in American labor organizations signifies a shift away from a "refugee" agenda (primarily concerned with return to the mother country) and toward an "immigrant" agenda (concerned with domestic policy issues). Becoming assimilated into the American labor movement is an expression of immigrant dreams of the future, not refugee desires for the past.

Throughout this century, as in today's Miami, unions with the strongest tradition and commitment to interethnic cooperation are the ones that benefit the most from this process of organizational assimilation. So it was that the garment unions of New York and Chicago established themselves as vehicles to the promised land for thousands of Poles and Slavs. So it is that Cuban women in the Miami garment industry put their children through college and watch as new workers from Haiti and Central America begin their long road to becoming American.

It is significant that Portes and Bach (1985) report that of the Cubans in their sample, 65.5 percent became union members when joining a union was an option. Yet, only 13 percent of the Cubans in their sample reported knowledge of the possibility of joining a union. While this is a strong indictment of the ambivalence of labor unions for organizing Cubans, it is a strong message that Cuban-Americans are organizable.

Just as second-generation Poles served to form the backbone of the United Automobile Workers during the 1930s and 1940s, so too is there hope that second-generation Cubans will see the labor movement as a vehicle for upward mobility while still being able to maintain an ethnic identity. At least that is the goal of the current Cuban-American labor leadership in Dade County. It is leadership's goal to replace the perception of a common political fate that emphasizes common class objectives with the understanding that it is within the American social system that the Cuban-American working-class voice will find its full expression.

Notes

1. Recent survey data identifying 10.6 percent of the population as union families point to an even higher proportion statewide (Institute for Public Policy Opinion Research 1988).

2. Some of the data presented were gathered as part of an ongoing project, funded by the Ford Foundation, on the changing relations between immigrants and established residents. Co-investigators on that project were Alex Stepick, Marvin Dunn, and Max Castro.

3. An important methodological point differentiates this study from most studies of

the Cuban community in Miami. For the past two years, I have served as the director of Florida International University's Center for Labor Research and Studies. This center is charged with the study and analysis of the changing situation of workers and their organizations in the state. I have been actively participating in the formulation and implementation of a Cuban/Latin union worker agenda. Thus, while part of my research properly can be termed "participant observation," I prefer to use the phrase "observation through participant activism" (Bookman 1988), since my participation does not take a backseat to observation, as is usually the case in participant observation methodology.

4. While the number of employees in Hispanic firms is growing, currently the top 140 Hispanic-owned firms in Dade County in 1988 only report 18,261 employees.

5. Although no figures exist for Cuban participation in exclusionary unions, the U.S. Equal Employment Opportunity Commission (EEOC) reports an increase of Hispanics in the apprenticeship programs of the trades from 1969 to 1975 of 2.4 percent to 3.9 percent (Gould 1977).

6. Hispanic surname identification from the original membership lists is the method I used to establish the ethnicity of union members. Previous research on the Mexican-American population (Gottlieb 1983) indicates that the use of surname identifiers is an accurate method of measuring ethnic representation within a population.

7. At one of the very first meetings I attended, I repeatedly used the term "Cuban" to refer to the membership. It was politely suggested that I use "Latin" or "Hispano," since the Cubans want to solidify the Latin workers under one banner.

8. Each organization has its roots in the prerevolutionary period of the Cuban labor movement and remains closely tied to the ideology of the old-guard Cuban leadership, even to the point of carrying over old divisions and alliances. For example, the historic split between Cofino and Salamea continues to express itself within the Plantas Eléctricas organization.

9. Even among the old guard, there is evidence that new coalitions need to be developed to solve the domestic issues facing Cuban-American workers. While the discourse of these groups on foreign policy issues aligns them with the Republican party, there is a recognition that domestic issues and Democratic party policies should begin to influence Cuban-American organizational behavior. As one of the oldest Cuban labor leaders, a registered Republican, reported: "Since Roosevelt, the only party that has shown interest in the well-being of the worker has been the Democratic Party. The Republican, forget it. You will see this (Republican) party collides now when the Cuban people remember that."

References

Alba, Victor. 1968. Politics and the Labor Movement in Latin America. Stanford, Calif.: Stanford University Press.

Amaro, N., and Alejandro Portes. 1972. "Una sociologia del exilio: situación de los grupos cubanos en los Estados Unidos." *Aportes* 23: 6–24.

Appel, John C. 1956. "The Unionization of Florida Cigarmakers and the Coming of the War with Spain." *Hispanic American History Review* 36, no. 1: 38–49.

Bookman, Ann. 1988. "Unionization in an Electronics Factory: The Interplay of Gender, Ethnicity, and Class." In *Women and the Politics of Empowerment*, edited by Ann Bookman and Sandra Morgen, 159–79. Philadelphia: Temple University Press.

Carlson, Leonard A., and Caroline Swartz. 1988. "The Earnings of Women and Ethnic Minorities, 1959–1979." *Industrial and Labor Relations Review* 41, no. 4 (July).

Dewar, Heather. 1988. "Union Support Vital in Casas' G.O.P. Win." *Miami News*, September 7: 9A.

Díaz, G. M., ed. 1980. *Evaluation and Identification of Policy Issues in the Cuban Community*. Miami: Cuban National Planning Council.

Dominguez, Jorge I. 1978. *Cuba: Order and Revolution*. Cambridge, Mass.: Harvard University Press.

Dubofsky, Melvyn. 1968. *When Workers Organize: New York City in the Progressive Era*. Amherst, Mass.: University of Massachusetts Press.

Ferree, M. M. 1979. "Employment without Liberation: Cuban Women in the United States." *Social Science Quarterly* 60: 35–50.

Florida AFL-CIO. 1987. *Final Legislative Reporter and Voting Record*. United Labor Lobby.

———. 1988. *Final Legislative Reporter and Voting Record*. United Labor Lobby.

Gallagher, Patrick Lee. 1980. *The Cuban Exile: A Socio-Political Analysis*. Salem, N.H.: Arno Press.

Gobel, Thomas. 1988. "Becoming American: Ethnic Workers and the Rise of the CIO." *Labor History* 29, no. 2.

Gottlieb, Karen. 1983. "Genetic Demography of Denver, Colorado: Spanish Surname as a Marker of Mexican Ancestry." *Human Biology* 55, no. 2, 227–34.

Gould, William B. 1977. *Black Workers in White Unions: Job Discrimination in the United States*. Ithaca, N.Y.: Cornell University Press.

Greene, Victor R. 1968. *The Slavic Community on Strike, Immigrant Labor in Pennsylvania Anthracite*. Notre Dame, Ind.: University of Notre Dame Press.

Gutman, Herbert G. 1976. "The Negro and the United Mine Workers of America." In *Work, Culture and Society in Industrializing America*, edited by H. G. Gutman. New York: Random House.

Hall, Richard. 1969. *Occupations and the Social Structure*, Englewood Cliffs, N.J.: Prentice-Hall.

Institute for Public Policy Opinion Research (IPPOR). 1988. *FIU/Florida Poll*. Miami: Florida International University Press.

Instituto de Historia del Movimiento Comunista y la Revolución Socialista de Cuba. 1975. *El Movimiento Obrero Cubano: Documentos y Artículos*.

Jordan, George. 1988. "Voters' Anti-Metro Mood Doomed Oesterle, Redford." *Miami News*, September 7: 1A.

Jorge, Antonio, and Raul Moncarz. 1982. "The Future of the Hispanic Market: The Cuban Entrepreneur and the Economic Development of the Miami Standard Metropolitan Statistical Area." Discussion Papers in Economics and Banking, International Banking Center and Department of Economics, Florida International University, Miami.

Jorge, Antonio, Raul Moncarz, and Robert A. Cruz. 1983. "An Examination of Hispanic Occupational Mobility, Wage Earnings, and Discrimination in Employment Opportunities in South Florida." Paper presented at the Equal Employment Opportunity Commission hearing, Miami, June 17, 1983.

Long, Durward. 1965. "'La Resistencia': Tampa's Immigrant Labor Union." *Labor History* 6, no. 3: 193–213.

Malone, Joseph. 1985. *Hispanics in the Electoral Process of Dade County, Florida: The Coming of Age.* Miami: Metro-Dade Elections Department.

Marshall, Ray, and Vernon V. Briggs, Jr. 1967a. *The Negro and Apprenticeship.* Baltimore: Johns Hopkins University Press.

———. 1967b. "Negro Participation in Apprenticeship Programs." *Journal of Human Resources* 2: 51–59.

Marshall, Ray, and Charles B. Knapp. 1978. *Employment Discrimination: The Impact of Legal and Administrative Remedies.* New York: Praeger.

Marshall, Ray, Charles B. Knapp, Malcolm H. Liggett, and Robert W. Glover. 1976. *The Impact of Legal and Administrative Remedies to Overcome Discrimination in Employment.* Austin: Center for the Study of Human Resources, University of Texas.

Moncarz, Raul. 1978. "The Golden Cage: Cubans in Miami." *International Migration* 16: 160–73.

Newman, M. J. 1978. "A Profile of Hispanics in the U.S. Work Force." *Monthly Labor Review* 101, no. 12: 3–14.

Olson, James S. 1970. "Race, Class, and Progress: Black Leadership and Industrial Unionism, 1936–1945." In *Black Labor in America*, edited by Milton Cantor. Westport, Conn.: Greenwood Press.

Pérez, Lisandro. 1986. "Immigrant Economic Adjustment and Family Organization: The Cuban Success Story Reexamined." *International Migration Review* 20, no. 1, 4–18.

Portes, Alejandro. 1969. "Dilemmas of a Golden Exile: Integration of Cuban Refugee Families in Milwaukee." *American Sociological Review* 34: 505–18.

———. 1981. "Modes of Structural Incorporation and Present Theories of Labor Immigration." In *Global Trends in Migration: Theory and Research of International Population Movements*, edited by M. M. Kritz, C. B. Keely, and S. M. Tomasi, 279–97. New York: Center for Migration Studies.

———. 1982. "Immigrants' Attainment: An Analysis of Occupation and Earnings among Cuban Exiles in the United States." In *Social Structure and Behavior: Essays in Honor of William Hamilton Sewell*, edited by R.M. Hauser et al., 91–111. New York: Academic Press.

———. 1984. "The Rise of Ethnicity: Determinants of Ethnic Perceptions among Cuban Exiles in Miami." *American Sociological Review* 49: 383–97.

Portes, Alejandro, and R. L. Bach. 1980. "Immigrants' Earnings: Cuban and Mexican Immigrants in the United States." *International Migration Review* 14, no. 3: 315–41.

———. 1985. *Latin Journey: Cuban and Mexican Immigrants in the United States.* Berkeley: University of California Press.

Portes, Alejandro, and Cynthia Truelove. 1987. "Making Sense of Diversity: Recent Research on Hispanic Minorities in the United States." *American Review of Sociology* 13: 359–85.

Portes, Alejandro, J. M. Clark, and R. L. Bach. 1977. "The New Wave: A Statistical Profile of Recent Cuban Exiles to the United States." *Cuban Studies/Estudios Cubanos* 7: 1–32.

Portes, Alejandro, Juan Clark, and Robert Manning. 1985. "After Mariel: A Survey of the Resettlement Experiences of 1980 Cuban Refugees in Miami." *Cuban Studies* 15, no. 2 (Summer): 37–59.

Poyo, Gerald. 1986. "The Impact of Cuban and Spanish Workers on Labor Organizing in Florida, 1870–1900." *Journal of American and Ethnic History* (Spring): 46–63.

Prieto, Y. 1987. "Women, Work and Change: The Case of Cuban Women in the U.S." Latin American Monograph Series, Northwestern Pennsylvania Institute for Latin American Studies.

Rogg, E. M. 1974. *The Assimilation of Cuban Exiles: The Role of Community and Class.* New York: Aberdeen Press.

Schutt, Russell K. 1987. "Craft Unions and Minorities: Determinants of Change in Admission Practices." *Social Problems* 34, no. 4: 388–402.

Strategy Research Corporation. 1989. *Southeast Florida Latin Market Study.* Washington: U.S. Department of Labor.

U.S. Department of Commerce. 1990. *1987 Economic Censuses: Survey of Minority-Owned Business Enterprises.* Washington: Bureau of the Census.

U.S. Department of Labor. 1985. *Employment and Earnings*, pp. 208–11. Washington: Bureau of Labor Statistics.

———. 1986. *Employment and Earnings*, p. 213. Washington: Bureau of Labor Statistics.

———. 1987. *Employment and Earnings*, pp. 219–22. Washington: Bureau of Labor Statistics.

———. 1988. *Employment and Earnings*, pp. 222–25. Washington: Bureau of Labor Statistics.

Wilson, K. L., and Alejandro Portes. 1980. "Immigrant Enclaves: An Analysis of the

Labor Market Experiences of Cubans in Miami." *American Journal of Sociology* 86: 295–319.

Wilson, K. L., and W. A. Martin. 1982. "Ethnic Enclaves: A Comparison of the Cuban and Black Economies in Miami." *American Journal of Sociology* 88: 135–60.

8

The Reform Tradition and Ethnic Politics: Metropolitan Miami Confronts the 1990s

John F. Stack, Jr., and Christopher L. Warren

As the 1990s begin, any analysis of ethnic politics in Miami must emphasize the way in which Miami's[1] complex local government system has helped to shape the contours of the conflicts that have made south Florida a national symbol for ethnic and racial unrest. This chapter argues that the events of the 1980s that brought Miami to the forefront of the national media, especially the rioting in black areas and the problems associated with massive Latin immigration, have taken on a particularly vivid cast because of the inability of Miami's local political system to deal with the problems and subtleties associated with ethnicity and race. Miami's future prospects, therefore, depend in large part on how the political system responds to the challenges posed by ethnicity.

The Reform Tradition and the Creation of Miami Metropolitan Government

With the creation in 1957 of Dade County's two-tiered metropolitan form of government, a complex governmental structure designed to implement the central assumptions of the reform tradition in urban politics was created (Hofstadter 1935; Riordon 1948; Hayes 1964; Higham 1963; Lowie 1976). The reform model categorically rejected big-city machine politics with its neighborhood and partisan orientations, its reliance on the control of ethnic voters, and the perceived legacy of political corruption.

In contrast the reform model, as epitomized in the creation of Metropolitan Dade County government in 1957, was based on the progressive reform tradition of urban politics. The reform model embraced the assumptions of the Good Government movement that arose in the first three decades of the twentieth century. Like other reform movements of this period, the Good Government movement was motivated by a moralistic, if simplistic, view of the causes of urban decay. This movement also had as its focal point a powerful missionary zeal (Strong 1891; Steffens 1904). Consequently the reform tradition sought to sanitize urban politics through structural and functional changes. Among other things, it emphasized a council-manager form of government; nonpartisan, at-large elections; the creation of a merit-based civil service; a reliance on a technocratic bureaucracy that would emphasize economy, efficiency, and responsiveness; and the attempt to create an "at-large community interest" in local government policy-making (Banfield and Wilson 1963). As a result, the service-delivery function of local government was to be given priority over the management of political and group conflict.

The goal of the reform model was to deemphasize such perceived parochial allegiances as neighborhood, political party, and ethnic and racial interests.[2] Proponents of local government reform in Dade County sought the establishment of a countywide political system. Major business interests, in particular, saw the creation of a reformed metropolitan government as the most effective way to influence public policy throughout the area, as opposed to attempting to work through all of Dade County's twenty-six municipalities.

The emphasis these reformers of the 1950s placed on at-large elections epitomizes the attempt to dilute the political interests of existing municipalities, neighborhoods, or ethnic groups within the context of the broader policy goals they sought to attain. Further, in a community plagued by the typical social ills of one of America's most notorious playgrounds— gambling, prostitution, organized crime, smuggling—the reform tradition aspired to remake the political systems of Miami Beach, the city of Miami, and the city of Hialeah by investing Dade County with unusually broad and powerful political control of the twenty-six cities within its jurisdiction. Thus, a two-tiered system of government evolved, with overlapping county and municipal jurisdictions. This system was to provide a means of control in the hope that the excesses of Miami's rough-and-ready past

could be tamed and a more civilized and civic-minded political consciousness could be created.

Thus, the creation of Metropolitan Dade County had as its central
priority the coordination of existing city governments along with that of the
huge unincorporated sections of the county (Mohl 1984). The sharing of
power between Dade County and the twenty-six cities within its boundaries was worked out in a complex political and legal arrangement. Dade
County's role in this arrangement was predominant, and it became Florida's first home-rule county. Dade County was also the first metropolitan
form of government in the United States and was widely viewed as a model
for the successful application of the reform tradition because of the
innovative way in which power was shared.

In the metropolitan government, countywide policy-making authority is
vested in the Metropolitan "Metro" Commission (otherwise known as the
Dade County Commission) in such important areas as mass transit, public
health, parks, and recreation. In addition the Metro Commission establishes minimum standards of performance for those services still provided
by the twenty-six cities within the commission's jurisdictional boundaries.
These cities, however, retain control over their police departments,
establish city tax rates, and may exceed county standards in zoning and
service delivery among other narrower powers (Mohl 1983). The Metro
Commission possesses exclusive authority over the sprawling areas of
unincorporated Dade County, which is larger and has a population greater
than all of the municipalities combined.

In an attempt to depoliticize policy-making, the reform tradition as
applied to Dade County provided for the establishment of a council-
manager form of government. The eight commissioners and the mayor,
who as a council member is in theory first among equals, are elected in
countywide, at-large, nonpartisan elections. The commissioner's terms of
office run for four years, but elections are staggered so that one-half of the
seats are filled every two years. The county manager is hired and fired by
the commission and holds administrative authority to run Dade County's
large and complex bureaucracy.

Many of Dade's cities also opted for the reform model of government.
The largest, the city of Miami, has a council-manager form of government
with a five-member council that includes the mayor. The city of Miami
commissioners are also chosen in nonpartisan, at-large elections, while
the city manager possesses authorities similar to those of the county
manager.

At present the highly variable political fortunes of each of Dade

County's three major ethnic groups are both reflected in and reinforced by the structure of metropolitan government. Historically Anglos exercised pervasive dominance at both the county and municipal levels. Today the county government remains the most important base of non-Hispanic, white power complemented by continuing control over many of the most important downtown economic and civic institutions. Several city commissions are also still dominated by non-Hispanic whites.

Black political power remains fragmented and diluted at the county level. As analyzed in subsequent sections of this chapter, the prospects for even a moderate increase in the political power of black Dade Countians depends on major structural alterations of the county government. Despite decade-long discussions about the feasibility and increasingly the desirability of district elections and even the incorporation of a predominantly black city in unincorporated sections of northwest Dade County, these structural reforms have been opposed by the county commission (Mohl 1989).

Hispanic (mainly Cuban) voting strength and representation at both the municipal and county levels have gradually evolved such that the Latin voting bloc promises to be the new dominant force in south Florida politics in the near future. The Hispanic political presence has steadily expanded outward from those cities in which Cubans have come to constitute a voting majority: Hialeah, Sweetwater, West Miami, and increasingly the city of Miami itself. This trend has also continued in political contests for legislative seats in the Florida house and senate. And although only one Hispanic, Alex Penelas, holds a seat on the county commission (out of nine available seats), with each subsequent election Latin political clout increases. It is only a matter of time before Hispanics become the dominant bloc even in at-large county elections.

As discussed in the next section, two consequences of Dade County's political system are most relevant. First, the primary beneficiaries of the area's reformed metropolitan government have been the area's major Anglo-dominated business and economic interests. Second, effective political mobilization at the countywide level has been hindered for blacks and Hispanics.

The Socioeconomic Context of Dade County Governance

In dramatically expanding the power of the county's political system and in emphasizing the importance of professionalism, efficiency, and

bureaucratic rationality as the central sine qua non for rational administrative decision making, Dade County explicitly made a partnership with
major business and civic groups capable of speaking the new technocratic
lingua franca of county governance. These groups included the larger law
firms, developers, mid- to large-size companies engaged in tourist-related
industries, and the county's growing manufacturing sectors committed to a
new and better Miami. Despite the good government and civic pride
rhetoric of the reformers, the establishment of Dade County's metropolitan
form of government benefited Dade County's business elite at the expense
of neighborhood, sectional, and ethnic/minority interests (Sofen 1966b).
As Professor Edward Sofen (1966) observed in 1961: "The business
community had no real competitors in the political arena. Moreover, since
the cause of 'good government' groups coincided with the desires of the
more powerful Miami business organizations, the latter were quite content
to allow the newspapers, professional groups, the university professors,
and the League of Women Voters to assume positions of catalytic leadership in civic affairs."

Viewed from the perspective of 1957 and even the early 1960s, it is not
surprising that the architects of Dade County's political system were
insensitive to the needs of the black and Hispanic communities. The
system was created in the years just prior to the civil rights movement and
massive Cuban immigration. Miami's black population was relatively
small (approximately 13 percent of the total) and severely disenfranchised. The Hispanic population was virtually nonexistent. Given the
rather homogeneous population, the primary local political conflicts at the
time of Metro's creation were between "turf-conscious" municipal politicians and those who supported the creation of Metro. Ethnic or other forms
of group conflict were simply not part of the political calculus.

The tensions characterizing the relations among Dade County's blacks,
Hispanics, and Anglos therefore need to be evaluated within the context of
the reformist nature of metropolitan government. Indeed, to explain ethnic
and racial conflict without reference to the political system that fosters
zero-sum expectations and in fact exacerbates conflicts between blacks
and Hispanics overlooks and distorts a critically important aspect of
contemporary Miami.

Miami's International Context

There are of course other factors beyond the workings of Miami's local
government that have influenced interethnic and racial conflicts in Miami.

Of great significance has been the area's progressive internationalization (Levine 1985; Didion 1987; Rieff 1987). However, an analysis of such issues falls outside the scope of this chapter. We will limit our discussion of the international dimensions of Miami politics, emphasizing the critical ways that Miami's destiny is tied to international issues and events that make local governance difficult and exacerbate the area's ethnic and racial tensions.

The forces of international politics and economics have had an enduring impact on Miami for at least the past thirty years. These events include the Cuban revolution of 1959 and the massive influx of Cuban refugees throughout the 1960s, 1970s, and 1980s. The successful establishment of the Cuban community served as a magnet, attracting Latin Americans who could pursue business endeavors in a hospitable environment in which Spanish language and culture were encouraged. Miami's progressive internationalization was accompanied by high levels of economic growth in the 1970s. In the period between 1960 and 1981, Miami's job market grew by 74 percent over the national average. Between 1956 and 1977 the number of jobs in wholesale and retail industries increased by 103 percent, while the number of new businesses increased by 90 percent (Wilkins 1980; Roussakis 1981).

Further, Miami's growing economic prosperity and its cosmopolitan culture drew both legal and illegal immigrants (Maingot 1986; Warren and Stack 1986). Miami found itself increasingly drawn into a web of political and economic interactions that made events in the Caribbean, Central America, and South America both immediate and relevant to fundamental questions of local politics and economics. Miami's political and economic dependence on Latin America in the banking, real estate development, manufacturing, tourism, and drug trafficking industries integrated south Florida in a regional economic system that had both positive and negative effects on the Miami economy.

The 1970s and 1980s demonstrated just how dependent and vulnerable Miami was to the political and economic currents flowing through the Caribbean from Central and South America. Miami found itself directly connected to powerful international issues and events in ways that most American cities have not experienced.[3]

Geopolitically, economically, and culturally Miami is more closely connected with the Caribbean and Central America than with Florida's capital, Tallahassee. If one moves outward from Miami in concentric circles, its geographical proximity to Latin America becomes even more apparent. For the past thirty years, international issues and events have shaped the political agenda and much of the demographic change that Miamians have confronted but could not control.

The resulting ethnic and racial tensions of the 1980s illustrate in large measure the degree of frustration that blacks, Cubans, and non-Hispanic whites have confronted as local government seemed powerless to address problems created by international issues and events—especially the mutually reinforcing perceptions that Anglos, blacks, and Hispanics were each losing out to one another. The 1982 report of the United States Commission on Civil Rights analyzing the 1980 McDuffie riots specifically cited the economic exclusion of blacks as a cause of the rioting in the context of Miami's internationalization and impressive economic growth. "Black exclusion from the economic renaissance translates into low earnings, high unemployment rates, reduced job opportunities, and the absence of a capital formation base" (U.S. Commission on Civil Rights 1982). The ethnic and racial conflicts of the 1980s thus illustrate a zero-sum outlook that characterizes intergroup relations in Miami. The initial conceptualization, structure, and functioning of the local political system are major parts of the problem.

Since Dade County's political system was designed to reduce its responsiveness to political pressure from ethnic groups and other localized influences, as noted above, ethnic grievances have at times been expressed in nontraditional ways. Throughout the 1980s, Dade County government and the political processes of several of its larger cities have sidestepped the difficult issues posed by proposals calling for structural change. These proposals have emphasized a shift to district elections and the incorporation of new cities in order to give ethnic and neighborhood interests greater influence. The result has been increased frustration and ultimately higher levels of polarization among blacks, Cubans, and non-Hispanic whites.

As noted in the subsequent analysis, Dade County's black neighborhoods have played an increasingly marginal role in the county's complex governmental system. The economic and political benefits of the civil rights movement, evident in many cities throughout the United States, had not been realized in south Florida. To many it seemed the massive federal assistance throughout the 1960s and 1970s was primarily directed at the social and economic needs of Dade County's newly established immigrant community rather than at the needs of blacks. Black perceptions emphasized the lack of responsiveness and racism inherent in Miami's political, economic, and judicial systems. The repeated patterns of violent upheaval and rioting that have occurred in black neighborhoods on four separate occasions—1980, 1982, 1984, and 1989—attest to the feelings of anger, frustration, and powerlessness of many segments of the black community. This is what we refer to as the "Miami syndrome."

The Politics of Black Protest: The Miami Syndrome

For want of a better descriptive phrase, we use the phrase "Miami syndrome" to denote the futility of black attempts to alter or amend a political system that is fundamentally unresponsive to black needs. Use of the term is meant to convey high levels of black frustration in a stagnant political system combined with a crisis of rising expectations that is often expressed in rioting and other acts of nontraditional political protest. The Miami syndrome also refers to the continuing weakening of black political strength within a dynamic political environment. Blacks find themselves pitted against Hispanics in what amounts to a zero-sum relationship with the surging political, economic, and cultural power of Hispanics as the central force transforming Dade County politics. The result of increased Hispanic political power is the further erosion of black political strength—limiting the emergence of strong black political leaders with grass roots bases of political support. Despite repeated official public pronouncements by Anglo and Hispanic elites (especially following each of the riots of the 1980s) that the community would mobilize to meet black needs and demands, no meaningful reforms of the political and economic system have occurred. As black-Hispanic and black-Anglo tensions continue to rise, the gulf separating communities was larger as the 1980s ended than when the decade began. Violence and other nontraditional manifestations of protest thus are symptomatic of the Miami syndrome.

Figure 8.1 illustrates the findings of a February 1989 *Miami Herald* poll of racial and ethnic attitudes in south Florida. Fully 34 percent of the black respondents reported that they or someone they knew have faced discrimination in seeking a job or a promotion, in contrast to 14 percent of Anglos and 13 percent of Hispanics. In response to a question that asked respondents to indicate if another group would discriminate against them, 32 percent of black respondents blamed Hispanics, and 40 percent of black respondents blamed Anglos.

These perceptions underscore the marginal roles that blacks play in Dade County's economic and political systems. These perceptions would also seem to limit the ability of black leaders to extract concessions from

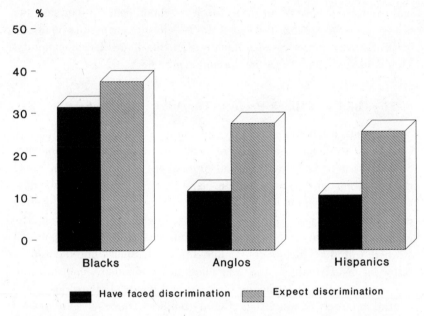

Fig. 8.1. South Florida racial and ethnic attitudes, 1988–89. *Source: Miami Herald*, February 27, 1989.

the dominant Anglo and Hispanic elites. Thus, it is not surprising that Miami has emerged in the 1980s as a national symbol of the failure to involve blacks in any meaningful way in issues of local governance. Levels of dissatisfaction and frustration find expression in the intensity of black rioting, which constitutes one of the few available forms of political protest—however nontraditional, menacing, or counterproductive.

The Political Disenfranchisement of Dade's Black Community

The disenfranchisement of black voters at the founding of Metro was neither unintended nor unprecedented in Miami. Many of Dade's geo- graphically scattered black neighborhoods had been excluded in the formation of the various municipalities (Porter and Dunn 1984; Mohl 1987, 1989). At the time of Metro's founding in 1957, none of the municipalities had black majorities. Thus, the tendency of reformed government to overlook the representational needs of ethnic minorities converged with an already racist and exclusionary political environment to prevent effective participation by blacks.

Further the technocratic and bureaucratic (as opposed to more political) forms of decision making in Dade County masked basic political choices relating to the allocation and distribution of costs and benefits. The new countywide political agenda supported by Metro's advocates was so overwhelming that the needs of Dade County's black citizenry and black neighborhoods are often lost in the political process.

Today Dade County elections still have an aura of unreality about them. Many citizens do not understand the substantial political power of the commission. The seeming remoteness of the Dade County Commission is only further exacerbated by the nonpartisan, at-large elections. It is difficult to determine who the players are in any meaningful sense and how they are different from other candidates. Most importantly, the economic costs of running countywide elections are so great and the necessary electoral base so large that candidates must win support from the county's private sector and civic elites in order to finance viable campaigns.

By and large black candidates have not been attractive candidates for Miami's business and good-government elites precisely because their election campaigns have been poorly financed and their voter support comes from neighborhoods that are politically less important in a countywide contest. Moreover the practical necessity of raising campaign funds and thus being acceptable to private-sector interests makes it especially difficult for black candidates who might otherwise appeal to grass roots needs in black neighborhoods. In Dade County many of the most important business interests revolve around issues of development. Thus, when the Miami Dolphins settled on the site for the new Joe Robbie Stadium adjacent to a middle-class black neighborhood in northern Dade County, the county's only black commissioner, Barbary Carey, felt compelled to vote in favor of the stadium's development despite the deleterious impact that such development would have on a solid, middle-class, black neighborhood.

The way in which Dade County's black population has settled into distinctive neighborhoods has also diluted black voting strength (Mohl 1989). Despite the fact that blacks currently comprise one-quarter of the population of the city of Miami and now constitute significant majorities in two small cities, Opa-Locka and Florida City, more than 60 percent of the black population live in unincorporated Dade County. Further, blacks have not been able to build viable political bases, even in the ethnically divisive environment of the city of Miami, where ethnic bloc voting is encouraged.

Black voters were decisive in the 1981 election when then-Mayor Maurice Ferre (who is Puerto Rican) defeated a Cuban, Manolo Reyboso (Bayor 1989). But in Miami's highly charged ethnic environment, black voters could never take political loyalty from public officials for granted, particularly in the case of Mayor Ferre. In 1984 Ferre joined forces with two Cuban members of the city commission and voted to fire the popular black city manager, Howard Gary (Mohl 1989). Resulting frustrations in the black community ran so high that there were fears that a riot might occur (Mohl 1989). The black community launched a drive to recall Mayor Ferre; this drive was killed when the county's supervisor of elections threw it out because of the presence of several thousand invalid signatures on the recall petition (Mohl 1989). The ensuing struggle to choose a new city manager was resolved when the only black city commissioner, Miller Dawkins, cast the decisive vote to hire a Cuban city manager, thus breaking the impasse on the thirty-sixth ballot in March 1985 (Mohl 1989). As the Hispanic bloc became more decisive in city of Miami elections, Ferre was defeated in his next bid for reelection by Xavier Suarez, a Cuban-American candidate. Commissioner Dawkins received campaign support from the political action committee of the Cuban American National Foundation in subsequent elections.

The frustrations of black residents of the city of Miami were also evident most recently when blacks failed to turn out in large numbers in the special congressional election to fill the unexpired term of the late member of Congress Claude Pepper (in contrast to Anglo and Hispanic voters). The Democratic challenger, Gerald Richman, lost to Cuban-American Republican Ileana Ros-Lehtinen. The low black turnout and high rates of Latin participation were the keys to Ros-Lehtinen's victory. The election saw 58 percent of Latin voters participating, as compared to 46 percent of Anglos and only 33 percent of blacks. In some Little Havana precincts, Cuban voter turnout approached the 70 percent level, something normally only encountered in a presidential election (Fiedler 1989; Soto 1989).

The fact that the majority of the black population resides in highly segregated yet spatially isolated neighborhoods throughout sprawling Dade County, as is discussed in chapter 3, makes it difficult for any effective grass roots political mobilization to occur (Tasker 1982). Black neighborhoods range from the high-density housing projects of Liberty

City, which is adjacent to the city of Miami, to smaller neighborhoods and ghettos throughout Dade County, ultimately reaching into the agricultural sections of southern Dade County.

Despite the preponderance of black voters in Florida City and Opa-Locka, these cities have played marginal roles in local affairs because they are among the poorest of all suburban incorporated areas in the United States (Johnson 1987). Thus, as a voting bloc Dade County's black population remains too small and dispersed to exert a major impact on countywide politics, even if high levels of voter turnout could be assured.

The facts that blacks constitute nearly 20 percent of the total population of Dade County and 25 percent of the total population of the city of Miami, as figures 1.2 and 1.3 illustrate, and that both Dade County commissioners and city of Miami commissioners are elected at-large also contribute to a profound sense of black political powerlessness. A recent suit against Metro (*Meek et al. v. Dade County*) in the United States District Court for the Southern District of Florida to overturn the county's at-large elections, which was overwhelmingly supported by black political organizations, will soon be determined.

In the wake of the riots of the 1980s, local political and economic notables repeatedly established study commissions that issued proposals for neighborhood development, improved service delivery, and better means of dealing with "violence-prone police officers" in black neighborhoods. Still, considerable skepticism persists given the past pattern in Miami of such commissions being appointed only to have their recommendations ignored.

The failure of the Metro Miami Action Plan (MMAP), which was funded by key public and private support following rioting in 1980 and 1982, after five years of operation, is a case in point. Its recommendations for change have been ignored, corporate funding has disappeared, and county and city governments have gradually reduced their levels of support. As one former board member, Eduardo Padron, pointed out: "MMAP has been abandoned by almost everyone. There is not a sense of urgency about black problems. . . . A lot of prominent corporate leaders began to disappear after the second year. In Miami, you only get the corporate world to react in times of crisis. There's not a conscience that endures" (Dugger 1987).

Ultimately the political status of Miami's black community must also be viewed against the area's rapidly changing demography. In the city of Miami, for instance, the shift to Hispanic, mostly Cuban, predominance has been likewise striking. As figure 1.3 documents, in the period between 1970 and 1990 the Hispanic population increased from 45.3 percent to 63 percent, whereas the black population underwent a very slow increase from 21.9 percent to 25 percent. The Anglo population underwent the most dramatic transformation, declining from 32.6 percent in 1970 to 12 percent in 1988. Changes countywide, as illustrated in figure 1.2, have only been slightly less dramatic.

The problems that limit the political empowerment of black neighborhoods in Metropolitan Dade County are similar to those in the city of Miami. Black neighborhoods have been fragmented by downtown development and freeway construction and/or gentrification. The once cohesive and comparatively vibrant Overtown neighborhood disintegrated as greater Miami's freeway system dissected the neighborhood and as an expanding downtown began to encroach. Despite current attempts to lure middle-income residents back to Overtown, the proliferation of crack houses, slums, and the presence of hundreds of homeless make Overtown a less desirable place to live. The equally historic black neighborhood south of Overtown in Coconut Grove has undergone a similar fate. Expensive housing and inflation of real estate, fueled by the gentrification of the area, has pushed blacks out of Coconut Grove, adding to the density of already crowded areas such as Liberty City. The isolation and fragmentation of black neighborhoods has increased.

Political Indifference and the Politics of Protest in Miami's Black Communities

When racial violence again erupted in January 1989 following the shooting deaths of two black men, Clement Lloyd and Allan Blanchard, by a Hispanic (Colombian) city of Miami police officer, William Lozano, Miami's image-sensitive civic leadership immediately launched an extensive effort at damage control. From the perspective of Miami's elite, the fourth episode of racial violence in the long decade of the 1980s was doubly unfortunate. In the mid-1980s, there had been some success in rehabilitating Miami's image as the drug, crime, and riot capital of the United States. Miami's problems—refugees, illegal immigrants, racial conflicts, and drug wars—were repackaged. Much was made of innovations in architecture, the emergence of the downtown skyline, the redevelopment of south Miami Beach's art deco hotel district, and the cosmopolitan flavor that Spanish language and culture emphasized, not to mention the stylized portrait presented on "Miami Vice." Even the presence of sizable exile communities from Central America was romanticized in journalistic accounts, with parallels being drawn between Casablanca and the new Miami.

Miami's civic elite found the racial violence of January 1989 especially embarrassing because it stood in direct contrast to the area's emergent new image. The violence also occurred when the national media were focused on Miami during the week immediately preceding Super Bowl XXIII, which was being held in the newly opened Joe Robbie Stadium. Miami's boosters had expected that the Super Bowl hoopla would showcase a revitalized and attractive metropolitan area.

These hopes were quickly dashed by three days of rioting that marred Miami's national image. Despite intensive efforts at damage control by civic leaders and the major local media, who have consistently attempted to minimize the recurrent outbreaks of violence by referring to them as "disturbances,"[4] the decade-long impact of Miami's racial violence is striking. The cumulative effects of four riots resulting in 1,800 people arrested, 25 killed, nearly 500 injured, and probably more than over $200 million in property damage suggest something more serious and intractable than a series of sporadic outbreaks of mild disorder.

A common thread in each of the riots has been either the killing of one or more blacks by city of Miami or Dade County police or the acquittal of those same police officers. The fact that the precipitating events for the killings have been either traffic violations or routine arrests has added greatly to the sense of outrage among many in the black community. The often dismal relations between police and the black community, while not unique to metropolitan Miami, are generally acknowledged to be compounded by the variable effects of racism, poverty, drugs, and the general social and economic decline of the largest predominantly black neighborhoods: Overtown and Liberty City. Just as important, Dade County's massive Hispanic immigration has at once created severe competition for entry-level jobs; an enclave economy largely closed to blacks; and continuing resentment over federal, state, and local aid to political refugees that is not available to native blacks. That the 1980 riots coincided with the Mariel boatlift from Cuba, and that the most recent violence took place at a time when thousands of Nicaraguans were coming to Miami, reinforced the perception that there has been a connection between rioting and Hispanic immigration.

At the same time, many who live in Overtown and Liberty City are increasingly frustrated by the destruction of businesses and property in their own neighborhoods. Many neighborhood residents condemned what was seen as unjustified police violence, while at the same time they called for a stronger police or National Guard response to the rioting—especially when looting, arson, and attacks on whites driving through the affected neighborhoods were involved.

The last weeks of 1989 were dominated by the manslaughter trial of city of Miami police officer William Lozano, whose actions precipitated the January riot. As the trial proceeded to its conclusion, Miami mobilized for expected violence. Parallels were continuously drawn with the other incidents that had resulted in riots in the 1980s. When the jury's verdict finding the officer guilty of manslaughter was announced, it was as if some segments of the community (especially blacks and non-Hispanic whites) breathed a collective sigh of relief. For some Hispanics, however, the conviction raised the troubling question of whether a Hispanic police officer on trial for the killing of black citizens could ever be given a fair trial when the potential of civil disturbances overshadowed the issues of the trial. Miami escaped a fifth episode of urban violence as the decade closed.

The widespread belief throughout south Florida was that violence would be the likely consequence of an acquittal of the officer involved in the case. This belief underscores the generalized perception that conditions have not materially changed for blacks who took to the streets earlier in the decade. Such a perception also illustrates the tendency of non-blacks to see the primary cause for racial violence as one best addressed by changes within the black community itself. This is not a surprising perspective. Throughout the 1980s, it has been much easier for Miami's political elite and its white and Hispanic citizenry to view the episodes of violence in 1980, 1982, 1984, and 1989 as simply the work of the criminal element in the black community. It would be more difficult to address more fundamental questions regarding the reform of the political structure and changes in the distribution of resources. Thus, proposals for the structural change of local government in Metropolitan Dade County or the city of Miami, whether through the incorporation of new predominantly black municipalities or a shift to district elections, could be dismissed much more easily when the primary causes of the rioting were argued to be the actions of thugs and criminals.

Yet, as the work of community psychologist Marvin Dunn and the report of the United States Commission on Civil Rights following the 1980 rioting state, the causes of urban violence in Miami are rooted in the political, judicial, socioeconomic, and cultural institutions that have shut blacks out (Porter and Dunn 1984). The lack of responsiveness of Miami's political elite and the racist patina that easily colors discussions about the reform of the structure and function of government in south Florida obscures the fundamental issues at stake among blacks, non-Hispanic whites, and Anglos.

The Hispanic Ascendance

Until the mid-1980s, Hispanic candidates also had fared poorly in local elections—especially at the county level. Several factors account for their lack of success. The exile status of first-generation Cuban-Americans discouraged involvement in local politics because it required exiles to become registered voters. They thus had to become American citizens and symbolically affirm that a return to the homeland was unlikely at best. By definition exile status connotes a temporary stay. At the least, exile status is a mindset that sees the fall of Castro in Cuba as possible.

The transformation of Dade County and increasing tensions between Anglos and Cubans throughout the 1970s ushered in a decade of conflict, as is discussed in chapter 6. The Mariel boatlift and the subsequent resettlement of approximately 100,000 refugees in Dade County led to a sharp Anglo backlash. Perceptions of zero-sum relations led to an upsurge in anti-Cuban sentiments. These sentiments were especially evident in the increased concern placed by both groups on what were essentially symbolic political issues. Bilingualism and local anticommunism became particularly potent issues. These issues had significant symbolic importance for Anglos, who increasingly felt under siege in "their own" city, and for Latins, who were beginning to assert themselves politically—as well as economically and socially. Ironically perceptions of rising anti-Cuban sentiments helped to mobilize the Cuban community politically to an unprecedented degree.

Symbolic politics in Dade County throughout much of the 1980s became collective expressions of ethnic concerns by both Anglos and Hispanics. This citizen preoccupation with largely symbolic issues initially required very little of substance from Dade County's local governments and politicians. Yet, the promotion of anti-Cuban policy stances, especially in a 1980 antibilingualism referendum, became a pivotal point in the political transformation of the Cuban community. The community moved away from the apolitical policy stances of exiles, at least on local issues, to the active shaping of a policy agenda that suggested the emergence of ethnic politics.

Moreover in the context of Dade County's governmental system, political symbols have at times been manipulated to avoid addressing some of the more difficult substantive policy concerns that are especially related to the problems of poverty and ethnic conflict. In the process, the gulf separating Cubans from Anglos and blacks has often been reinforced. Non-Cuban resentments continue to build over the perception of local government preoccupation with several symbolic issues of singular concern to Cubans.

Especially illustrative of this phenomenon is the 1980 antibilingualism referendum, in which Dade County voters were asked to affirm the primacy of the English language and American culture in Dade County. This heated campaign was fought over a county ordinance, which was passed on April 15, 1973, and which established Metro-Dade County as "officially bilingual." The 1973 ordinance was a pragmatic attempt to recognize the cultural and economic role that the county's growing Latin population played in Dade County's internationalized economy (Jacobs 1973). Further, the ordinance reflected a concrete reality in a community in which it was estimated that in 1980 over 40 percent of the area's Hispanic population had "no" or "poor" English language skills (Tasker 1980). For years the ordinance remained on the books, receiving little attention and having even less substantive impact on policy. Of greater political significance was the fact that the ordinance was seen by many Cubans as a symbolic gesture made by a nine-member county commission that had never had any Hispanic representation, recognizing the breadth and depth of the Hispanic presence and the gradual empowerment of the Cuban citizenry.

The citizen-generated antibilingualism initiative in 1980 stated that "the expenditure of county funds for the purpose of utilizing any language other than English, or promoting any culture other than that of the United States" would be prohibited (Tasker 1980). Support for the measure was a clear expression of the frustrations of the non-Hispanic community with the increasing Latinization of the area. A *Miami Herald* poll indicated that nearly half of those voting for the initiative did so in order to express their "protest" and "frustration" with Dade's Latins and not because they thought the ordinance itself was a good idea (Tasker 1980). Ultimately ethnicity seemed to be the primary determinant in how most people voted.

Among non-Hispanic whites who voted, 71 percent supported the anti-bilingualism initiative; 85 percent of the Latin voters opposed it (Tasker 1980).

Although the 1980 antibilingualism initiative had little substantive impact on actual policy or services, it clearly played an important role in enhancing Latin (especially Cuban) political mobilization on local political issues. That the 1980 vote coincided with the Mariel boatlift and the Liberty City riots, events which further reinforced both ethnic group identity and ethnic grievances, only highlighted the extent to which emergent Cuban ethnic identity had distinct political implications for the Miami community (Governor's Dade County Citizens' Committee on the Liberty City Riots 1980).

The referendum also had particular importance in terms of the political development of the Cuban community. Cuban organizations such as the Spanish American League Against Discrimination (SALAD) and the Cuban American National Foundation were created to fight back. From that point on, even token straw votes that invoked issues with powerful symbolic significance were at times fought over and campaigned for as vigorously as if an important mayoralty were at stake. The Cuban community began to mobilize on a mass level. Elected officials in Dade County and those cities with large Cuban populations suddenly became anxious to placate an increasingly vocal Cuban citizenry. Non-Cuban elected officials found themselves placing controversial issues on the public ballot, ostensibly as important barometers of public opinion, but also as a way to appeal to the Cuban vote in their own electoral contests.

In the city of Miami where the strength of the Cuban vote was now obvious, the City Commission began to place on the ballot purely symbolic issues concerning whether representatives of "Communist-Marxist" governments should be allowed to participate in a number of international conferences to be held in the city.[5] Controversy even surrounded the inclusion of representatives of Poland and Yugoslavia in Miami's Miss Universe pageant. During the sixteen-month period preceding May 1983, the Miami City Commission passed twenty-eight formal resolutions, ordinances, and motions dealing with U.S. foreign policy, most of which were strictly symbolic expressions of Latin anticommunism (Tomb 1983). Dade's smaller cities with Hispanic majorities (such as Hialeah, Sweetwater, and West Miami) also engaged in extensive symbolic politics (Stack and Warren 1990).

National issues and political figures have also played a role in local

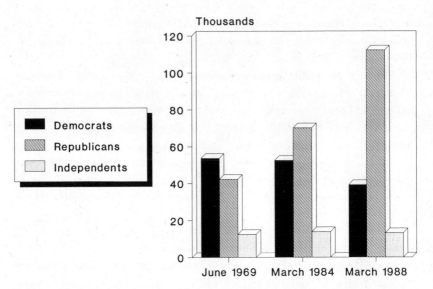

Fig. 8.2. Hispanic voters by party registration, Dade County, 1969–88 (Hispanic category contains only those born outside of the United States or Puerto Rico). *Source*: Metro-Dade Elections Department.

Hispanic mobilization. For instance the appeal of the Reagan administration's conservative foreign policies, at least until 1987, struck a resonant chord in Cuban Miami. Increased rates of naturalization led to numerous ceremonies, such as the one held in the Orange Bowl on July 4, 1986, when 14,200 immigrants became citizens (Mohl 1989). The Republican party has been the chief beneficiary of Miami's new Cuban voters (see fig. 8.2).

The political power of Cuban voters is now evident at all levels of local politics, especially in the cities with Cuban majorities. It is increasingly a force to be reckoned with in county politics. The rapid rise of Hispanic elected officials is noteworthy. At the dawn of the 1980s, only four Hispanics held elective office in the Miami area. In 1990 over forty Hispanics held elective office, including seven mayoralties as well as majorities on the city commissions of the city of Miami, Hialeah, West Miami, and Sweetwater. Cuban-Americans also occupy ten of the twenty-eight positions on the Dade delegation of the Florida legislature. There is only one Hispanic member on both the Dade County Commission and the Dade County School Board, but as the number of Hispanic voters increases, more Hispanics will undoubtedly be elected.

Indeed, the most recent races for countywide office have underscored the importance of the Hispanic vote. Campaigns have been increasingly oriented to Hispanic voters in terms of a tilt to the right in campaign rhetoric, especially when it appears in the Spanish mass media. Anti-Communist rhetoric is now part and parcel of the campaign oratory in Hispanic-Hispanic, Hispanic-Anglo, and even Anglo-Anglo races. The fact that Cuban-American turnout is usually higher than that of blacks or non-Hispanic whites only serves to enhance Latin clout (Warren, Corbett, and Stack 1990).

The recent victory of member of Congress Ileana Ros-Lehtinen illustrates just how starkly ethnic battlelines can be drawn and how essential high rates of Cuban-American voter turnout can be for the success of a Hispanic candidate. Ros-Lehtinen received 94 percent of all Latin votes. The district comprises 46 percent Hispanic voters, of whom most are Cuban-Americans. The district also comprises 36 percent Anglo voters and 19 percent black voters. Latins outvoted Anglos and blacks by three-to-two and two-to-one, respectively, providing Ros-Lehtinen with 53 percent of the total votes cast. Latin voter turnout was the key to Ros-Lehtinen's victory. As stated earlier, in some Little Havana precincts Cuban voter turnout approached the 70 percent level.

The district split along ethnic lines, with 88 percent of all Anglo voters (including the majority of Anglo Republicans) and 96 percent of black voters supporting the Democratic challenger (Fiedler 1989). The bruising campaign and the prospect of a growing number of Cuban-American victories in countywide races has revitalized proposals to alter the at-large structure of Dade County politics, something that Dade County's Anglo establishment was adamantly opposed to before the prospects of ascendant Latin political power became so likely.

Structural Change and the Possibilities of Political Reform

Historically, structural tinkering has been variously utilized in local governmental affairs to exclude certain groups of participants (through gerrymandering); undercut existing political organizations, such as political machines (through the institution of at-large and nonpartisan elections); and raise the level of professional participation (through council-manager models of local government). People also have sought to utilize structural reform to increase representation of particular groups, such as through the creation of ethnically cohesive districts (affirmative gerrymandering) and the consolidation of political power in a particular area, such as through new incorporations.

The story of structural reform in Dade County has chapters devoted to each of these more broadly defined purposes. The current proposals for structural change, however, are primarily rooted in the last two descriptions. County and municipal government in Greater Miami has faced numerous proposals either to scrap the existing at-large Metro and City of Miami electoral configurations and institute district elections with lines drawn so as to almost assure "balanced" Latin, black, and non-Latin white representation; or to incorporate new municipalities in the now unincorporated Liberty City, Kendall, Key Biscayne, and Westchester areas.[6]

While space does not permit an elaborate analysis of each of these proposals, all available evidence points to the following observations. The effort to institute district elections for the Dade County Commission can be best understood as a strategy to boost black and Hispanic representation on the commission. Interestingly in the long run, district elections also may come to preserve non-Hispanic, white representation on the county commission of an area that may soon see a Latin voting majority.

The City of Miami Commission, with its own at-large election system, has been the subject of similar proposals for reform. District elections in this municipality would most directly serve to institutionalize and legitimize the politics of ethnic turf already so evident in this body's proceedings. It may also be the best way to preserve the one "black seat" as well as the one "Anglo seat" on this five-member body. To the extent that many blacks and Hispanics continue to push for this reform and non-Hispanic whites come to see their own representation best secured through the adoption of district elections, it would seem that this proposed change (or minimally a compromise with a mixture of at-large and district elections) could well become a reality.

A new round of discussions on the issue of district elections was set off when a detailed proposal was unveiled in 1984 (Hertz 1984). In 1986 the *Miami Herald* put forth a proposal that would graft district elections onto the at-large system (Mohl 1989). Most recently a panel reviewing the structure of Metro, headed by the widely respected former county manager, Merrett Stierheim, called for a stronger mayor and the establishment of an expanded Metro Commission elected from mostly district elections (Soto 1990). The most recent round of discussions followed a fifteen-month period in which civic leaders discussed plans to make Metro government "more accountable, more sensitive to minorities and less vulnerable to special interests" (Soto 1990).

Less certain of success are the proposals for the new incorporations mentioned above. Since the establishment of the Metro Charter, new incorporations have been particularly difficult to realize. Only one new municipality, Islandia, has been established.

The most recent attempts to incorporate parts of Dade County seem to have been motivated by one of two purposes. In the case of the proposed incorporation of the mostly black Liberty City area, the call was for "community control" in the wake of the 1980 riots. It was argued by advocates that the area's needs could be more effectively and sensitively met by a government, a bureaucracy, and a police force constituted of Liberty City residents (New City Political Action Committee:1–6). As compelling as this argument may have been, the Metro Commission voted down the proposal and branded the plan "fiscally unsound," given the weak tax base of the area. The commission ultimately did not have to address the more elusive but fundamental question of political representation (Cottman 1981).

Conclusion

Proposals to incorporate the affluent suburban communities of Kendall, Key Biscayne, and Westchester have not gotten past the county commission either. Some observers suggest that these plans constitute a "circling of the wagons" mentality in the interest of preserving and protecting the communities as they are by giving them control over their own zoning and services (Silverman 1983).

Incorporation of the more affluent communities of Kendall, which has a growing Hispanic plurality, and Westchester, which is predominantly Hispanic, would no doubt anger the advocates of the Liberty City incorporation. But incorporation could also serve as an important precedent for those predominantly black sections of Dade that have remained largely disenfranchised at both levels of Metro's two-tiered system.

There is every reason to believe that through structural reform, especially through the institution of district elections, ethnic representation on important county and municipal governing bodies could be "balanced." In the interests of representative government, this achievement alone would stand as quite an accomplishment. Yet, healthy skepticism is probably called for in considering the effectiveness of such changes in altering this community's political and economic agenda in any substantial way. It is doubtful that the fundamental issues relating to the distribution of public- and private-sector resources can be addressed through structural tinkering. At best, structural reform may come to represent the community's last best chance to deal with its problems through largely symbolic reassurances.

Notes

1. Throughout this paper "Miami" is used interchangeably with the area encompassed by Dade County, Florida. Any reference to Dade County's largest city, the city of Miami, will be specifically noted.

2. As Theodore Lowie (1976:313) has observed: "Politics under Reform are not abolished. Only their form is altered. *The legacy of Reform is the bureaucratic city-state.* Destruction of the party foundation of the mayoralty cleaned up many cities but also destroyed the basis for sustained, central, popularly-based action. This capacity, with all its faults, was replaced by the power of professionalized agencies. But this has meant creation of new bases of power. Bureaucratic agencies are not neutral; they are only independent" (Lowie's emphasis).

3. Joan Didion's (1987: 83–151) survey of exile politics and the special role that Miami has played in these intrigues since the Bay of Pigs fiasco in April 1962 is as illuminating as it is sobering.

4. The public-relations approach is embraced by civic leaders. It draws attention away from fundamental issues involving the needs of the black community and reform of Dade's political system in the decade-long pattern of rioting and upheaval in black neighborhoods. Perhaps the best example of the public-relations approach is a statement attributed to Tom Ferguson, president of the Beacon Council, a prominent organization of business and civic leaders. When rioting broke out in 1989 less than a week before the Super Bowl, he said, "If it wasn't for the fact that the Super Bowl is down here it [the riots] wouldn't be more than a blip in the news. . . . We still have a good product to sell, and we still need to be selling it more than ever before" (Resnick and Croghan 1989).

5. An example of these tactics occurred when the Miami City Commission voted to put the following question to the city's voters in November 1982: "Should funds of the City of Miami be expended to finance in whole or in part, any multinational commercial or cultural conference or convention where representatives of Communist-Marxist countries have either been scheduled to participate or invited to attend?" (Silva 1982:7–B).

6. The following discussion is largely drawn from these and other sources: Zaldivar 1982; Betancount 1982; Martinez 1982; New City Political Action Committee

1980; Inter-University Committee on Dade County Government 1981; Mohl 1982: 9–13, 21–31.

References

Banfield, Edward C., and James Q. Wilson. 1963. *City Politics.* New York: Vintage Books.

Bayor, Ronald. 1989. "Race, Ethnicity, and Political Change in the Urban Sunbelt South." In *Shades of the Sunbelt,* edited by R. M. Miller and G. E. Pozzetta, 127–42. Boca Raton, Fla.: Florida Atlantic University Press.

Betancourt, Marie. 1982 "Kendall Group Starts Study of Incorporation." *Miami Herald,* April 22, 3NS.

Cottman, Michael. 1981. "Metro Rejects New City Idea by a 7–1 Vote." *Miami Herald,* September 23, 1B, 2B.

Didion, Joan. 1987. *Miami.* New York: Simon and Schuster.

Dugger, Celia. 1987. "MMAP Losing Punch." *Miami Herald,* July 17.

Fiedler, Tom. 1989. "Lopsided Latin Vote Doomed Richman Bid." *Miami Herald,* August 30, 1A, 12A.

Governor's Dade County Citizens' Committee on the Liberty City Riots. 1980. "Report." Mimeo. Miami, October 30.

Hayes, Samuel P. 1964. "The Politics of Reform in Municipal Government in the Progressive Era." *Pacific Northwest Quarterly* (October): 156–67.

Hertz, David B. 1984. *Governing Dade County: A Study in Alternative Structures.* Miami: University of Miami.

Higham, John. 1963. *Strangers in the Land: Patterns of American Nativism, 1860–1925.* New York: Atheneum.

Hofstadter, Richard. 1935. *The Age of Reform: From Bryan to FDR.* New York: Alfred A. Knopf.

Inter-University Committee on Dade County Government. 1981. "Alternative Approaches to Dade County Government." Photocopy. Miami.

Jacobs, Sam. 1973. "Bilingual Bill Passed by Dade." *Miami Herald,* April 16, 3B.

Johnson, Dirk. 1987. "The View From the Poorest U.S. Suburbs." *New York Times,* April 30, 10.

Levine, Barry B. 1985. "The Capital of Latin America." *Wilson Quarterly* (Winter): 46–69.

Lowie, Theodore J. 1976. "Machine Politics—Old and New." In *The City Boss in America,* edited by Alexander B. Callow, Jr., 310–18. New York: Oxford University Press.

Maingot, Anthony P. 1986. "Ethnic Bargaining and the Noncitizen: Cubans and Haitians in Miami." In *The Primordial Challenge: Ethnicity in the Modern World,* edited by John F. Stack, Jr., 81–113. Westport, Conn.: Greenwood Press.

Martinez, Guillermo. 1982. "Dade Commission's Ethnic Realities." *Miami Herald*, January 9, 19A.

Mohl, Raymond A. 1982. "Miami Metro, Charter Revisions, and the Politics of the Eighties." *Florida Environmental Urban Issues* 10 (October): 9–13, 21–31.

———. 1983. "Miami: The Ethnic Cauldron." In *Sunbelt Cities: Politics and Growth since World War II*, edited by Richard M. Bernard and Bradley R. Rice, 58–99. Austin: University of Texas Press.

———. 1984. "Miami's Metropolitan Government: Retrospect and Prospect." *Florida Historical Quarterly* (July): 24–50.

———. 1987. "Trouble in Paradise: Race and Housing in Miami during the New Deal Era." *Prologue* 19: 7–21.

———. 1989. "Ethnic Politics in Miami, 1960–1986." In *Shades of the Sunbelt: Essays on Ethnicity, Race, and the Urban South*, edited by Randall M. Miller and George E. Pozzetta, 143–60. Boca Raton: Florida Atlantic University Press.

New City Political Action Committee. 1980. "The New City: A Proposal." Photocopy. Miami, September 16.

Porter, Bruce, and Marvin Dunn. 1984. *The Miami Riot of 1980: Crossing the Bounds*. Lexington, Mass.: Lexington Books.

Resnick, Rosalind, and Love Groghan. 1989. "After the Storm." *Miami Herald*, January 22, 1F.

Rieff, David. 1987. *Going to Miami: Exiles, Tourists, and Refugees in the New America*. Boston: Little, Brown.

Riordon, William L. 1948. *Plunkitt of Tammany Hall*. New York: Alfred A. Knopf.

Roussakis, Emmanuel. 1981. *Miami's International Banking Community: Foreign Banks, Edge Act Corporations and Local Banks*. Miami: Peat Marwick, Mitchell and Co.

Silva, Helga. 1982. "Anti-Red Vote Saved Convention Ferre Says." *Miami Herald*, November 7, 7B.

Silverman, Steve. 1983. Interview with author, January. Miami.

Sofen, Edward. 1966a. *The Miami Metropolitan Experience*. 2d ed. Garden City, N.J.: Doubleday Anchor.

———. 1966b. "Problems of Metropolitan Leadership: The Miami Experience." *Midwest Journal of Political Science*, no. 1: 21.

Soto, Luis Feldstein. 1990. "Panel Urges Changes in Dade Charter." *Miami Herald*, January 6, 1B.

———. 1989. "It's Ros-Lehtinen, 53–47%, Cuban GOP Winner Is First for Dade." *Miami Herald*, August 30, 1A, 12A.

Stack, John F., Jr., and Christopher L. Warren. 1990. "Ethnicity and the Politics of Symbolism in Miami's Cuban Community." *Cuban Studies* 20: 11–28.

Steffens, Lincoln. 1904. *The Shame of the Cities*. New York: McClure, Phillips and Co.

Strong, Josiah. 1891. *Our Country*. New York: Baker and Taylor Co.

Tasker, Fredric. 1982. "Dade Neighborhoods Stay Segregated as Residents Seek American Dream." *Miami Herald*, August 30, pp. 1A, 2A.

———. 1980. "Anti-Bilingualism Approved in Dade County." *Miami Herald*, November 5, 1A, 11A.

Tomb, Geoffrey. 1983. "City Makes World Affairs Its Business." *Miami Herald*, May 2, 1C, 2C.

U.S. Commission on Civil Rights. 1982. *Confronting Racial Isolation in Miami.* Washington: Government Printing Office.

Warren, Christopher L., and John F. Stack, Jr. 1986. "Immigration and the Politics of Ethnicity and Class in Metropolitan Miami." In *The Primordial Challenge: Ethnicity in the Modern World*, edited by John F. Stack, Jr. Westport, Conn: Greenwood Press.

Warren, Christoper L., John G. Corbett, and John F. Stack, Jr. 1990. "Hispanic Ascendancy and Tripartite Politics in Miami." In *Racial Politics in American Cities*, edited by Rufus P. Browning, Dale Rogers Marshall, and David H. Tabb. New York: Longman.

Wilkins, Mira. 1980. *New Foreign Enterprise in Florida*. Miami: Greater Miami Chamber of Commerce.

Zaldivar, R.D. 1982. "Give Miami Mayor More Power Committee Urges." *Miami Herald*, May 20, 10D.

9

Ethnicity and Partnership: The Eighteenth Congressional District in Miami

**Dario Moreno
and Nicol Rae**

The persistence of ethnic voting in the United States continues to defy the predictions of political scientists who predicted its demise. Robert Dahl (1961:34–51) presented a three-stage model in which immigrant groups would gradually become "assimilated" as their social mobility increased. When a large segment of the group has entered the "middle class," economic factors would become more politically relevant than ethnic factors in their political choices: "To these people, ethnic politics is often embarrassing or meaningless. Political attitudes and loyalties have become a function of socioeconomic characteristics" (Dahl 1961:35).

Yet Dahl's conclusions were challenged by Raymond Wolfinger, a fellow participant in Dahl's study of New Haven, Connecticut. Wolfinger found that Dahl's model did not work for New Haven's Italian community, since its level of ethnic voting had actually risen, while its socioeconomic status had improved (Wolfinger 1965). In contrast to Dahl's assimilation theory, Wolfinger (1965:905) posited a "mobilization theory" of ethnic voting: "The strength of ethnic voting depends on both the intensity of ethnic identification and the level of ethnic relevance in the election. The most powerful and visible sign of ethnic political relevance is a fellow-ethnic's name at the head of the ticket, evident to everyone who enters the voting booth."

Wolfinger's criticism of the assimilation model was reinforced by a broader critique of the entire "melting pot" concept. It seemed clear that ethnic consciousness and identification were still very much alive in the 1960s and had not disappeared as members of immigrant groups moved up the social scale and moved to suburbia (Parenti 1967; Moynihan and Glazer 1970).

The recent special election in Florida's Eighteenth Congressional District—held for twenty-eight years by Congressman Claude Pepper—is one of the clearest examples in recent years of a campaign and election in which ethnic factors predominated over all others. This election largely corroborates Wolfinger's mobilization theory by demonstrating the capacity of ethnicity to override partisanship and all other issues in a particular context. It is even more interesting that this should occur in south Florida, which has been one of the areas of the United States where the impact of recent Hispanic immigration has been greatest.

From the results of the Eighteenth District's election and other recent contests in the Greater Miami area, it seems clear that there has been a genuine secular realignment (Key 1959) of partisan forces in south Florida, which has taken place on the basis of both local and national concerns. However, in this process the Democratic and Republican parties in Dade County have become little more than "front organizations" for the interests of particular ethnic groups. If this assessment is correct, then ethnicity will likely remain the most important factor determining electoral outcomes in south Florida for some time to come.

The Context

Florida's Eighteenth Congressional District is the House district based on the cities of Miami and Miami Beach. It also includes the upper-income city of Coral Gables and portions of the heavily Cuban city of Hialeah. Fifty percent of the district's population in 1980 were of "Spanish origin," 13 percent black, 1 percent Asian, and the remainder non-Hispanic white (Barone 1987).

The district's voters live in neighborhoods that are usually dominated by one ethnic group or the other. Blacks are concentrated in the inner-city ghetto areas of Overtown and Liberty City, which exploded in rioting three times during the 1980s (see chapter 3). The Cuban population is concentrated in Little Havana and Hialeah. Miami Beach and the contiguous communities of Surfside, Bal Harbour, and Bay Harbour are mainly

Jewish, but the southern part of Miami Beach has been increasingly penetrated by Cubans and other Latins in recent years. Coconut Grove, Coral Gables, and Key Biscayne are "upper-income" communities with a more mixed ethnic profile than the other parts of the district.

Since 1961 House elections in the district had been dominated by a Democrat, Congressman Claude Pepper. Pepper was a living reminder of the New Deal era. He had served as a U.S. senator during the 1930s, where he acquired a reputation as the South's leading supporter of Franklin Roosevelt (Key 1949:605–6). Defeated by an infamous "red-baiting" Democratic primary campaign in 1950, Pepper returned as a member of Congress from the Miami-based district in 1961. He had a second congressional career in the House, which culminated in his accession to the chairmanship of the powerful House Rules Committee in 1982.

Despite often appearing as a figure from another era, Pepper was nevertheless a canny politician regarding Miami politics. His voting behavior in the House was well-attuned to the changing demands of his constituents. His national leadership on issues affecting the elderly earned him the devotion of the elderly Jewish voters in Miami Beach. His impeccable civil rights record and New Deal credentials made him popular among the black population, and the more conservative Cuban voters were appeased by Pepper's strong anti-Castro stands. In recent years Pepper had been instrumental in establishing Radio Martí, and he had supported Contra aid—both issues dear to his Cuban constituency.

While House incumbents are generally invulnerable these days, Pepper was even more invulnerable than most. His only serious reelection challenge came in 1978, when a Cuban Republican challenger actually outspent him. Yet Pepper still secured 63 percent of the vote. No serious Republican challenge could be mounted as long as Pepper held the seat.

Yet beneath Pepper's aura of impregnability, the demographics of his district were changing rapidly. Figure 9.1 illustrates the rapid rise of Hispanic registration in the Eighteenth District and the switch of these voters to the Republican party during the 1980s.

As the Hispanic population continued to grow and as these voters became increasingly Republican in their voting behavior, Democratic candidates at other levels of electoral competition began to lose out. This was especially true for offices that have great symbolic power such as the presidency and the U.S. Senate. Thus, Ronald Reagan twice carried the district easily in his bid for the presidency, and George Bush carried it

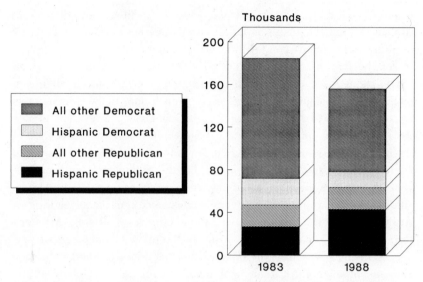

Fig. 9.1. Voter registration breakdown by party and ethnicity, Eighteenth Congressional District, 1983 and 1988. *Source*: Metro-Dade Elections Department.

again in 1988. In fact both Reagan and Bush received nearly 90 percent of the vote in the Little Havana portion of the district. Republican Senate candidates Paula Hawkins and Connie Mack also carried the Eighteenth, and even in state races an increasingly Republican identification became evident. Pepper's coalition was personal and unique to U.S. House races; at other levels the Eighteenth was slipping away from the Democratic party. It became generally assumed that if and when the seat did fall vacant, it would probably fall to a Cuban Republican.

The Candidates and the Parties

The Republican nomination in the race to succeed Pepper was more or less settled at a very early stage in the contest. There were basically only three serious potential contenders: Miami Mayor Xavier Suarez, State Senator Ileana Ros-Lehtinen, and State Representative Lincoln Diaz-Balart—all prominent Cuban-Americans. Suarez (a former Democrat registered as an Independent) had no particular interest in going to Washington (*Miami Herald*, June 6, 1989). After a meeting between the three contenders and Republican state committee member Al Cardenas (also Cuban), Diaz-Balart decided to step aside for Ros-Lehtinen in the congressional race and to run instead for her vacated state senate seat (Ramos 1989a).[1] That left Ros-Lehtinen with businessman Carlos Perez as her only viable opposition for the GOP nomination.

For the Republicans there was no alternative to a Cuban-American candidate in this seat. Indeed the opportunity to further solidify their grip on the Cuban vote and impress other Hispanic groups in the United States by sending the first Cuban-American to Congress was evident to Lee Atwater, GOP national chair. Atwater appeared before the convention of the principal national Cuban lobbying organization, the Cuban American National Foundation, and announced that the Eighteenth Congressional District seat "belonged" to a Cuban-American (Searingen 1989). At face value this might appear as a fairly innocuous piece of partisan needling on Atwater's part. But in the vexed ethnic climate of Miami, Atwater's throwaway line became a major issue in the election campaign. It persuaded the most serious of the Democratic contenders to abandon the race and accentuated anti-Cuban sentiments among Miami's other ethnic groups. These sentiments would be exploited in the Democratic primary campaign.

On the Democratic side, the clear front-runner was State Senator Jack Gordon, a veteran Miami politician revered by Miami's increasingly beleaguered liberal community. Gordon by no means had the rapport with the Cuban community that Pepper had possessed, however. Indeed he had gone out on a limb politically by supporting better relations with the Castro regime, opposing aid to the Nicaraguan Contras, and opposing (successfully) a state budget proposal for an institute at Florida International University (FIU) to be administered by the Cuban American National Foundation. Gordon had thus engendered deep resentments in the Cuban community that would have made his candidacy controversial in any case. Atwater's statement raised the ethnic factor in the race even further. After looking at some polling data, Gordon decided that the price of victory for him in the Eighteenth District special election was too great to pay: "I think the only way that this election could be won by a Democrat, or will be won by a Democrat, is by virtue of raising ethnic divisiveness by saying 'Stop the Cubans' in one fashion or another. . . . I will not run a campaign that I am ashamed of" (Fiedler and Soto 1989a).

After Gordon's withdrawal the state Democratic chair, Simon Ferro (another Cuban), scrambled desperately to find a Democrat who could challenge Ros-Lehtinen. The logic of the district's demographics led Ferro to conclude that the strongest Democratic contender was likely to be a

Cuban Democrat. Such a candidate could win the election by cutting into Republican support among Cubans and holding onto the traditional Democratic constituencies of elderly Jews and blacks. The leading Cuban Democrat in south Florida, Hialeah Mayor Raul Martinez, was uninterested in a race that would earn him enemies within the Cuban community and that he appeared unlikely to win. That left Miami City Commissioner Rosario Kennedy, a powerful vote-getter in municipal elections, as the leading Cuban Democratic alternative. Ferro eventually cajoled Kennedy into running.

At the outset of the campaign, the opposition to Kennedy did not appear to be too serious within the Democratic camp. Marvin Dunn, a black professor of psychology at FIU, was widely respected for his intellect, but his somewhat eclectic issue positions stigmatized him as a maverick from the outset of the campaign, and he was never able to mount a really serious challenge. Sonny Wright, a black businessman, was unable to get any serious support outside the black community. Eastern Airlines pilot John Paul Rosser and Jewish millionaire Bernard Anscher never looked like serious contenders. Miami lawyer Gerald Richman, a previous president of the Florida Bar Association, was another political neophyte. Cuban banker Raul Masvidal looked as though he might pose some problems for Kennedy—at least among Cuban Democrats—but under pressure from state party officials, Masvidal was persuaded to withdraw. The final candidate was a surprise entrant: the late Congressman Pepper's niece, Joanne Pepper, a federal probation officer and another political newcomer who nevertheless hoped to be able to trade on the Pepper name.

After her reluctant entry into the race, Kennedy put together a strong campaign organization (with the tacit support of state chairman Ferro). She also picked up all the important endorsements—principally of the AFL-CIO and of the *Miami Herald* (1989a). For most of the primary race, it appeared that the main challenge to the front-runner would come from Joanne Pepper, whose name clearly evoked strong nostalgic support from black voters and many of the elderly in Miami Beach. In the week preceding the election, these two appeared most likely to get into the Democratic run-off primary.

Only in the last few days of the primary campaign did the picture begin to change as Jewish lawyer Gerald Richman emerged as a serious contender. Richman pumped $180,000 of his own money into the campaign and made a strong pitch for the support of Jewish Democrats by taking a strong pro-Israel stance. In addition Richman latched onto the "Cuban

seat" issue raised earlier by Lee Atwater and Jack Gordon. In the last
week of the primary campaign, he filled the airwaves with commercials
stressing his campaign slogan: "It's not a Jewish seat, or a black seat, or a
Cuban seat, it's an *American* seat" (Ramos 1989c). Richman evidently had
fewer qualms than did Jack Gordon about taking on the "ethnic" issue that
Atwater had introduced into the campaign. Richman's slogan was designed to appeal to those voters in the district who resented the notion that
the seat somehow "belonged" to a Cuban-American, whether Republican
or Democrat.

Sensing danger from Pepper and Richman, over the campaign's final
weekend Kennedy saturated the district with pamphlets that derided the
credentials of both her main opponents for public office. Pepper and
Richman retaliated by holding a joint press conference on the Saturday
prior to the poll, condemning Kennedy's "negative campaigning."

In the meantime Republican front-runner Ros-Lehtinen continued on
her almost regal march toward certain nomination in the first Republican
primary. In the polls she was outpolling the hapless Carlos Perez by three-
to-one among Republicans. So confident was the Ros-Lehtinen camp of
victory, that the candidate—with a view to the general election—was
dispatched on a series of "fact-finding" trips to Israel and Central America. The Republican party and the Cuban political elite had ensured that
the Republican nominee would win with the solid support of the Republican constituency in the district. By contrast, despite Ferro's efforts, it was
clear that there was little unity in the Democratic camp and that the
infighting would be prolonged into a run-off primary. It appeared that the
race had already become the Republicans' to lose.

The Primaries and the Runoff

The results of the Republican primary were not surprising. Although
the Republican race was extremely one-sided while the Democratic contest was close, 35 percent of the district's Republicans turned out to vote
compared to under a quarter of the registered Democrats (Fiedler 1989a).
Ileana Ros-Lehtinen won with 83 percent of the Republican vote. The
intensity of Cuban-American support for Ros-Lehtinen was indicated by
turnouts of over 40 percent in the first primary in some Little Havana
precincts (*Miami Herald*, August 2, 1989). Even more interestingly,
despite the fact that the Republican race was dead while that of the
Democrats was very much alive, and despite the fact that the district

contained 100,198 registered Democrats to 71,620 Republicans, the total primary vote for the Republicans (20,482) was almost equal to that of the Democrats (20,897) (Fiedler 1989b). This small Democratic advantage in overall turnout was a further indication of the erosion of the Democrats' electoral advantage in the Eighteenth District.

In the Democratic race the winners were Kennedy (as expected) and Richman (more surprisingly). Richman in fact topped the poll among Democrats with 28 percent to Kennedy's 27 percent. Joanne Pepper finished with 24 percent, and none of the other candidates got into double figures. Kennedy did well in the Cuban precincts. Richman's base was elderly Jewish voters in Miami Beach. Although Pepper did well among blacks, their turnout was too low to carry her into the runoff.

The run-off campaign between Kennedy and Richman became a bitter ethnic confrontation. Indeed, apart from ethnicity, there was little else to divide the candidates. Kennedy took particular exception to Richman's "American Seat" slogan, regarding it as a subtle exploitation of resentment against Cuban-Americans like herself. She picked up valuable endorsements from Joanne Pepper and from defeated black candidates Dunn and Wright. Richman, by contrast, found himself condemned by Dade's Fair Campaign Practices Committee (a bipartisan, quasi-official, "watchdog" body), the *Miami Herald* (which backed Kennedy), and the Spanish American League Against Discrimination for his "divisive" "American Seat" slogan (*Miami Herald*, editorial, 1989b). He was also embarrassed by revelations that he and his wife had contributed to Republican George Bush's 1988 presidential campaign.

All of this was of little account when the returns of the run-off election came in on August 15. Richman trounced Kennedy with over 60 percent of the vote—mainly due to his lock on the Miami Beach Jewish vote and the relatively small number of Cuban Democrats (Fiedler 1989c). Kennedy's labor and black endorsements were insufficient to withstand the groundswell of Democratic support for Richman, whose campaign benefited from the surprising degree of Anglo discontent with Miami's increasingly dominant Cuban-American political establishment. Indeed, in Richman's success there were some ominous echoes of Jack Gordon's withdrawal statement at the outset of the campaign. Only by exploiting anti-Cuban resentments among Anglos and blacks could an Anglo Democrat stand any chance of success in the Eighteenth District.

Another interesting factor in Kennedy's defeat was the utter failure of the local Democratic party machinery to "deliver" the nomination for her.

Moreover, the Democratic nomination had been secured by a political unknown, who had been backing the Republican presidential campaign a year previously. In view of the strong support for Kennedy from state chair Ferro and virtually all prominent local Democrats, Richman's victory was almost an insult to Miami's traditional Democratic party establishment. One could not have better evidence for the irrelevance of party considerations when ethnic issues come to the fore to the extent that they did in this campaign. The Dade County Democratic leadership was drowned in a tidal wave of ethnicity.

The General Election Campaign

The general election campaign was even more dominated by the "ethnic issue" than the primary had been. Richman failed to get the endorsement of an embittered Rosario Kennedy and of Dade's only other prominent Cuban Democrat—the mayor of Hialeah. Mayor Raul Martinez was forthright in his condemnation of Richman's campaign tactics: "If you really care about the community, you cannot vote for this man. I do not think that his campaign is what the Democratic party stands for" (Fiedler and Soto 1989b).

Ros-Lehtinen—assisted by a personal visit from President Bush on the day after the Democratic runoff—also attacked Richman as a "bigot" and announced that she would not engage in any face-to-face debates with him during the campaign: "Principle is more important than political gain, and a seat in Congress is not worth dignifying for even a moment Gerald Richman's racist view of America and of me. I will not dignify the bigoted campaign of Gerald Richman by appearing with him at any event, forum or debate" (Ramos 1989b).

The campaign subsequently became extremely embittered. Ros-Lehtinen largely evaded other issues and concentrated her attacks on Richman's "bigotry." Richman accused Ros-Lehtinen of using bigotry as an excuse for not facing up to a debate on issues such as abortion and gun control—on which his views were more in line with those of the district than were hers: "She has a lot of issues she does not want to talk about. She has a voting record that is completely out of step with this district and this country" (Ramos 1989b). It is interesting to note that having capitalized on ethnicity to win the primary, the Richman campaign now sought to emphasize issues in the general election. Ros-Lehtinen's refusal to debate, however, blunted the effectiveness of this strategy.

The campaign strategies of both campaigns were based purely on ethnic calculations. The race came down to a pure ethnic conflict, despite Richman's attempt to back away from his earlier rhetoric. Richman realized that to win he needed to do more than just mobilize the voting potential of the non-Cuban groups in the district. He needed to penetrate Ros-Lehtinen's support in the Hispanic community. In addition he sought the vote of upper-income, Anglo Republicans who might be alienated by the fanatical Cuban support for their first serious congressional contender and who might also feel put out by Ros-Lehtinen's strong anti-abortion record. Certainly Richman lost no opportunity to use the abortion issue to his advantage, and he associated himself with pro-choice forces at every available opportunity (Soto 1989a).

Ros-Lehtinen abandoned attempts at "bridge-building" with Jews and blacks and instead concentrated on mobilizing her Cuban base. However, polls indicated that Richman's cultivation of the ethnic issue had turned what initially appeared likely to be an easy election for the Republicans into a very close race. *Miami Herald* polls showed the two candidates to be neck-and-neck, with the whole election largely to be decided by the ethnic turnout factor (Fiedler 1989d).

Only Chicago in recent years has witnessed an election in which voters were so clearly divided along ethnic lines as in this election. All of Miami's institutions were affected. The *Miami Herald* endorsed Ros-Lehtinen, but on the same day of the endorsement the paper also carried a story describing how publisher Dick Capen had overruled his editorial board, which favored Richman (Fiedler and Soto 1989c). The credibility of the Dade County Fair Campaign Practices Committee was undermined when it too was torn apart by the ethnic conflict. On the Sunday prior to the poll, committee members condemned Ros-Lehtinen for distributing a leaflet designed to rally Cuban-American support against Richman. The following day, however, a Hispanic member of the committee claimed that the committee had come under pressure from the Richman campaign to issue a condemnation of Ros-Lehtinen and that proper procedures had not been followed in issuing the Sunday statement (Fiedler and Ramos 1989). No institution could evade the ethnic issue.

The Results

Election day in Miami saw Gerald Richman and the Democratic party defeated by a large and monolithic Cuban-American vote. Richman's

"American Seat" slogan, which was the key to victory in the Democratic runoff, proved to be a two-edged sword. Cuban-Americans offended by the perceived racism of the Democrat party candidate voted for Ros-Lehtinen by the remarkable margin of 94 to 6 percent (Soto 1989b).

The mobilization of the Cuban community around the Republican candidate was overwhelming and impressive. Local Cuban media (five radio and two television stations) bombarded the airwaves on election day with anti-Richman propaganda, including the dubious claim that Fidel Castro himself had endorsed the Democratic candidate. Richman carried all of the other blocs of voters (Jews, Anglos, and blacks), but they represented only 47 percent of the electorate. High Cuban turnout—some Little Havana precincts reported a 70 percent turnout in the general election—provided Ros-Lehtinen with the margin of victory: 53 percent of the votes. The Republicans won simply because more Cubans voted and almost all of them voted for Ros-Lehtinen.

The heavy Cuban-American vote and the high turnout for the Republican candidate were undoubtedly aided by the fact that Ros-Lehtinen was Cuban. However, her support in the congressional election must be put in the context of the dramatic trend toward the GOP among Dade County Cubans in recent elections.

Figure 9.2 illustrates the support that Dade's Hispanics have given to such conservative Republican candidates as President George Bush, Senator Connie Mack, and Governor Bob Martinez. Ros-Lehtinen thus received roughly the same support in the thirty most heavily Hispanic precincts[2] of the Eighteenth District as other Republican candidates.

The 1989 special election reinforced the trend of increasing Cuban-American support for the GOP. Cuban support for the Republican party and its candidate is reflected in the results of the correlations of the Hispanic variable with the vote received by Republican candidates: Bush (.8590), Mack (.9303), Martinez (.8575), Ros-Lehtinen (.9630), and Republican party registration (.8898). These figures suggest that Hispanics in Miami will support conservative candidates whether they are running for president, senator, governor, or representative.[3] The Cuban community's strong anticommunism, the formation of a viable ethnic enclave community, the economic incorporation of the expansive Cuban middle and upper classes, the opportunity to use the previously under-utilized state Republican machinery as a vehicle for political mobilization, and the emergence of other institutional bases of influence such as the Cuban American National Foundation all serve to explain this remark-

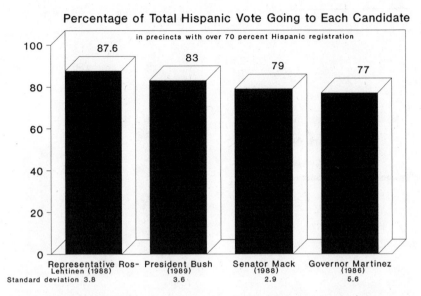

Fig. 9.2. Hispanic support for GOP, Eighteenth Congressional District, 1986–89. *Source*: Metro-Dade Elections Department.

able level of Cuban support for the Republican party (Moreno and Warren 1991). The election of Ros-Lehtinen also continued the process of Cuban empowerment in Dade County. This empowerment began in 1982 and has witnessed Cubans win seven seats in the state house of representatives; three seats in the state senate; plus the mayoralty of Miami, West Miami, North Miami, Sweetwater, and Hialeah Gardens. This empowerment by Dade Cubans has come about almost exclusively under the Republican banner.

The electorate in Miami became divided along ethnic lines not because Cubans changed their voting behavior but because other groups rallied around the Democratic candidate in a futile attempt to "stop the Cubans." The tragedy of the 1989 special election was that Richman's coded call to U.S.-born voters ("this is an American seat") to stop the Cuban candidates, which included Kennedy in the Democratic primary and Ros-Lehtinen in the general election, worked. In the general election, Richman carried all the non-Cuban groups in the district (Anglos, blacks, and Jews). According to one exit poll, he even won among Republican Anglos by 55 to 45 percent (Soto 1989b).

Figure 9.3 illustrates the wide difference in support that non-Hispanic whites gave to conservative candidates. Ros-Lehtinen, while not differing

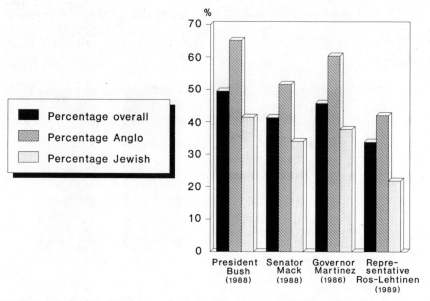

Fig. 9.3. Support for GOP among non-Hispanic whites, Eighteenth Congressional District, 1986–89. *Source*: Metro-Dade Elections Department. *Note*: In precincts with over 70 percent non-Hispanic registration.

in any significant policy issue with Bush, Mack, or Martinez, did very poorly among their non-Hispanic supporters in the Eighteenth District. The Cuban Republican candidate ran nearly 20 percent behind Anglo Republicans in the non-Hispanic, white precincts of Dade County.

Two communities reflect just how effective Richman's "American Seat" slogan was among non-Hispanic groups. Bal Harbour, an affluent Jewish city that gave President Bush 50 percent, Mack 44 percent, and Martinez 52 percent of the vote, gave Ros-Lehtinen only 16 percent. Similarly on the heavily Republican island of Key Biscayne, Ros-Lehtinen received barely 48 percent of the vote, while Bush received 70 percent, Mack 59 percent, and Martinez 68 percent.

The anti-Latin nature of Richman's support is reflected in its close correlation to the "yes" vote on Proposition 11 in the 1988 election. Proposition 11 was the "English as official language" amendment to the Florida Constitution. Hispanics were the only group that consistently opposed the amendment, voting over 80 percent against the measure (see also chapter 6).

A districtwide analysis shows that the Ros-Lehtinen votes correlated more closely with the "no" vote on Proposition 11 than with that of any

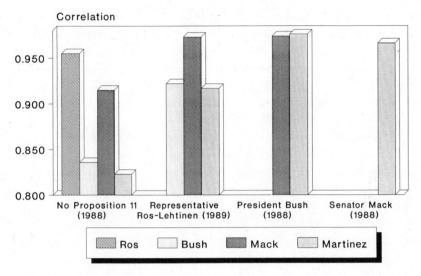

Fig. 9.4. Correlations of voting behavior, Eighteenth Congressional District, 1988–89. *Source*: Metro-Dade Elections Department.

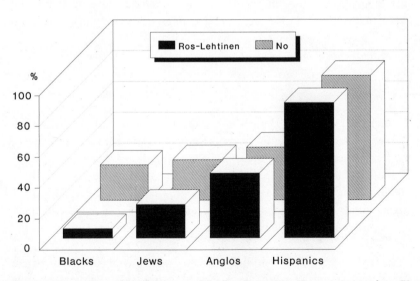

Fig. 9.5. Comparison of Ros-Lehtinen and "no" on Proposition 11 in precincts at least 70 percent uniform, Eighteenth Congressional District, 1988–89. *Source*: Metro-Dade Elections Department.

other Republican candidate (see fig. 9.4). This trend is even more pronounced in the non-Hispanic precincts, where Ros-Lehtinen votes only correlated with the "no" vote on Proposition 11 (.8132), compared with very low correlation between her vote and the votes of other recent GOP hopefuls: Bush (.2659), Mack (.5810), and Martinez (.0355).[4] Figure 9.5 illustrates a comparison between Ros-Lehtinen support and the "no" vote on Proposition 11 among the district's ethnic groups.

Richman was able to mobilize the district's non-Hispanic groups in a campaign to stop the Cubans. In so doing, he turned what had looked like an apparent stroll for the Republicans into a very close race. However, in turning the election into a referendum on Cuban empowerment, Richman also guaranteed that he would eventually lose the election. Hispanic voters, while estimated to comprise only 43 percent of the district's registered voters, actually comprised a majority of the electorate. Dade County only counts those Hispanics born outside the United States and in Puerto Rico in its registration figures. The growing number of native-born Latins in Miami, especially the children of Cubans who came during the 1960s and are now able to vote, are not included in these figures, resulting in an underestimation of approximately 10 percent in the size of the Hispanic bloc. This, combined with the traditional 5 percent higher voter turnout among Cuban-Americans, helped to guarantee the election of the first Cuban-American to Congress. Richman's "American Seat" slogan made it an election about power. As salsa singer Celia Cruz yelled into the microphone at the Ros-Lehtinen victory party: "The Cubans won!"

Conclusion

Recent elections in Dade County have largely confirmed Raymond Wolfinger's mobilization theory with regard to ethnic voting. In the case of the Dade Cubans, all the important criteria for ethnic voting according to Wolfinger's model are met: Dade's Cubans have an intense level of ethnic identification; ethnicity has been a salient issue in elections; and in the Eighteenth District's 1989 special election, there was a Cuban at the head of one party's ticket with a real chance of becoming the first Cuban elected to Congress.

Instead of becoming thoroughly assimilated, middle-class, suburban Americans, Miami's Cubans have aligned themselves even more strongly with the Republican party as their socioeconomic status has improved. The second generation of Cuban-Americans appears to be even more Republican in its voting behavior than the first. The election of Ileana Ros-

Lehtinen to Congress and the context in which she got elected will undoubtedly consolidate even further the Cubans' overwhelming and passionate identification with the Republican party.

The success of this Cuban-Republican alliance was underscored by the comfortable fashion in which Ros-Lehtinen defeated businessman Bernard Anscher in the 1990 election. Her 64-to-36 percent victory margin was made possible by the fact that seven out of every eight Hispanics supported her (Goldfards 1990). Ros-Lehtinen's overwhelming victory to secure her first full term illustrates the continuing saliency of ethnic voting in Dade County. The 1990 election was far more subdued than her contentious special election victory in 1989, so much so that her opponent complained of a media "conspiracy of silence."

The Wolfinger theory is further confirmed by the fact that in the Eighteenth District special election, Cubans were not the only group voting ethnically. Cubans had already become overwhelmingly Republican. The most dramatic shifts in voting patterns occurred not among Cubans, but rather among Jewish and non-Jewish Anglos whose level of support for the Republican candidate dropped dramatically from the 1980s norm. For these voters, it seems clear that the criteria for ethnic voting were also met (particularly for the Jewish voters): there was a high level of ethnic identity and ethnic salience in the race, and the Democratic candidate was Jewish. Anglos appeared to have been voting ethnically to an even greater degree than Cubans.

The longer-term consequences for politics in Miami are potentially serious, particularly as the party labels in Dade County have been virtually appropriated by different ethnic groups, with Republican Cubans opposing Democratic blacks and Anglos. Although the Democrats appeared to make significant gains among Anglo voters in the special election, longer-term demographic trends in Dade are not on their side. As is noted in the introduction, the Anglo population of the county is gradually diminishing as Anglos move north to Broward (Fort Lauderdale) and Palm Beach counties. The Latino electorate of Dade County is likely to continue to grow. Although much of this growth will be among non-Cuban Latins, by far the largest of these groups—the Nicaraguans—is likely to adopt an equally strong Republican identification. Dade County might well be left with an economically powerful Republican Latino majority facing an economically deprived and politically weak black Democratic minority, which has already expressed its frustration in civil violence four times in this decade.

Ethnicity thus remains as a potent force in American electoral politics, and its power should never be underestimated. The continuing migration of new ethnic groups into the United States from East and South Asia and Latin America is likely to open up further dimensions of ethnic voting and ethnic conflict in the twenty-first century.

Notes

1. Florida law compels holders of legislative and local government seats to surrender their seats when running for other elective offices.

2. "Heavy Hispanic" is described as precincts in which over 70 percent of the registered voters are Hispanics. It should also be noted that the Hispanic category only contains those Hispanics born outside of the United States or in Puerto Rico.

3. It should be noted that non-Cuban Hispanics in Dade do not support Republican candidates to the same extent as do Cuban-Americans. However, their numbers are not politically significant.

4. The correlation is taken from the forty-three precincts in the district that have over 70 percent non-Latin, white inhabitants.

References

Allman, T. D. 1987. *Miami, City of the Future*. New York: Atlantic Monthly Press.

Barone, Michael. 1987. *The Almanac of American Politics, 1988*. Washington, D.C.: National Journal.

Dahl, Robert A. 1961. *Who Governs? Democracy and Power in an American City*. New Haven, Conn.: Yale University Press.

Fiedler, Tom. 1989a. "Turnout Is Big Edge for GOP." *Miami Herald*, August 2: 1A.

————. 1989b. "Democratic Runoff is Likely to Have Donors Hedging Bets." *Miami Herald*, August 3: 1B.

————. 1989c. "Richman Slogan May Backfire in August 29 Vote." *Miami Herald*, August 18: 22A.

————. 1989d. "Poll: Ethnic Groups Turnout Is Key to Tight Race." August 23: 1A.

Fiedler, Tom, and Ronnie Ramos. 1989. "It's D-Day in Fight for Pepper Seat." *Miami Herald*, August 29: 1B.

Fiedler, Tom, and Luis Feldstein Soto. 1989a. "Irate Gordon Won't Seek Pepper Seat." *Miami Herald*, June 16: 1A.

————. 1989b. "Kennedy Won't back Richman." *Miami Herald*, August 18: 1B.

————. 1989c. "Herald Recommendation was Publishers Choice." *Miami Herald*, August 27: 3B.

Goldfards, Carol. 1990. "Incumbents Returned to Congress: Fascell, Lehman, and Ros-Lehtinen Win in Walks." *Miami Herald*, November 7: 1B.

Key, V. O., Jr. 1949. *Southern Politics in State and Nation*. New York: Knopf.

————. 1959. "Secular Realignment and the Party System." *Journal of Politics* 21: 198–219.

Malone, Joseph. 1988. *Hispanics in the Electoral Process of Dade County, Florida: The Coming of Age.* Miami: Metro-Dade Elections Department.

Metro-Dade Planning Department. 1986. *Hispanic Profile: Dade County's Hispanic Origin Population.* Miami.

Miami Herald. 1989a. Editorial, "For U.S. Congress: The Herald Recommends." July 23: 2C.

Miami Herald. 1989b. Editorial, "It Is Bigotry Sir." August 13: 16A.

Miami Herald. 1989c. Editorial, "For U.S. Congress: The Herald Recommends." August 27: 2C.

Moreno, Dario. Forthcoming. *Latinos in the 1988 Election.* Boulder, Colo.: Westview Press.

Moreno, Dario, and Christopher L. Warren. 1991. "The Conservative Enclave: Cubans in Florida." Forthcoming.

Moynihan, Daniel P., and Nathan Glazer. 1970. *Beyond the Melting Pot: The Negroes, Puerto Ricans, Jews, Italians and Irish of New York City.* 2d ed. Cambridge, Mass.: MIT Press.

Parenti, Michael. 1967. "Ethnic Politics and the Persistence of Ethnic Identification." *American Political Science Review* 61: 717–26.

Ramos, Ronnie. 1989a. "Race Is on for Pepper's Seat." *Miami Herald,* June 6: 1B.

————. 1989b. "Ros-Lehtinen Refuses to Debate Racist." *Miami Herald,* August 18: 1B.

————. 1989c. "Ros-Lehtinen, Richman Attempt to Make Peace." *Miami Herald,* September 1: 1B.

Searingen, Jacquelyn. 1989. "Atwater: Pepper's Seat Is for a Cuban American." *Miami Herald,* June 14: 10A.

Soto, Luis Feldstein. 1989a. "Richman Ads Hit on Crime, Abortion." *Miami Herald,* August 22: 1B.

————. 1989b. "It's Ros-Lehtinen 53–47%." *Miami Herald,* August 30.

Steinberg, Stephen. 1981. *The Ethnic Myth: Race, Ethnicity and Class in America.* Boston: Beacon Press.

Strategy Research Corporation. 1988. *The 1989 South Florida Latin Market.* Miami: Strategy Research Corporation.

Wolfinger, Raymond E. 1965. "The Development and Persistence of Ethnic Voting." *American Political Science Review* 59: 896–908.

Contributors

Max J. Castro is a principal investigator in a study of relations between African-Americans and Hispanics in Miami, sponsored jointly by the Social Science Research Council and the Inter-University Program for Latino Research. He was born in Havana, Cuba, and has lived in the United States since 1961. He received a Ph.D. in sociology from the University of North Carolina at Chapel Hill. His recent writings include "The Official English Movement in Florida" (with Margaret Haun and Ana Roca) in *Perspectives on Official English* (1990) and "On the Curious Question of Language in Miami" in *Sourcebook on Official English* (forthcoming). From 1988 to 1991, he was the executive director of Greater Miami United.

Marvin Dunn is an associate professor of community psychology at Florida International University. He is also executive director of the Institute for Innovative Interventions, Inc., a community-based group which operates the Academy for Community Education, an alternative high school in Coral Gables, Florida. His primary area of interest is race and ethnic relations. He is coauthor of *The Miami Riot of 1980: Crossing the Bounds* (1984).

Guillermo J. Grenier is the director of the Florida Center for Labor Research and Studies and professor of sociology at Florida International University. Born in Havana, Cuba, he received his Ph.D. from the University of New Mexico in Albuquerque. He is the author of *Inhuman Relations: Quality Circles and Anti-Unionism in American Industry* (1988) and of numerous other articles on labor and ethnic issues in the United States. His forthcoming books include *Employee Participation and Labor Law in the American Workplace* and *This Land Is Our Land: An Ethnography of Immigrant and Ethnic Interrelations in Miami*.

Anthony P. Maingot is professor of sociology and editor of *Hemisphere*, a magazine of Latin American and Caribbean studies, at Florida International University. His research and publications have focused on the social history and political sociology of Caribbean Basin societies. His most recent book is *Small Country Development and International Labor Flows: Experiences in the Caribbean* (1991).

Dario Moreno is assistant professor of political science at Florida International University. He has written various pieces on Cuban-American electoral behavior and published *U.S. Policy in Central America: The Endless Debate* (1990).

Lisandro Pérez was born in Havana, Cuba, and migrated to the United States in 1960 at the age of eleven. He is associate professor of sociology and director of the Cuban Research Institute at Florida International University. He received his Ph.D. in sociology from the University of Florida and taught for eleven years at Louisiana State University before joining FIU in 1985. His research has focused primarily on demographics and social change in Cuba and on the dynamics of the Cuban community in the United States. His writings have appeared in *International Migration Review*, *The Annals of the American Academy of Political and Social Science*, *Cuban Studies*, and *The Harvard Encyclopedia of American Ethnic Groups*. He is a member of the Board of Contributors of the *Miami Herald* and is a contributing editor for the *Handbook of Latin American Studies*, published by the Library of Congress.

Nicol C. Rae is assistant professor of political science at Florida International University. He was born in Scotland and has degrees from Edinburgh and Oxford universities. His publications include *The Decline and Fall of the Liberal Republicans: From 1952 to the Present* (1989).

John F. Stack, Jr., is professor of political science at Florida International University. He is the author of *International Conflict in an American City: Boston's Irish, Italians, and Jews, 1935–1944* (1979) and editor of *Ethnic Identities in a Transnational World* (1981) and *The Primordial Challenge: Ethnicity in the Modern World* (1986). He has written extensively on the linkages between ethnicity and world politics with special emphasis on ethnic conflict in Miami. His articles have appeared in *Ethnicity*, *PS*, and *Cuban Studies*, as well as in edited books.

Alex Stepick III is associate professor of sociology and anthropology and director of the graduate program in comparative sociology at Florida International University. In 1988, he earned the Margaret Mead Award for his work with Haitian refugees. He is coauthor of *Social Inequality in Oaxaco: A History of Resistance and Change*, with Arthur Murphy, and is completing another book, *City in the Sun: Miami and the Immigrants*, with Alejandro Portes. Along with Guillermo Grenier, Max Castro, and Marvin Dunn, he is also working on *This Land Is Our Land: An Ethnography of Immigrant and Ethnic Interrelations in Miami*.

Christopher L. Warren is associate professor of political science at Florida International University, where he teaches urban and American politics. His research and publications have focused primarily on Miami politics, reform of local governmental structures, and the politics of ethnicity and class in urban areas.

Index

Abortion, as 1989 election issue, 194, 195
Acculturation, enclave and, 93
AFL (American Federation of Labor): influence on Cuba of, 138–39; and "unorganizable" immigrants, 153
AFL–CIO, 136, 145–47, 148, 149; and LCLAA, 150; nativism in, 153; R. Kennedy backed by, 191
African National Congress. *See* Mandela, Nelson
Afro-Americans. *See* Native blacks
AIDS, Haitians and, 65, 72
Airlift, Cuba to U.S., 85–86, 87, 96, 98
Airlines, 2, 8, 9, 84
Alemán, José Manuel, 85
Allapattah, 51
Allman, T.D., xivn.1
Alvarez, Luis, 44
Amalgamated Clothing and Textile Workers Union, 143–44
American Institutes for Free Labor Development (AIFLD), 148
Amnesty, for illegal immigrants, 20
Amnesty International, 64
Anglos. *See* Whites, native
Anscher, Bernard, 191, 201
Anti-Americanism, in Caribbean, 29
Antibilingualism, 16, 109–10, 119–30, 175–77. *See also* English Only movement
Anticommunism: Cuban-American, 16, 95, 96, 135, 136, 148, 175, 179, 196 (*see also* Castro, Fidel, as Cuban-American Satan); Dade Co. official, 177, 182n.5
Aristide, Jean Bertrand, 62
Arizona, English Only in, 128, 129

Arson, in Miami riots, 174
Arts, Dade Co. Hispanics and, 126
Aruba, 28
Asians, 187, 202; of Chicago, xiii; as U.S. immigrants, 27
Assimilationism, 186–87; "enlightened," 115–18
Atwater, Lee, 190, 192
Aviño, Joaquín, 125

Bach, Robert L., 90, 91, 92, 154
Bahamas, Haitians of, 33
Bahamians, 3, 4–5, 8, 48–49, 54
Bal Harbour, Fla., 187, 198
Bananas, Central American, 28
Banks, 2, 9, 165; Cuban-run, 10
Barbados, 27, 28, 32, 33
Barbados Development Plan, 1979–83, 32
Batista, Fulgencio, 83
Bay Harbour, Fla., 187
Bay of Pigs, 5, 182n.3
Bazin, Marc, 73
Beacon Council, 182n.4
Bennett, William J., opposes bilingual education, 129
Biamby, Roger, 72–73
Biculturality, 103–4
Bilingualism, 16, 109–10, 112, 127, 130, 175; among Cuban-Americans, 104; in Dade Co. schools, 115–18, 124; as employment prerequisite, 121; federal support of, 124. *See also* Antibilingualism; Citizens of Dade United; English Only movement; Spanish (lang.)
Birth rate, Cuban-American, 97
Bishop, Maurice, 28
Black Lawyers Association, 53

209

Wolfinger, Raymond, 186–87, 200, 201
Women, Cuban-American working,
   91–93, 138, 143–44, 154
Workers' organizations, Cuban, 147–48

Wright, Phillip Irwin, 42
Wright, Sonny, 191, 193

Ybor City, Fla., 84

About the Editors

Guillermo J. Grenier is director of the Florida Center for Labor Research and Studies and chairman of the Department of Sociology and Anthropology at Florida International University. He is the author of *Inhuman Relations: Quality Circles and Anti-Unionism in American Industry* and coauthor of *Employee Participation and Labor Law in the American Workplace.*

Alex Stepick III is director of the comparative sociology graduate program and associate professor of anthropology and sociology at Florida International University. In 1988 he earned the Margaret Mead Award from the American Anthropological Association for his work with Haitian refugees. He is coauthor of *Social Inequality in Oaxaca: A History of Resistance and Change.*

Library of Congress Cataloging-in-Publication Data

Miami now: immigration, ethnicity, and social change / Guillermo
Grenier and Alex Stepick, editors.
      p.   cm.
   Includes index.
   ISBN 0–8130–1154–X (cloth: alk. paper). —ISBN 0–8130–1155–8
   (paper: alk. paper)
   1. Minorities—Florida—Miami.   2. Miami (Fla.)—Race relations.
3. Miami (Fla.)—Ethnic relations.   4. Miami (Fla.)—Social
conditions.   I. Grenier, Guillermo J.   II. Stepick, Alex.
F319.M6M639 1992   92–10100
305.8′009759′381—dc20   CIP